THE SUPERNOVA ERA

CIXIN 刘慈欣 LIU

TRANSLATED BY JOEL MARTINSEN

HEAD ZEUS

An Ad Astra Book

Originally published as 超新星纪元 in 2004 by
Sichuan Science & Technology Press in Chengdu.
First published in the United States of America in 2019 by
Tor, an imprint of Tom Doherty Associates LLC

First published in the UK by Head of Zeus Ltd in 2019
Copyright © 2004 by 刘慈欣 (Liu Cixin)

This paperback edition first published in the UK by Head of Zeus in 2021
An Ad Astra book

English translation copyright © 2019 by
China Educational Publications Import & Export Corp., Ltd

Translation by Joel Martinsen

9 7 5 3 1 2 4 6 8

A catalogue record for this book is available from
the British Library.

ISBN (PB): 9781800248960
ISBN (E): 9781788542418

Typeset by Adrian McLaughlin

Printed and bound in Great Britain by
CPI Group (UK) Ltd, Croydon CR0 4YY

Head of Zeus Ltd
5–8 Hardwick Street
London EC1R 4RG

WWW.HEADOFZEUS.COM

THE
ERA

CIXIN LIU is China's #1 SF writer and author of *The Three-Body Problem* – the first ever translated novel to win a Hugo Award. Prior to becoming a writer, Liu worked as an engineer in a power plant in Yangquan.

Translator **JOEL MARTINSEN** is also the translator (with Alice Xin Liu) of *The Problem With Me*, a collection of essays by Han Han. His translations of short fiction have appeared in *Pathlight*, *Chutzpah* and *Words Without Borders*. He lives in Beijing.

BY CIXIN LIU

THE THREE-BODY TRILOGY
The Three-Body Problem
The Dark Forest
Death's End

Ball Lightning
The Supernova Era
Of Ants and Dinosaurs

SHORT STORY COLLECTIONS
The Wandering Earth
Hold Up the Sky

For my daughter, Liu Jing.
May she live in a world of fun.

Cast of Characters

Adults

Zheng Chen, homeroom teacher for a graduating middle-school class

Zhang Lin, agent with the Central Extraordinary Commission

The president of China

The premier of China

Chinese Children

Huahua, a handsome, charismatic boy

Specs, an introverted boy with a keen mind

Xiaomeng, a quiet, respected girl mature beyond her years

The preceding three make up the central leadership

General Lü Gang, chief of general staff of the People's Liberation Army

Du Bin, ambassador to the United States

Lieutenant Wang Ran, tank driver

Second Lieutenant Wei Ming, armored infantry

Air Force Major Jin Yunhui, J-10 fighter pilot
Yao Rui, power station engineer
Feng Jing, Yao Pingping, nursery staff
Li Zhiping, letter carrier
Chang Huidong, barber
Zhang Xiaole, cook

Other Children
Secretary General Will Yagüe (UN)
President Herman Davey (USA)
Secretary of State Chester Vaughn (USA)
Chief of Staff Frances Benes (USA)
Major General Dowell (USA)
Vice President William Mitchell (USA)
General Harvey (USA)
Prime Minister Nelson Green (UK)
President Jean Pierre (FR)
Prime Minister Ōnishi Fumio (JP)
President Ilyukhin (RUS)
Marshal Zavyalova, chief of general staff (RUS)
Prime Minister Jairu (IND)
Prime Minister Lê Sâm Lâm (VIE)

Contents

Prologue

In those days, Earth was a planet in space.

In those days, Beijing was a city on Earth.

In the sea of lights of this city was a school, and in a classroom in that school, a class was holding a middle-school graduation party where, as in all such events, the children were talking about their aspirations.

"I want to be a general!" said Lü Gang, a skinny kid who gave the impression of power disproportionate to his size.

"Boring!" someone said. "There won't be any fighting, so all a general can do is lead troops in drills."

"I want to be a doctor," a girl named Lin Sha said in a quiet voice, to mocking laughter.

"Yeah, right. Last time we went to the countryside, even the sight of cocoons freaked you out. And you want to cut people open?"

"My mom's a doctor," she said, either as proof she wasn't frightened, or to explain her reason for wanting to be one.

Zheng Chen, their young homeroom teacher, had been staring out the window at the city lights, lost in thought, but now turned her attention back to the class.

"What about you, Xiaomeng. What do you want to do when you grow up?" she asked the girl next to her, who had also been staring out the window. The girl was plainly dressed, and her large, spirited eyes revealed a melancholy and maturity beyond her years.

"My family's not well-off. I'll only be able to go to a vocational high school," she said with a small sigh.

"What about you, Huahua?" Zheng Chen asked a good-looking boy whose large eyes were always lit up with delight, as if the world was perpetually a riot of newly exploded fireworks.

"The future's so cool I can't decide. But whatever I do, I want to be the best!"

Someone said they wanted to be an athlete, someone else a diplomat. When one girl said she wanted to be a teacher, Zheng Chen said gently, "It's not easy," and then turned back to stare out the window.

"Did you know Ms. Zheng's pregnant?" a girl whispered.

"That's right. And the school has cutback layoffs scheduled for right around the time she'll be giving birth next year, so things don't look good," said a boy.

At this, Zheng Chen laughed. "I'm not thinking about that right now. I'm wondering, what will the world be like when my kid is your age?"

"This is boring," said a small, scrawny kid. His name was Yan Jing, but everyone called him "Specs" because of the thick glasses he wore for nearsightedness. "No one knows what the future holds. It's unpredictable. Anything could happen."

"Science can make predictions," said Huahua. "Futurologists can."

Specs shook his head. "It's science that tells us that the future's unpredictable. Any predictions from those futurologists are imprecise, because the world is a chaotic system."

"I've heard about that. When a butterfly flaps its wings, there's a hurricane on the other side of the world."

"That's right," Specs said, nodding. "A chaotic system."

Huahua said, "My dream is to be that butterfly."

Specs shook his head again. "You don't understand at all. We're all butterflies, just like every butterfly. Every grain of sand and every drop of rain is a butterfly. That's why the world is unpredictable."

"You once talked about an uncertainty principle . . ."

"That's right. Microparticles can't be predicted. They only exist as a probability. So the whole world is unpredictable. And there's the theory of multiple worlds, where when you flip a coin the world splits in two, and the coin lands heads in one world and tails in the other . . ."

Zheng Chen laughed. "Specs, you yourself are proof enough. When I was your age, I'd never have imagined that one day a middle school student would know so much."

"Specs has read lots of books!" said another child, and others nodded.

"Ms. Zheng's baby is going to be even more amazing. Who knows—maybe genetic engineering will let him grow a real pair of wings!" Huahua said, and everyone laughed.

"Students," their teacher said as she stood up, "take a last look at your campus."

They left the classroom and strolled with their teacher through the grounds. Most of the lights were off, and the city lights that shone in the distance lent the campus an air of hazy calm. They passed two classroom buildings, administration, the library, and finally the row of Chinese parasol trees before reaching the athletic field. The forty-three children stood in the center surrounding their young teacher, who opened her arms to the sky, its stars dim under the lights of the city, and said, "Now, children, childhood is over."

In those days, Earth was a planet in space.

In those days, Beijing was a city on Earth.

It may seem like an insignificant story. Forty-three children leaving their peaceful school and continuing their respective life journeys.

It may seem like an ordinary night, a moment in the flow of time between the endless past and the limitless future. "One can't step twice in the same river" is nothing more than the babbling of an ancient Greek, for the river of time is the river of life, and this river flows endlessly at the same unchanging speed, an eternal flow of life and history and time.

That's what the people of this city thought. That's what the people of the plains of northern China thought. That's what the people of Asia thought. And that's what the carbon-based life-forms called humans everywhere on the planet thought. On this hemisphere, they were being lulled to sleep by the flow of time, convinced that the sacred eternal was unbreakable by any force, and they would wake up to a dawn identical to that of countless previous mornings. That faith, lurking in the depths of their consciousness, granted them the same peaceful dreams woven for untold generations.

It was an ordinary school, in a peaceful corner of a brilliant night in the city.

Forty-three thirteen-year-olds and their homeroom teacher looked up at the stars.

The winter's constellations, Taurus, Orion, and Canis Major, were already below the western horizon, and the summer's, Lyra, Hercules, and Libra, had been up for a while. Each star was like a distant eye blinking at the human world from the depths of the universe. But on this night, the cosmic gaze was somewhat different.

On this night, history as known to humanity came to an end.

1

The Dead Star

![divider]

The End

In the space within a ten-light-year radius of Earth, astronomers discovered eleven stars: the triple-star system formed from Proxima Centauri, Alpha Centauri A, and Alpha Centauri B; two binary-star systems, Sirius A and Sirius B, and Luyten 726-8 A and Luyten 726-8 B; and four single stars, Barnard's Star, Wolf 359, Lalande 21185, and Ross 154. Astronomers have not ruled out the possibility that other stars, either especially dim or obscured by interstellar dust, are waiting to be detected.*

Astronomers had noticed in this area the presence of a large amount of cosmic dust, like a dark cloud floating in the black night of space. When UV sensors on a satellite

---

* Stars discovered after this book's original date of publication include the dwarf stars Luhman 16A and Luhman 16B (announced in 2013), and sub-dwarf WISE 0855–0714 (in 2014).

were trained on this distant cloud, a peak of 216 mm was found on the absorption spectrum, suggesting that the cloud was likely formed from carbon microparticles; the cloud's reflectivity suggested that these particles were covered in a thin layer of ice. The particles were in the 2–200 nm range, roughly the same as the wavelength of visible light, rendering it opaque.

It was this cloud that blocked a star eight light-years from Earth. Twenty-three times the diameter of the sun and sixty-seven times its mass, the star was no longer main sequence but was in the final phase of its long evolution, its waning years. We'll call it the Dead Star.

Even if it had a memory, the Dead Star would not remember its childhood. It was born five hundred million years ago out of a mother nebula. Atomic motion and radiation from the galactic center disrupted the stillness of the nebula, whose particles congealed around a center under gravitational attraction. This stately dust storm endured for two million years, while in its center, hydrogen atoms began to fuse into helium. The Dead Star was born out of this atomic furnace.

After a dramatic childhood and rocky adolescence, fusion energy arrested the collapse of the stellar crust, and the Dead Star entered a lengthy middle age, an evolution that took place over hundreds of millions of years instead of the hours, minutes, and seconds of its childhood, bringing a new point of calm light to the galaxy's vast starry ocean. But a flyby of the Dead Star's surface would have revealed that this calm was illusory. It was an ocean of atomic fire, enormous waves of searing flames that churned red and flung high-energy particles out into space like a storm swell. Tremendous energy erupted from the star's depths and surged in blinding waves in that sea, over which an endless nuclear storm of constant hurricanes raged, and dark red plasma undulated under a strong magnetic field in million-kilometer tornadoes reaching into space like the tendrils of a red tide. . . . No human mind could grasp the sheer size of the Dead Star; against that sea of fire, Earth was like a basketball tossed into the Pacific Ocean.

The Dead Star ought to have been bright in the visible sky. With an apparent magnitude of −7.5, if not for the interstellar dust incubating another star that sat three light-years distant and blocked its light from reaching Earth, it would have shone on human history with a light more than five times brighter than Sirius, the brightest star in the heavens, bright enough to cast shadows on a moonless night, a dreamy blue adding a dose of sentimentality to human history.

The Dead Star burned a glorious existence without incident for 460 million years, but the cold hand of the law of conservation of energy made certain internal changes unavoidable: the fusion fire depleted hydrogen, and the helium by-product sank to the star's center and accumulated over time. This change was an exceedingly slow process for such a giant object, one for whom the whole span of human history was the snap of a finger, but after 480 million years, the depletion had a tangible effect: enough of the more inert helium had accumulated that the source of the star's energy waned. It had grown old.

But other, more complicated physical laws determined that the Dead Star would end its life in a blaze of glory. The density of the helium at its center increased, and the fusion that continued in the surrounding hydrogen produced temperatures high enough to initiate fusion in the helium, consuming nearly all of it at once in a nuclear inferno. The helium fusion caused the Dead Star to shine with a powerful light, but since its energy was only a tenth of that of hydrogen, the effort only further weakened the star. Termed a helium flash by astronomers, the phenomenon's light reached the patch of interstellar dust three years later, where the relatively long-wavelength red light penetrated the cosmic barrier. That light traveled for another five years before arriving at a far smaller, ordinary star, the Sun, as well as the handful of cosmic dust attracted by its gravitational pull, known to humans as Pluto, Neptune, Uranus, Saturn, Jupiter, Mars, Venus, Mercury, and of course Earth. This took place in 1775.

That evening, in Earth's northern hemisphere, in the English spa town of Bath, outside a high-end music hall, a German-born organist by the name of Frederick William Herschel was gazing hungrily into the universe through a telescope of his own design. The glittering Milky Way so called to him that he poured his entire life into telescopes, to the extent that his sister Caroline had to spoon him his meals while he continued observations. During the lifetime the most distinguished of eighteenth-century astronomers spent in front of the lens, he marked seventy thousand stars on the map, but he overlooked the one that became most significant to humanity. That night a red body suddenly appeared in the western sky in the constellation Auriga, at the midpoint between Capella and Beta Aurigae. An apparent magnitude 4.5, it wasn't bright enough for a casual observer to pick out even if they knew its location, but to an astronomer, the red star was nothing less than an enormous lantern that Herschel might have discovered, were he viewing the heavens with the naked eye like pre-Galilean astronomers rather than being glued to the lens. And that discovery might have altered the course of human history some two centuries later. But his attention was entirely commanded by that telescope, just two inches in diameter, pointed in an entirely different direction, as, unfortunately, were telescopes at the observatories in Greenwich and Hven, and everywhere else in the world, for that matter. . . .

The red star in Auriga shone for the whole night, but the next night it had disappeared.

That same night in that same year, on the continent called North America, eight hundred British soldiers crept along a road to the west of Boston, their red uniforms giving them the look of a line of ghosts in the night. Clutching muskets in the chilly spring wind, they hoped to reach the town of Concord, twenty-seven kilometers from Boston, before daybreak, and were under orders from the Massachusetts governor Thomas Gage to wipe out the minutemen's arsenal and arrest their leadership. But when the sky turned gray and the woods, huts, and pasture fences took shape as silhouettes against the growing light, the soldiers looked about them and found they had only gotten as far as the town of Lexington. From a thicket ahead of them came a sudden flash, and an earsplitting crack broke the stillness of the North American dawn, closely followed by the whoosh of bullets: the quickening in the womb of the embryonic United States of America.

*

On the vast continent on the other side of the Pacific, a civilization had already endured for five thousand years. Now, in that ancient land, people were heading day and night toward the capital of that age-old kingdom carrying huge quantities of ancient books collected from every corner of the land. The imperial edict to compile the *Sikuquanshu* had been issued two years ago, and books were still streaming endlessly toward the capital. In a massive wooden hall in the Forbidden City, the Qianlong Emperor was constantly making the rounds of the rows of bookcases holding the works amassed for the library project, now divided into four general categories, Classics, Histories, Masters, and Collections, and stored on these huge shelves.

Leaving his attendants outside the door, the emperor carefully entered the archives, three scholars wearing peacock feathers on their hats,* Dai Zhen, Yao Nai, and Ji Yun, leading the way carrying lanterns. It was they, not the titled imperial clansmen, who were the true compilers of the encyclopedia. The tall cases slipped slowly past the four men, like black city walls in the dim lantern light. They came to a pile of bamboo slips; the emperor picked up one bundle in trembling hands, the wavering yellow light making him feel as if he were at the dark floor of a book canyon, the canyon of time's mountain, and beneath the book cliff face, countless ghosts from across five thousand years took silently to the air.

* The peacock feather was an honor bestowed on high-ranking officials.

"How time flows onward, Your Majesty,"* whispered one compiler.

Unimaginably far out in space, the Dead Star continued its march toward doomsday. There were more helium flashes, but smaller in scale than the first, and helium fusion produced a new core of carbon and oxygen. Then that core ignited, producing neon, sulfur, and silicon, and then a huge number of neutrinos appeared in the star, spooky particles that carried off the core's energy without interacting with any matter.

Over time, the center of the Dead Star grew unable to support its heavy crust, and the gravity that had given it life now worked the reverse. Under gravity's pull, the Dead Star collapsed into a dense ball, its constituent atoms shattered under the impossibly huge stresses, neutron crushing into neutron. Now a teaspoon of matter from the Dead Star had a mass of a billion tons. First the core collapsed, and then the unsupported crust smashed into the tightly packed center, triggering a final fusion reaction.

An epic of gravity and fire spanning 500 million years came to an end in a cosmos-splitting snow-white blast, and the Dead Star shattered into trillions of fragments and a giant quantity of dust. Its enormous energy, converted into a torrent of EM radiation and high-energy particles, surged outward in all directions. Three years after the explosion, the tide of energy slipped easily through that cosmic dust cloud, heading for the sun.

When the Dead Star exploded, humanity was flourishing

* Quotation from the *Analects*, 9.17.

eight light-years away. Though they knew they were living on but a speck of dust in the cosmos, they had not truly come to accept this fact. In the millennium that had just ended, they had harnessed the immense power of nuclear fission and fusion and had created complex thinking machines using electrical impulses confined in silicon, imagining they had the power to conquer the universe. No one knew that the energy from the Dead Star was making its inexorable way toward their small blue planet at the speed of light.

After passing the three stars of Centaurus, the Dead Star's light spent another four years in vast, lonely outer space until at last it reached the outskirts of the solar system. In that region, inhabited only by tailless comets, the energy from the Dead Star had its first encounter with humanity: More than a billion kilometers away from Earth, a man-made body was making its lonely sojourn into the Milky Way—*Voyager,* an interstellar probe launched from Earth in the 1970s. It was shaped like a weird umbrella, its parabolic antenna opened toward the Earth. The probe carried humanity's calling card, a lead-alloy plate inscribed with two naked humans, a disc bearing the UN secretary general's greeting to alien civilization, recordings of Earth's oceans, birdcalls, and the traditional Chinese tune "Liu Shui."

Earth had its first taste of the grimness of the cosmos when its emissary to the galaxy passed into the light of the Dead Star and turned immediately into a hunk of blazing metal. Its umbrella antenna warped as its temperature suddenly shot up from near absolute zero. The intensity of the high-energy radiation overloaded a Geiger counter and caused it to read out only zeros. The UV probe and magnetic-field instruments remained operational, and in the just two seconds before the circuits were fried by radiation, *Voyager* sent back to its creators on Earth a stream of unbelievable data that, owing to the damage to its antenna, would never be received by the high-sensitivity arrays in Nevada and Australia. No matter; humanity would soon be able to measure the unbelievable for themselves.

The Dead Star's beam crossed the boundary of the solar system and kicked up steam on the blue crystalline solid-nitrogen ground of Pluto, and then met Neptune and Uranus, turning their rings crystal clear. The storm of high-energy particles passed Saturn and Jupiter, phosphorescing their liquid matter, just after the Beijing schoolchildren began their graduation party. The energy traveled for another half hour at light speed and reached the moon, shedding blinding light on Mare Imbrium and the crater of Copernicus. It lit up the set of footprints left behind by Neil Armstrong and Buzz Aldrin four decades earlier under the watchful eyes of hundreds of millions of television viewers on the nearby blue planet, who in that moment of excitement were convinced that the cosmos had been put there for them.

One second later, the Dead Star's light completed its eight-year journey across space to Earth.

The Midnight Sun

It was midday!

That was the children's first reaction when their vision returned. The light had come so suddenly it was like the flip of some cosmic light switch, and they had been momentarily blinded.

CIXIN LIU

It was 8:18 in the evening, but the children were standing in the blazing light of noon. They looked up into the blue and took in a cold breath. This was most definitely not the same blue as usual; the sky was a startling blue-black, like color recorded on ultrasensitive film. And it seemed unusually clean, as if a grayish-white layer of skin had been peeled off and the sky's pure-blue flesh was liable to start bleeding at any moment. The city was lit bright by the light, and the sight of the sun made the children cry out in alarm.

This was not humanity's sun!

The light that had broken into the night sky was too powerful to look at directly, but through the gaps in their fingers they caught glimpses of a sun that wasn't round—it was a shapeless point like other visible stars, an intense white light emitting from some point in the universe, but it didn't seem small. It had an extremely high brightness of −51.23, almost an order of magnitude greater than the sun, and its light scattered in the atmosphere, turning it into an enormous, blinding poison spider hanging in the western sky.

The Dead Star appeared suddenly and reached peak brightness in a matter of seconds. Earth's eastern hemisphere was the first to see it, and the largest panic began almost immediately. Everyone lost all capacity for normal reason and action; the entire world was paralyzed. The spectacle was grandest for viewers in the Atlantic, and on the west coast of Europe and Africa. Here is an eyewitness account from an observer in the Atlantic:

At daybreak we discovered an anomaly: after the sun rose

above the ocean, light continued to pour over the eastern horizon, white light, radiating from some unknown source below the surface of the water, as if a huge lamp were hidden beneath the eastern ocean. The light intensified. It was so strange it unsettled everyone on board. There was nothing but static on the radio. The second daybreak grew brighter and brighter, and "dawn" clouds shone with a blinding light, like lightbulb filaments. . . . Our fear grew with the light. We all knew that the light source would rise at some point, but no one knew what we would see. At last, three hours after dawn, we saw a second sunrise. The captain later offered this apt description of the new sun: "It's like a giant cosmic welder!" Of the two suns in the sky, it was our old one that was the most frightening: it was so much dimmer than the new one that it looked black by comparison! Not everyone could handle the nightmare, and some people tore madly about the decks, or jumped overboard. . . .

From Albert G. Harris,
A Witness to the Dead Star. London, SE 6.

Before the children on the field had recovered their senses, lightning broke out as the atmosphere ionized under the Dead Star's radiation. Long purple arcs crossed the sky, and grew denser as earsplitting thunder rolled.

"Quick! Into the classroom!" Zheng shouted, and they all raced back, shielding their heads against the thunder that split the sky and threatened to split the world in two. Once inside, the trembling children clustered around their teacher. The Dead Star's light shone through the windows on one side casting clear rectangle patterns on the floor; lightning through the windows on the other side flashed that side of the classroom with purple electricity. Static filled the air, metal attachments on their clothing clicked with tiny sparks, their hair stood on end, and they could feel their skin tingling all over, as if their clothing had grown spikes.

Below is a transcript of transmissions between the Russian space station *Mir*, the Baikonur Cosmodrome in Kazakhstan, and the American space shuttle *Zeus*, by *Mir*'s final crew before its deorbiting:

Commander: D. A. Vortsev
Flight engineer: B. G. Tinovich
Mechanical engineer: Y. N. Bykovsky
Environmental engineer: F. Lefsen
Station doctor: Nikita Kasyanenko
Crew: Joe La Mure, solid state physicist; Alexander Andrev, astrophysicist

EM COMMUNICATIONS:
10:20'10", MIR: Don calling Baikonur! Don calling Baikonur! Base, acknowledge. Base, acknowledge.
(No response. Static.)
10:21'30", BASE: This is Baikonur base! Baikonur calling Don. Please respond.
(No response. Static.)

INFRARED COMMUNICATIONS:
10:23'20", MIR: Base, this is *Mir*. Main system interference is too high, so we've initiated backup communications. Please respond.

10:23'25", BASE: We hear you, but the signal isn't stable.

10:23'28", MIR: Difficulty with orienting the transmission and reception units. Orientation control circuit chips have failed due to radiation, so we've resorted to manual optical orientation.

10:23'37", BASE: Fix the transmission and reception units in place. We will take over control.

10:23'42", MIR: Done.

10:23'43", BASE: Signal normal!

10:23'46", MIR: Base, can you tell us what happened? What should we call the thing that appeared all of a sudden?

10:23'46", BASE: We know as much as you do. Call it "Star X" if you want. Please send us the data you've obtained.

10:24'01", MIR: We will transmit observation data beginning at ten o'clock for the integrated radiometer, ultraviolet and gamma ray instruments, gravimeter, magnetometer, Geiger counter, solar wind meter, and neutrino detector, as well as 136 visual spectrum and infrared images. Prepare to receive.

10:24'30", MIR: *(Data transmission)*

10:25'00", MIR: Our space telescope has been tracking Star X since it first appeared. Given our level of sensitivity, we cannot estimate its angular diameter, nor have we found any clear parallax. Dr. Andrev believes that those two points together with the energy we've received mean that Star X is outside the solar system. This is just a hypothesis of course. Data is insufficient, and there's lots to be done by ground-based observatories.

10:25'30", BASE: What have you seen on Earth?

10:25'36", MIR: A large-scale hurricane in the equatorial region is moving northward with an estimated wind speed of 60 meters per second, judging by our observations of the changes in clouds over the equator. This may be due to the unevenness of the sudden influx of heat on Earth from Star X. Oh, and a large amount of ultraviolet radiation and blue flashes, possibly lightning, in the polar regions and currently expanding to lower latitudes.

10:26'50", BASE: Report on your own status.

10:27'05", MIR: Not good. The onboard flight control computer has been entirely fried by the high-energy rays, backup systems too. Their lead shielding is inoperative. Monocrystalline silicon solar batteries are totally fried, and chemical batteries are severely damaged. We are now entirely reliant on in-cabin isotope batteries, which are woefully underpowered, so we've had to shut down life support in the main cabin. Life support is functioning abnormally in the living cabin. We're close to having to put on our space suits.

10:28'20", BASE: The base feels that under the present circumstances it is inadvisable to remain in orbit, but also that a soft landing is impossible given the damage to the systems. The US space shuttle *Zeus* is in low orbit 3340; it was in Earth's shadow and suffered only light damage and is still capable of reentry. We have made contact with them, and the Americans have decided to carry out the provisions of the Outer Space Treaty concerning rescue of astronauts and take you on board. Parameters for speed reduction and engine operation to follow . . .

10:30'33", MIR: Base, the station doctor wishes to speak with you.

10:30'40", MIR: This is the station doctor. I believe there's no point to the transfer. Cancel it.

10:30'46", BASE: Please explain.

10:30'48", MIR: All astronauts aboard the station have received an ultralethal 5100 rad dose of radiation. We have only hours left to live, so even if we returned to Earth, the outcome would be the same.

10:31′22″, BASE: (Silence)

10:31′57″, MIR: This is the commander. Please allow us to remain on Mir. This station is humanity's farthest outpost for observing Star X. In our final few hours, we'll carry out our duties to the full. We will be the first astronauts to die in space; if the opportunity presents itself in the future, please return our remains to our homeland.

From Vladimir Konev, *A History of the Russian Space Program in the Common Era*, vol. 5. Moscow, SE 17.

The Dead Star lit up the cosmos for an hour and twenty-five minutes before it vanished abruptly. Only then were radio telescope arrays able to detect its remains: a swiftly revolving neutron star emitting a precisely separated EM pulse.

Faces pressed to the classroom window glass, the children watched the sunset that wasn't, as the blue-black of night descended on this peculiar evening. The light of the Dead Star faded into a twilight that occupied half the sky before quickly shrinking down to a small outlining circle, its color transitioning to white. Most of the sky was dark now, and scattered stars were visible. The halo around the Dead Star continued to contract until it finally vanished, leaving just a point where there once had been a gleaming light source. Once the night sky returned to normal, it was the brightest of the stars, but continued to dim until it was just another star in the galaxy, and five minutes later, the Dead Star had completely vanished into the depths of the cosmos.

When the lightning had stopped, the children ran out of the classroom, where they found themselves in a phosphorescent world. Everything beneath the night sky, the trees, the buildings, the ground, all glowed blue-green, as if the ground and everything on it had been transformed into translucent jade and a green moonlike source deep beneath the ground was flooding light through everything. Green-lit clouds hung in the air as flocks of startled birds sped by like glowing fairies. Most frightening to the children was that they were phosphorescent, too, like images from a photo negative, or a group of ghosts.

"Like I said," said Specs, "anything can happen."

The classroom lights turned back on, as did the lights of the city, and the children realized that there had been a blackout. The glow faded as the lights came on, and they initially thought the world had returned to normal. But they soon found to their shock that the episode was not over.

A red light emerged in the northeast, and before long clouds glowing dark red rose in that part of the sky, as if heralding the dawn.

"It's daybreak for real this time!"

"Idiot! It's not even eleven!"

The red clouds marched across half the sky, at which point the children realized that they were glowing with their own light. When they were directly overhead, the children could see they were composed of huge bands of light, like strips of slowly twisting red drapes hanging from the sky itself.

"Northern lights!" someone shouted.

The aurora soon covered the whole sky, and for the next week, night skies across the whole world danced with red bands of light.

★

When the auroras disappeared for good a week later and the glittering stars returned, one final, glorious movement of the supernova's symphony was left: A shining nebula appeared at the very spot where the Dead Star had been just days before. The explosion's dust cloud was excited by the high-energy pulse of the star's remains and emitted synchronized radiation in the visible spectrum for humanity to see. The nebula grew until it was roughly the size of two full moons in the sky. This rosette-shaped radiant body, later given the name "Rose Nebula," emitted a strange, harsh blue light into the heavens that shone over the earth with a moonlight-like silver, illuminating every detail on the ground with the brightness of a full moon, washing out the glow of the cities below.

The Rose Nebula would shine over human history until the day the inheritors of the dinosaurs' rule over the planet were wiped out, or were reborn.

2

The Selection

A World in a Valley

The Dead Star was unquestionably a major event in human history. The earliest recorded supernova was on an oracle bone inscription from 1300 BCE; the most recent from 1987, a supernova outside the galaxy in the direction of the Large Magellanic Cloud, at a distance of roughly 170,000 light-years from us. In astronomical terms, it was imprecise to call this latest supernova "neighboring"; it was practically on top of us.

Still, the world's fascination endured for just a fortnight. As science was just beginning its investigation, and with the worlds of philosophy and the arts well below a critical mass of inspiration, ordinary people had already turned back to their ordinary lives. Their interest in the supernova was limited to how large the Rose Nebula might grow and how its shape might change, but this attention was mostly casual in nature.

Two of the most important discoveries, as far as humanity was concerned, went practically unnoticed.

In an abandoned mine shaft in South America, an enormous cistern holding more than ten thousand tons of still water was monitored day and night by a host of precise sensors, part of humanity's neutrino-detection effort. The neutrinos, after penetrating five hundred meters of rock, would cause minute flashes in the cistern water, detectable only by the most sensitive of instruments. On duty in the mine that day were Anderson, a physicist, and Nord, an engineer. Bored out of his mind, Nord was counting the water stains that glittered under the dim lights on the rock walls and breathing in the dank subterranean air, imagining he was in a tomb.

He took a bottle of whiskey out of a drawer as Anderson extended a glass. The physicist used to hate drinking on duty and had once fired an engineer for it, but now was past caring. During their five years half a kilometer beneath the surface, not a single flash had made itself known, and they had lost all faith. But now the flash buzzer went off, heavenly music to their ears after the five-year wait.

The whiskey bottle fell to the ground and shattered as they threw themselves over to the monitor. It was totally black. They gaped at it for several seconds, and then the engineer recovered enough to race out of the control room to the side of the cistern, which resembled a tall, windowless building. Peering through a small porthole, he saw with his own eyes the ghostly blue spark in the water, so powerful it had oversaturated the sensitive instruments, which was why nothing was visible onscreen. The two men returned to the control room, where Anderson bent over another instrument for a closer inspection.

"Neutrinos?" the engineer asked.

Anderson shook his head. "The particle's got obvious mass."

"There's no way it would make it here. It would stop after interacting with the rock."

"It did interact. We detected its secondary radiation."

"Are you insane?" Nord shouted straight at Anderson. "How powerful would it need to be to produce secondary radiation through five hundred meters of rock?"

At the Stanford University Medical Center, hematologist Grant arrived at the lab to pick up the test results for two hundred samples he had submitted the previous day. Handing Grant a stack of forms, the lab chief said, "I didn't know you had so many beds."

"What do you mean?"

The chief pointed at the forms. "Where'd you come across all those poor bastards? Chernobyl?"

Grant inspected a few pages, and went into a rage. "Did you screw this up again! Aiming to get fired? These were control samples from normal people, for a statistical study!"

The chief stared at Grant for a moment, his eyes betraying a growing terror that made Grant's skin crawl. Then he seized Grant and dragged him back into the lab.

"What are you doing! You imbecile!" Grant protested.

"Draw blood! I'll do mine. And you all!" he shouted to the technicians. "Blood samples from everyone!"

*

Two days before school restarted after the summer holiday, halfway through a faculty meeting, the principal was summoned away for a phone call. He returned wearing a grave expression, motioned to Zheng Chen, and the two of them exited the conference room as the other faculty looked on in shock.

"Xiao Zheng," the principal said, "gather your class at once."

"Why? Classes haven't even started yet."

"Your graduating class, I mean."

"That's even harder. They're split up among five different high schools, and I don't know if they've even started class. Besides, how are we still involved with them?"

"The registration office will assist you. The director of education called in person."

"Did Director Feng say what to do after I've gotten them together?"

Realizing Zheng Chen hadn't fully understood, the principal added, "Not Director Feng. The director of the national Ministry of Education!"

Assembling the graduating class was not as hard as Zheng Chen imagined, and it wasn't long before the forty-three students returned to their school, spurred by an urgent notice when they arrived to register at their high schools. The children were overjoyed at this reunion of their disbanded class.

Zheng Chen and the children waited in their classroom

for around half an hour, unsure of what was to happen. Eventually a coach and two cars pulled up outside and three people got out. The principal introduced their leader as Zhang Lin, and said they were from the Central Extraordinary Commission.

"Extraordinary Commission?" said Zheng Chen.

"It's a newly established agency," Zhang Lin said without elaborating. "The students in your class will be away from their families for a while. We'll assume responsibility for notifying their guardians. Since you know the class pretty well, you'll come along. There's no need to take anything. We'll leave at once."

"What's the hurry?" Zheng Chen asked in surprise.

"Time is of the essence."

Carrying the forty-three students, the coach left the city headed west. Zhang Lin sat next to Zheng Chen, began examining the student register as soon as he boarded, and stared straight ahead without speaking once he finished. The two other men did the same. Zheng Chen noticed their solemn expressions but felt awkward mentioning it. The atmosphere infected the children, who said little along the way. They passed the Summer Palace and continued westward toward the Western Hills, and then traveled a ways down a forested road farther into the mountains until they entered a large compound whose gate was guarded by three armed sentries. In the center of the compound was a cluster of buses identical to theirs, and groups of children disembarking. They looked roughly the same age as her class.

Zheng Chen had just stepped out of the bus when she

heard someone call her name. It was a teacher from Shanghai she had met once at a conference. She took stock of his charges: clearly another class of middle school graduates.

"That's my class," the teacher said.

"You came from Shanghai?"

"Yes. We were notified late last night, and spent the night calling up every house to gather the children together."

"Last night? How'd you get here so fast? Even a plane would take longer."

"Charter plane."

They stared at each other silently for a moment, and then the Shanghai teacher said, "I don't know anything else."

"Neither do I," Zheng Chen said. She remembered that the Shanghai teacher was in charge of a pilot class in the Ministry of Education's character program. Four years ago, the ministry had launched Project Star, a large-scale education experiment for which classes were chosen in major cities across the country to adopt instructional methods well removed from the mainstream; the program was primarily intended to foster children's overall competence. Zheng Chen's class had been one of them.

She looked around her. "These all seem to be Star classes."

"That's right. Twenty-four in all. Around a thousand kids from five cities."

That afternoon, staffers gathered more information from the classes and drew up a detailed register for each student. The evening was mostly unplanned, so the children phoned home and told their families they were at summer camp, even though the summer was over.

Before daybreak the next morning, the children boarded the buses and set off again.

After a forty-minute drive through the mountains, they reached a valley ringed by gentle slopes. Come autumn the hills would be ablaze with red, but now they were still green. A stream ran down the valley floor, shallow enough to cross with trousers hiked up. The children exited their buses and gathered in an open area beside the road, a thousand of them in a big group. One of the leaders stood on a boulder and began to speak.

"Children, you've come here from all over the country. Now let me tell you the purpose of this journey: We're going to play a big game!"

He clearly was not someone who frequently interacted with kids. His manner was severe, nothing of the feel of a game, but his words prompted rustles of excitement among the children anyway.

"Look," he said, pointing at the valley. "That's where we'll play. Each of your twenty-four classes will be given some land around three to four square kilometers. That's not a small plot! Every class will use that land—now listen—every class will establish a little country!"

That last line seized the children's attention. A thousand pairs of eyes focused on him.

"The game will last for fifteen days. For fifteen days you'll live off the territory you've been granted!"

The children cheered.

"Quiet down and listen. These twenty-four territories have been stocked with necessities like tents, camp cots, fuel, food, and drinking water, but these goods haven't been equally divided. One territory, for example, might have more tents but less food; another might be the opposite. But be certain of one thing: the total amount of provisions on these territories is insufficient for so many days. You have two avenues at your disposal to obtain provisions:

"First, trade. You can trade your own surplus materials for those in short supply. But even so, your little countries won't be able to last the full fifteen days, because the total quantity is insufficient. This means:

"Second, engage in production. This is your country's primary duty and chief activity. Production means opening up undeveloped land on your territory, and then planting seeds and irrigating them on the cleared land. It's not feasible to wait for grain to grow, of course, but based on your land clearing, sowing, and irrigation figures, you'll be able to obtain equivalent food from the game's directorate. The twenty-four countries are distributed along this stream, which will serve as your water source. You'll use that water to irrigate your cleared land.

"You'll choose your own national leaders, three paramount leaders to share power equally. They will jointly exercise the highest decision-making authority. You will set up your country's own administrative organs, and make all the decisions for your country, development plans, foreign policy, and so forth. We will not interfere. Citizens have free mobility; you can choose to go to any country you think best.

"Now we'll divvy up territory for you. First thing, choose a name for your country and report it to the directorate. The rest is up to you. I'll only tell you that the game has very few rules. Children, the fate and future of these countries is in your hands. I hope that you'll make your little countries flourish and grow strong!"

It was the grandest game the children had ever seen, and they raced off toward their own territories.

Zheng Chen's class followed Zhang Lin to their territory, an area surrounded by a white fence straddling the riverside and a slope, with tents and various provisions neatly stacked where the two met. The children ran on ahead to tear through the supplies, and then Zheng Chen heard exclamations of surprise as they crowded round. She hurried over and made her way forward through the children, and what she saw left her momentarily stunned.

On a square of green canvas lay a neatly arranged row of machine guns.

Although she was unfamiliar with weapons, she was still certain they were not toys. She bent down and picked one up, felt its heft, caught a whiff of gun oil, saw the cold blue glint of its steel barrel. Three green metal boxes sat next to the canvas; a child had opened one to reveal gleaming golden bullets inside.

"Are the guns real, uncle?" a child said to Zhang Lin, who had just arrived.

"Of course. These submachine guns are the army's newest issue. They're small and lightweight. Their foldable stock makes them well-suited for children."

Children cooed with awe as they excitedly picked up the guns. But Zheng Chen shouted sharply, "Stop! No one is to touch those things." Then she turned to Zhang Lin. "What is the meaning of this?"

"Surely weapons are one of a country's essential supplies," he said lightly.

"You said they're well-suited for . . . use by children?"

"Oh, you needn't worry," he said with a chuckle, and bent down to lift a string of shells from the ammo case. "These bullets are nonlethal. They're actually just two small balls of wire stuck to a piece of plastic, light enough that they lose velocity rapidly after firing and won't cause any bodily injuries. But the balls of wire carry a strong static charge and will release tens of thousands of volts into the target upon impact, enough to cause a fall and momentary loss of consciousness. The current is quite low, so the target will recover quickly and will suffer no lasting harm."

"Electrocution won't cause any harm?"

"This ammunition was first developed for police use and has undergone numerous animal and human tests. Police in the West were first equipped with it in the 1980s, and there have been no casualties in the many times it has been used."

"And if they strike an eye?"

"Eye protection."

"If the person hit falls from a high place?"

"We've chosen a relatively level geography precisely for that reason. . . . I have to admit of course that it's impossible to guarantee absolute safety, but there will be minimal chances for harm."

"Do you really intend to give these weapons to the children, and permit them to use them on other children?"

Zhang Lin nodded.

Zheng Chen blanched. "Can't they use toy guns?"

He shook his head. "War is an indispensable part of a country's history. We have to create as real an atmosphere as possible to obtain reliable results."

"Results? What results?" She stared at him with fear in her eyes, as if he were some kind of monster. "What are you all really after?"

"Calm down, Ms. Zheng. We're being pretty restrained

already. Reliable intelligence says that some countries are allowing their children to use live ammo."

"Other countries? Is the whole world playing this game?"

She glanced absently around her, as if to ascertain whether or not she was dreaming. Then, with effort, she calmed herself down, straightened her hair, and said, "Please send me and the children back home."

"I'm afraid that's impossible. This region is now under martial law. I told you that this is extremely important work . . ."

She lost control of her calm again. "I don't care about that. I will not permit you to do this. I am a teacher. I have my own duty and conscience."

"We have the same conscience, and an even greater duty. And those are the two things that force us to act." He turned his sincere face toward her. "Please trust us."

"Send the children home!" she shouted.

"Please trust us."

A quiet voice from behind her sounded familiar, although she couldn't immediately place it. The children were staring in shock at a spot behind her, so she turned around to discover a sizable crowd of people who, once she took them all in, only increased her sense of being outside of reality. Paradoxically, this calmed her again. She could identify a few in back as senior national leaders who often appeared on television, but the first two she recognized were standing right in front of her.

The president and the premier.

"It's like having a nightmare, right?" the president asked gently.

She nodded, unable to speak.

The premier said, "That's nothing unusual. That was our feeling at first, too. But we adjusted quickly."

"Your work is very important, and involves the fate of the country and its people," the president said. "Later, we'll explain everything, and at that time, comrade teacher, you'll feel pride in the work you've done and are doing." His words eased her mind to an extent.

When the group started off toward a neighboring territory, the premier took a step back and said to Zheng Chen, "All you need to understand right now is this: The world isn't what it used to be."

"Let's give our little country a name, everyone," Specs said.

The morning sun was peeking over the ridge, painting the valley in gold.

"Let's call it Sunland!" Huahua said, and after unanimous approval, added, "We need to paint a flag."

So the children found a piece of white canvas among the supplies, and Huahua took a thick marker from his schoolbag and drew a circle with it. "That's a sun. Who's got a red one, so we can fill it in."

"Won't that be the Japanese flag?" a child asked.

Xiaomeng took the marker and drew a pair of large eyes and a laughing mouth on the sun, and added radiating lines for rays of light. The children approved of this flag. In the Supernova Era, this clumsily artful flag was preserved in the National History Museum as a priceless historic artifact.

"And a national anthem?"

"Let's use the song of the Young Pioneers."

When the sun had fully cleared the mountains, the

children held a flag-raising ceremony in the center of their land.

After the ceremony, Zhang Lin asked Huahua, "Why did you first think of setting out a flag and anthem?"

"A country needs them as . . . a symbol. The students have to be able to see the country in order for us to cohere."

Zhang Lin made a few notes in his notebook.

"Did we do something wrong?" a child asked.

"Like I said before, you will be making all the decisions. You do things as you see fit. My duty is to observe, but never to interfere." Then to Zheng Chen, he said, "That goes for you, too, Ms. Zheng."

Next, the children elected national leaders, choosing Huahua, Specs, and Xiaomeng in a painless process. Huahua had Lü Gang form a military, for which twenty-five children volunteered. Twenty of them received submachine guns, and Lü Gang consoled the five who were furious at not getting any that the guns would be rotated over the next few days. Xiaomeng appointed Lin Sha as health minister and put her in charge of all medication in their provisions, and of treating any patients. The children decided that other state institutions would be set up as needed.

Then they started to settle into their new territory. They cleared some space and went to work on the tents, but when a few kids entered the first one they set up, it collapsed on top of them and they had a tough time digging their way out of the canvas. But they were enjoying it. By noontime, they had managed to erect a few tents and move the cots inside, basically settling the lodging issue.

Before they started making lunch, Xiaomeng suggested that they ought to take an inventory of all food and water and come up with a detailed plan for its daily use: conserve on food the first two days, since once land clearing began, their workload would increase and they would need to eat more. And they had to keep in mind that if agriculture ran into problems, there would be delays in getting food from the directorate. The children had worked up a considerable appetite over the course of the morning and were quite upset that they couldn't dig in immediately, but Xiaomeng patiently explained the situation to them as best she could.

Zhang Lin stood quietly off to the side watching all of this, making more notes in his notebook.

After lunch, the children visited their neighbors to barter a few excess tents and tools to bolster their limited food supply, and took stock of their surroundings. Upstream from them was the Galactic Republic, downstream was Giant Country. Opposite them was Emailand, bordered upstream by Caterpillaria, and downstream by Blue Flower Land, both taking their names from local flora and fauna. There were eighteen other microcountries in the valley, but they were far enough away that the children weren't much interested in them.

The next day and two nights were the golden age for this valley world. The children overflowed with enthusiasm for the new life. On day two, all countries began clearing land on the hillside with simple tools—shovels and hoes—and carried water from the river in plastic buckets to irrigate the land. At night, campfires sprang up all along the riverbank, and the valley echoed with the children's songs and laughter. It was a veritable pastoral wonderland out of a fairy tale.

But the fairy tale soon evaporated as gray reality returned to the valley.

As the novelty wore off, the pace of land-clearing declined. Children returned from work utterly exhausted and collapsed into their cots as soon as they were back in their tents. No longer were there nighttime fires and singing in the valley. Silence reigned.

The resource gap between the countries was becoming apparent. Though they weren't far apart, some countries had rich, soft land that was easy to cultivate, while in others, the rocky ground refused to give up much usable land even after strenuous effort. Sunland was among the most barren, but even worse than the extremely poor quality of the hillside soil was the fact that their riverbank was incredibly broad. The directorate had stipulated that the level floodplain could only be used as residential land, and all cultivation had to be done on the hillside. Any cultivation on the floodplain would be excluded from the count. In some countries, the hillside was so close to the river that a chain of children could pass water buckets up for irrigation, a great labor-saving strategy. But Sunland's wide floodplain meant a huge distance between the river and the hillside, so individuals had to tire themselves out carrying buckets up on their own.

Then Specs made a proposal: Dam the river with large stones. The water could still flow over or between the stones, but the water level would be raised. Then a pit could be dug at the base of the hillside, and a small channel cut to bring in river water. So Sunland transferred ten hard workers to undertake the project. No sooner had it started, however, than it met with fierce protests from Giantland and Blue Flower Land downstream, and despite Specs's repeated explanations that the dam would raise the river level without blocking its flow, thus posing no threat to the downstream flow rate or water level, the two countries were staunch in their opposition. Huahua maintained that they should ignore the protests and proceed with the project. But Xiaomeng, after careful consideration, decided that they ought to work on improving relations with their neighbors, taking the long view so as not to lose out on bigger things for short-term gains. The river was a shared resource for all countries in the valley, so anything involving it was a sensitive matter. Sunland ought to work on establishing a favorable reputation.

Specs approached the issue from a strength standpoint, and although Lü Gang insisted that the army could guarantee national security in the case of a conflict with their downstream neighbors, he noted that it was irrational to recklessly provoke conflict with two countries at once. And so Sunland abandoned its original plan. Without building a dam, a channel twice as deep was dug, bringing far less water to the pit at the foot of the hill than originally intended. But it substantially increased the efficiency of cultivation nonetheless.

Sunland seemed to have caught the directorate's eye; another observer was now stationed next to Zhang Lin.

All manner of conflicts and disputes increased dramatically in the valley on the fourth day, mostly sparked by resource allocation and bartering. The children had little facility or patience for conflict resolution, and so shots began to ring out. Still, the conflicts remained limited in scale and had not spread to the entire valley. The situation remained relatively stable in Sunland's vicinity, but a conflict sparked by drinking water on the seventh day would completely upset this stability.

River water was stale and undrinkable, and although a quantity of drinking water had been included among the provisions, it was unevenly distributed, leaving some countries with ten or more times as much water as others, a difference far greater than any of the other provisions and clearly done by design. Cultivation figures could only be redeemed for food, not water, so by the fifth day, water had become a critical question for national survival, and hence a focal point for conflict.

Among the five countries in Sunland's region, the Galactic Republic had the largest share of water, nearly ten times the others. Caterpillaria, across the river, was the first to run out. Its children were wasteful and shortsighted, and even used drinking water to wash up when they were too lazy to fetch water from the river, eventually landing themselves in this predicament. Their only option was to hold talks with their opposite neighbor and propose bartering for water, but the Galactic Republic countered with an unacceptable solution: Caterpillaria had to trade its land for water.

That night, Sunland was informed by a child from Emailand that Caterpillaria had demanded a loan of guns, ten of them, as well as ammunition, threatening to attack if the loan was denied. Caterpillaria reckoned that with thirty-seven soldiers, its military was strong enough to take on Emailand, which had few military-minded children and wouldn't put up much of a fight. Not wanting trouble, Emailand reached a favorable agreement with Caterpillaria and lent them the weapons. Shots rang out at midday in Caterpillaria as its soldiers practiced shooting.

Sunland called an emergency State Council meeting where Huahua laid out the situation: "Caterpillaria is certain to start a war against the Galactic Republic. Looking at military power alone, the Galactic Republic is bound to lose, and will be taken over by Caterpillaria. Caterpillaria has a large expanse of fertile hillside, and it will be especially powerful with the Galactic Republic's drinking water and weapons. That means trouble for us, sooner or later. We should prepare for sooner."

Xiaomeng said, "We should form an alliance with Emailand, Giant Country, and Blue Flower Land."

Huahua said, "If that's our approach, then we should include the Galactic Republic in the alliance before war breaks out. That way Caterpillaria won't risk starting a war."

Specs shook his head. "Balance of power is a basic principle of the world order. You're violating that principle."

"Would you mind explaining that, professor?"

"An alliance is only stable when facing a threat comparable in strength. It will dissolve when faced with a threat that's too big or too small. The countries farther upstream are too far away, so the six of us form a relatively independent system. If the Galactic Republic joins the alliance, Caterpillaria has no one to ally with and is the absolute weakest power, posing no threat to the alliance. So the alliance will dissolve. Besides, the Galactic Republic has so much drinking water of its own it will arrogantly believe we're after its water, and won't join an alliance in earnest."

Everyone agreed with this assessment. Xiaomeng asked, "So will the other three countries be willing to ally with us?"

Huahua said, "Emailand's not a problem. They've already felt Caterpillaria's threat. As for the other two, let me persuade them. An alliance is to their benefit, and we left a good impression after the dam conflict, so I think it won't be a problem."

That afternoon, Huahua visited three neighboring countries where, with superlative eloquence, he quickly convinced the leadership. On the riverside at their common border, they held a meeting formally establishing the Four Country Alliance.

Another member joined the observers stationed in Sunland.

The directorate established itself inside a TV repeater station at the top of the hill, where it had a bird's-eye view of the entire valley. That evening, after the founding of the Four Country Alliance, Zheng Chen arrived at the repeater compound and looked out at the nighttime valley for a long while, as she had done on previous evenings. The children were asleep after an exhausting day of work, so a few scattered lanterns were all that was visible.

By this point she had thrown herself fully into the project and no longer asked what it all was for. Not a single one of the countless answers she had dreamed up made sense, and the previous day she had heard a few kids in Sunland discussing the issue, too.

"It's a science experiment," Specs said to a few other children. "Our twenty-four little countries are a model of the world, and the adults want to see how this model develops. Then they'll know what our country should do in the future."

"Then why don't they run the experiment with adults?" someone asked.

"If the adults know it's a game, they won't play it

seriously. We're the only ones who'll play a game seriously, and that's what makes the outcome real."

It was the most reasonable explanation Zheng Chen had heard. But the premier's words still echoed in her brain: "The world isn't what it used to be."

Now Zhang Lin walked out of the door to the cabin that once had served as the lodgings for repeater station workers and came over next to Zheng Chen to survey the valley. He said, "Ms. Zheng, your class has been the most successful of all of them. Those children are made of good stuff."

"What do you mean by success? As I hear it, at the western end of the valley there's a country that has absorbed its five neighbors and now has six times its original land area and population, and it's still expanding."

"No, Ms. Zheng. That's not important to us. What we're looking at is a country's success in building itself, in cohesion, and in its judgment of the makeup of the world it inhabits, as well as the long-term decisions those lead to."

The game in the valley allowed free exit, and over the past couple of days children from practically every country had come to the directorate to say they were finished playing, that the game was getting boring, that the work was too tiring, and that the gun fighting was too scary. The directors said the same thing to each of them: "That's okay. Go home." And they were returned home at once. When they later found out what they had missed, some of them stayed angry the rest of their lives, while others were secretly glad. Sunland was the only country that didn't lose any children, a key data point for the directors.

Zhang Lin said, "Ms. Zheng, I'd like to learn more about those three young leaders."

CIXIN LIU

Zheng Chen said, "They're from ordinary families. But if you look more closely, their families really are a little different."

"Start with Huahua."

"His father is an engineer with an architecture institute, and his mother's a dance instructor. He takes after his father, who also comes across as open-minded, taking the long view toward things with little regard for the details of his own life. When I went to their home, he held forth on global affairs and the strategy China ought to adopt in the future, but didn't ask any questions about his son's performance at school."

"He's aloof."

"No, not aloof. He wasn't discussing those things for disinterested amusement. He talked about national and world affairs with a powerful sense of participation. He had a strong initiative, and that excessive broad-mindedness and disregard for his immediate surroundings might be why he's been unsuccessful in his career. Huahua does take after him, but one major difference is that the kid has charisma and an inclination to action, enough to bring together other children to accomplish unbelievable things. For example, he's gotten the class to set up a street stall, to build and fly a hot-air balloon, and to take a boating trip on a river in the distant suburbs. He's got motivation and resourcefulness far beyond his years. His weakness is a tendency toward fantasy and impulsiveness."

"You know your students very well."

"They think of me as a friend. Yan Jing—that's Specs—comes from a typical family of intellectuals. His parents are college professors, his father in the humanities and his mother in science."

38

"He seems to me to be very knowledgeable."

"That's right. But his greatest strength is how thoroughly he considers a problem, far more carefully than other children. He can pick up things from all angles that no one else notices. You might not believe it, but when I'm preparing my lessons I'll often seek his feedback. His weakness is obvious: He's introverted and isn't good at social interaction."

"The other students in your class don't seem to mind that."

"True. His erudition appeals to them and wins him their respect. Specs is always involved in discussions of major problems, and in any decision-making. That's why they elected him."

"And Xiaomeng?"

"Her background is unusual. Her family was a good one: her father was a reporter, and her mother a professional writer. When she was in the second grade, her father died in a car accident pursuing a story, and then her mother had kidney failure and needed dialysis. And she had a grandparent in bed at home. Both of them died last year, but for the past three years Xiaomeng basically has had to run the household. Still, she managed to get the best marks in class. She was right in the worst of it when I came on as homeroom teacher, and each morning when I came into class I'd look for signs of fatigue on her face, but there never were. Just . . ."

"Maturity."

"Right. Maturity. You've seen her expression, mature beyond her years. One thing I remember most clearly was when I took the class on a tour of the Aerospace Command and Control Center in western Beijing last semester. The other kids immersed themselves in all the high-tech marvels, and during a forum with the center's engineers, they all said that we should put an astronaut in space, and then build a huge space station, and land on the moon, all at once. Xiaomeng was the only one who asked how much a space station would cost, and when she was given a rough estimate, said that the money could fund the education of every poor child in the country through middle school. Then she rattled off statistics for unschooled children, and how much it would cost to educate them through middle school, taking into account regional differences and price increases. All of the adults in the forum were stunned."

"Is there anything about her that makes her popular with the others?"

"Trustworthiness. She is the most trusted kid in class. She can sort out tons of problems the kids have, even complicated ones that have me stumped. She's got management talent. She's very methodical in carrying out her duties as the class's studies monitor."

"There's one more student I'd like to know a little more about: Lü Gang."

"I don't know him very well. He's a transfer from the second half of last semester. He comes from an unusual family, too. His father's a general. And under his father's influence, he likes weapons and the military. The one thing that impressed me most about him is that when he joined the sports committee after transferring to our class, in just one week he took our soccer squad from second-to-last to first. School rules prohibit adding extracurricular practices, but he didn't run any practices at all, he just made some adjustments to our strategy. The surprising thing is that his previous school lacked the facilities for him to have much exposure to soccer at all, and he doesn't really play. His indomitable spirit is another impressive characteristic. During a cross-country race, he twisted his ankle and his foot swelled up so big he couldn't put his shoe on, but he finished the race anyway, even though there was no one left at the finish line when he came in. You don't see that kind of resolve in many children."

"One last question, Ms. Zheng. . . . Ah, you go first."

"What I'd like to say is that if you think their little country is the most successful, then it's due to collective effort. There may be a few standout kids in the class, but their biggest advantage is their collective strength. They might not amount to anything if you divide them up."

"That's just the question I wanted to ask. I've gotten the same feeling, and it's a very important point. My greatest regret, Ms. Zheng, is that my son was never your student."

"How old is he?"

"Twelve. One of the lucky ones."

It was several days later that she found out what his words meant. The Rose Nebula was now rising over the eastern horizon, its blue light rendering the valley in sharp relief.

"It's gotten bigger. And the floral shape has changed," she said.

"It'll continue to grow for the next few decades. Astronomers predict that at its largest it will occupy a fifth of the sky, and will be as bright as an overcast day. Night will disappear."

"My god. What will that be like?"

"I'd really like to know, too. Take a look at this," Zhang Lin said, pointing to a nearby scholar tree whose flower-laden branches were visible in the nebula light.

"It shouldn't be blooming this time of year. The past few days I've seen a lot of weird stuff with the hillside vegetation. Lots of blooming flowers, in all sorts of strange shapes."

41

"We're sequestered from the outside world here so we haven't seen the news for a few days, but I've heard that bizarre fruits and vegetables have been turning up in the marketplace, like grapes as big as apples."

From the valley came a burst of gunfire.

"It's from Sunland!" Zheng Chen shouted in alarm.

"No," Zhang Lin said after a moment, "it's farther upstream. Caterpillaria is attacking the Galactic Republic."

The gunshots grew thicker, and they could see muzzle flashes in an area of the valley.

"Do you really intend to let things go on like this? I don't think I can take it," Zheng Chen said in a trembling voice.

"The entirety of human history is war. There are figures showing that in five thousand years of civilization, there's been a total of just one hundred and seven years of genuine peacetime. Even as we speak humanity is at war. But doesn't life still go on?"

"But they're only children!"

"Not for long."

That afternoon, Caterpillaria agreed to the Galactic Republic's demand to exchange the best parcel of its untilled land for drinking water, but proposed holding a land-handover ceremony to which each side would dispatch an honor guard of twenty children. The Galactic Republic agreed. As leaders for both sides and their honor guards were carrying out the ceremony, a dozen Caterpillaria soldiers lying in ambush staged a surprise attack on the Galactic Republic honor guard, and at the same time the Caterpillaria honor guard also opened fire, taking out all twenty guard members with their electric charges. They came to ten minutes later and discovered they were prisoners and their territory had fallen into enemy hands, for while they were unconscious, the Caterpillaria army had assaulted the Galactic Republic. Their guns had all been sent off with the honor guard, and their remaining six boys and twenty-odd girls were ill-equipped for even an unarmed fight.

As soon as Caterpillaria merged with the Galactic Republic, it demanded land from the Four Country Alliance. Unprepared to launch a military attack, it played the water card. The downstream countries didn't have much left, and Caterpillaria planned to squeeze the Four Country Alliance until they ran out of water.

Now Specs's vast store of knowledge found an application in a method he proposed. Tiny holes were punctured all across the bottom of five washbasins, which were then filled with layers of stones, decreasing in diameter top to bottom, to form a water filter. Lü Gang suggested a second method: Smashing grasses and leaves into a paste and stirring it into the water would leave the water clean once it settled. He said he'd learned the technique from his father during outdoor training. Water subjected to these two methods was sent to the directorate for testing, and it turned out to be drinkable. The Four Country Alliance now had access to so much water it could even export its surplus to Caterpillaria.

And so Caterpillaria started planning an attack on the alliance. Its children had no interest in agriculture and cared only for territorial expansion. But they soon discovered there was no need for this, either.

From upstream came the news that the Nebula Empire, at the westernmost edge of the valley, had absorbed thirteen other countries to form a superstate with an army four hundred strong that was now marching downstream on a mission to unite the valley. In the face of such a powerful enemy, the resolve Caterpillaria's leaders had shown toward the conquest of the Galactic Republic evaporated. They panicked, and without a plan their country collapsed into chaos and ultimately disbanded. Some of the children fled upstream to the Nebula Empire, but most went to the directorate to be sent home. In the Four Country Alliance, Giant Land, Blue Flower Land, and Emailand dissolved, and most of their children also exited the game apart from a minority that joined their ally, leaving Sunland to face a powerful enemy alone.

All citizens of Sunland were determined to defend it to the end. Over the past two weeks they had grown fond of the tiny country into which they'd poured their sweat, and this emotion gave them spiritual strength that amazed the adults in the directorate.

Lü Gang drew up a battle plan: Sunland's children would knock down all the tents on the broad floodplain and put in two defensive lines on the eastern and western sides, formed from various materials. On the western side, the first front the enemy troops would reach, only ten children would be stationed. Lü Gang instructed them, "When you've finished the first volley, shout 'We're out of ammo!' and then run back."

The defensive lines had just been completed when the army of the Nebula Empire came surging along the valley floor, and soon it covered the entire territory of the former Galactic Republic and Caterpillaria. A boy shouted through a loudspeaker, "Hey, Sunland kids! The Nebula Empire has united the valley. Do you losers still want to play? Surrender! Have some dignity!"

The challenge was met with silence. And so the Nebula Empire began its assault. The children on Sunland's front defense line opened fire, and the invading army hit the ground immediately and returned fire. Shots from Sunland's side petered out, and then a kid shouted, "We're out of ammo! Run!," and all the kids on the line beat a fast retreat.

"They're out of ammo! Charge!" The Nebula Empire army surged forward with a roar, but when they were halfway across the floodplain, the guns of Sunland's second defensive line let loose. The invaders were caught totally unaware and huge numbers fell. Those behind them turned and ran. The first assault was beaten back.

When the shocks wore off and the kids crawled to their feet, the Nebula Empire organized a second attack. This time, Sunland was actually running low on ammo. As they watched an imperial force ten times their size advance carefully along the river toward them, a kid exclaimed, "God, they've even got helicopters!"

A helicopter was approaching over the hill, and when it stopped and hovered over the battlefield, an adult's voice over a loudspeaker said, "Children! Hold your fire! The game is over!"

The State

It had just turned dark when three helicopters carrying fifty-four children took flight toward the city. Eight of the children on board, including Huahua, Specs, Xiaomeng, and Lü Gang, were from Zheng Chen's class, and they were accompanied by Zheng Chen and four other teachers.

They landed in front of a plain 1950s-style building whose lights were blazing. Zhang Lin and the leader of the valley-game directorate led the fifty-four children through the main gate and down a long corridor, at the end of which stood a large leather-covered door with a gleaming brass handle. When the children neared, two guards eased it open and they entered a huge hall, one that had witnessed so many historic events whose shadows even now seemed to dance between the columns.

There were three people in the hall: the president of the country, premier of the State Council, and chief of staff of the army. They seemed to have been there a while, and were talking in low voices when the door opened and they turned to look at the children.

The two leaders went on ahead to make a brief, whispered report to the president and premier.

"Hello, children!" the president said. "This is the last time I'll treat you as children. History requires that you grow from thirteen to thirty over the next ten minutes. The premier will outline the situation for you now."

The premier said, "As you're all aware, a month ago there was a supernova in the vicinity of Earth. You're all familiar with the details so I won't go into them. Instead, I'll tell you some things you don't know. After the supernova, health agencies the world over studied its effects on humans. We've received reports from authoritative medical institutions on all continents that match the conclusions of our own domestic institutions: namely, the supernova's high-energy radiation destroys chromosomes in human cells.

This radiation has a penetrative power never seen before. No one was unaffected, even if they were indoors or down a mine shaft. But in one population group, chromosomes have the ability to repair themselves when damaged, ninety-seven percent in thirteen-year-olds, and one hundred percent in those aged twelve and under. Damage suffered by everyone else is irreversible. They'll survive only for another ten months to a year at most. Visible light from the supernova lasted for a little over an hour, but the invisible radiation continued for an entire week—that's when the sky was filled with aurora borealis. The Earth completed seven revolutions during that time, so the whole world was affected identically."

The premier spoke with a calm solemnity, as if discussing something more ordinary. The children listened numbly for a while as his words sank into their minds. For a long time it didn't make sense, and then all of a sudden it did.

Decades later, when the second generation of the Supernova Era was growing up, they were curious about how their parents' generation felt when they first heard the news, since after all it was the most shocking piece of information in human history. Historians and astronomers had made countless attempts to re-create that scene, none of them accurate. The following conversation between a young reporter and an elder took place forty-five years after the incident:

REPORTER: Can you describe how you felt when you first heard the news?

ELDER: I didn't feel anything, because I still didn't understand.

REPORTER: How long did it take for you to understand?

ELDER: It depended on the person. No one got it immediately. Some people took half a minute, others several minutes, and others a few days. Some kids stayed in a trance all the way up until the Supernova Era actually began. It's weird thinking back on it. Why was such a simple piece of information so hard to digest?

REPORTER: And yourself?

ELDER: I was lucky. I got it in three minutes.

REPORTER: Can you describe the shock?

ELDER: It wasn't a shock.

REPORTER: Then . . . was it fear?

ELDER: No, not fear.

REPORTER: *(laughs)* That's what they all say. I do understand, of course, how it might be hard to put that degree of fear and shock into words.

ELDER: There were no feelings like shock and fear back then. Please believe me, even if it might be hard for you to understand now.

REPORTER: Then what did you feel?

ELDER: Unfamiliarity.

REPORTER: . . .

ELDER: Back in our day, we had this story: A man blind from birth accidentally fell down the stairs one day, and the impact somehow jostled the nerves in his brain enough to restore his sight. He looked at the world around him brimming with curiosity. . . . That's how we felt. The world was going to turn strange for us, as if we'd never seen it before.

From Ya Ke, *Born in the Common Era*.
Beijing, SE 46.

In the huge hall, the beating heart of the country, fifty-four children shared the experience of this powerful unfamiliarity, as if an invisible razor had dropped, severing the past from the future, and they were staring into a strange new world. Through the wide window they could see the newly risen Rose Nebula, which projected its blue radiance on the floor like an enormous cosmic eye staring into this inexplicable world.

For an entire week high-energy rays had traversed every part of the solar system, and high-energy particles battered the Earth like a rainstorm pouring down on land and sea, tearing through human bodies at unimaginably high velocity, penetrating every cell. And the tiny chromosomes in each of those cells were buffeted like fragile crystalline threads by those high-energy particles, which unraveled the DNA double helix and sent nucleotides spinning away. Damaged genes continued to operate, but the precise chain that had evolved through hundreds of millions of years of copying life had been snapped, and the mutated genes now spread death. Earth revolved humanity through a deadly shower, winding up the death clock in billions of bodies that now ticked slowly away. . . .

Everyone above the age of thirteen would die, and Earth would become a children's world.

The fifty-four children were different from the rest. A second piece of information would take the world that had just been made unfamiliar and shatter it into pieces, leaving them hanging in a bewildered void.

Zheng Chen came round first. "These children, Premier, if I'm not mistaken . . ."

The premier nodded, and said calmly, "You're not mistaken."

"That's impossible," she cried out in alarm.

The state leaders looked at her in silence.

"They're just kids. How can they . . ."

"What do you think we ought to do, young lady?" the premier asked.

". . . You at least ought to have held a nationwide search for candidates."

"Do you really think that's possible? How would we select them? Kids aren't adults. They don't belong to a hierarchical national social structure, so in such a short time frame it's frankly impossible to choose the most talented and best suited from among four hundred million children to take on this responsibility. Ten months is just an estimate; we might actually have far less time than that. The adult world could become inoperative at any moment. This is humanity's darkest hour. We must not leave our country headless at a time like this. Did we have any other choice? Like every other country in the world, we adopted exceptional methods to make the selection."

"My god. . . ." She was close to fainting.

The president came up to her and said, "Your students may not agree with you. You only know them in ordinary times, but not in extreme situations. In times of crisis, people, children included, can become superhuman."

The president turned to address the children, who had not yet entirely grasped the situation. "Yes, children. You're going to lead this country."

3

The Great Learning

The World Classroom

On the day the Great Learning started, Zheng Chen left the school to check in on her students. Out of her class of forty-three, eight had qualified in the valley for the central government; the remainder, distributed throughout the city, were now embarking on the toughest curriculum in history under their parents' tutelage.

Yao Rui was the first student Zheng Chen thought of. Out of her thirty-five remaining students, he had the toughest course of study. She took a quick subway trip to the thermal power station, shut down on environmental grounds prior to the supernova but now saved from dismantling and returned to operation as a classroom.

She saw her student outside the gate. He was with his father, the station's chief engineer. Chief Yao greeted her, and she replied out of a jumble of feelings, "It's like you're me teaching my first class six years ago."

Chief Yao smiled and nodded. "Ms. Zheng, I'm probably even less confident than you were."

"Back in parent-teacher conferences, you never were pleased with my teaching methods. Today we're going to see how you go about it."

They went through the gate alongside a host of other groups of parents and children.

"What a tall, thick smokestack!" Yao Rui shouted, pointing excitedly ahead of them.

"Silly boy. I've told you before, that's not a smokestack. It's a cooling tower. Over there, behind the plant, is a smokestack."

Chief Yao led his son and Zheng Chen up into the cooling tower, where water rained down into a circular pool. Pointing at it, Chief Yao said, "That's the cooled water that circulates in the generator. It's pretty warm. When I first came to the plant fifteen years ago, I used to swim in it." He sighed at the memory of his youth.

Then they came to several small mountains of black coal. "This is the coal yard. A thermal power plant produces electricity by burning coal. At full capacity, our plant will consume twelve thousand tons per day. I bet you have no idea how much that is. See that coal train with forty railcars? You'd need about six of those trains full of coal."

Yao Rui stuck out his tongue. He said, "That's scary, Ms. Zheng. I never used to think that Dad's job could be so awesome."

Chief Yao let out a long sigh. "Kiddo, this is all a dream for your dad, too."

They followed the long coal belt for a while until they reached a huge machine dominated by a large, rotating drum whose thunderous rumble set Yao Rui's and Zheng Chen's skin crawling. Chief Yao shouted, close beside their ears, "That's the pulverizer. The belt brings coal here where it's milled to a powder as fine as flour."

Then they came to the base of another tall steel building. There were four of them, all visible from a distance, just like the cooling towers and smokestacks. Chief Yao said, "This is the furnace. The coal dust milled by the pulverizer is sprayed by four nozzles into its belly where it burns in a fireball. The coal gets almost completely burned up; only a tiny amount is left behind. Look, here's what's left." He extended a palm and showed his son a smattering of objects that looked like translucent glass beads, which he had scooped up from a square pond along their path. Then they came to a small window through which they could see the blazing furnace fire. "The wall of this giant boiler is lined with an enormous number of long pipes. Water flowing through the pipes absorbs the fire's heat and turns to high-pressure steam."

Then they entered a cavernous building holding four huge machines, half cylinders lying on the ground. "These are the turbine generator assemblies. Steam from the boiler is piped here to turn the turbines, which drive the generators to produce electricity."

Finally they reached the main control room. It was clean and well-lit, with signal lights twinkling like stars on a tall instrument panel and a row of computer screens displaying complex images. In addition to the duty operator, a number of other parent-child pairs were in the room. Chief Yao said to his son, "We had only a drive-by look just now. A power plant is actually a highly sophisticated system that involves a host of separate disciplines, and requires the work of lots of people to operate. Dad's field is electrics. Electrics is divided into high and low voltage; I work in high voltage." He paused and looked quietly at his son for several seconds. "It's a dangerous field, involving currents that can fry a person in a tenth of a second. To keep that from happening, you've got to fully understand the structure and principles of the entire system. That begins now."

Chief Yao took out a roll of charts and peeled off one. "Let's start with the main wiring diagram. It's fairly simple."

"I don't think it's simple at all," Yao Rui said, staring in obvious disbelief at all of the lines and symbols crisscrossing on the chart.

"Those are generators," his father said, pointing at a diagram made up of four circles. "Do you know the principles of an electric generator?" Yao Rui shook his head. "Well, this is the bus bar. The generated electricity is sent out here. It's three-phase, you see. Do you know what three-phase is?" Yao Rui shook his head again, and his father pointed to four pairs of concentric circles. "Okay. These are the four MTs."

"MTs?" Yao Rui asked.

"Er, the main transformers. And these two are the auxes."

"Auxes?"

"Auxiliary transformers. . . . You know the principles of transformers?"

Yao Rui shook his head.

"What about the basics? The principle of electromagnetic induction?"

Another head shake.

"You've got to know Ohm's law, at least?"

Another head shake. Chief Yao let the charts drop. "Then what the hell *do* you know? Did you eat your lessons?"

His son started to cry. "I've never studied any of this."

Chief Yao turned to Zheng Chen. "Then what have you been teaching him for six years?"

"Your son's just out of middle school, remember. He's not going to learn anything with teaching methods like yours!"

"I've got ten months to take this kid through a complete course of study in electrics, and to hand over my own twenty years' work experience." He sighed and tossed the charts aside. "It seems like an impossible task, Ms. Zheng."

"But you've got to do it, Chief Yao."

He stared at her for a long while, and at last sighed, picked up the charts, and turned to his son. "Okay, okay. So you know about electric current and electric potential, right?" Yao Rui nodded. "Then what are the units for current?"

"It's a certain number of volts."

"Oh for the love of—"

"No! Right, that's the unit for potential. For current, it's . . . it's . . ."

"Amps! Very well, we'll start from there, my boy."

Just then Zheng Chen's mobile rang. It was the mother of another student, Lin Sha. The two families were neighbors, so she knew them quite well. Lin Sha's mother told her that she was having trouble teaching her daughter, and asked Zheng Chen to give her a hand. And so after bidding a hasty farewell to Yao Rui and his father, she hurried back into the city.

At the major hospital where Lin Sha's mother worked, the two of them were heatedly discussing something outside a room with a large red sign over the door reading AUTOPSY.

"I can't stand that smell," Lin Sha said, screwing up her eyebrows.

"It's formalin, a kind of preservative. For soaking the bodies used in dissection."

"I'm not going to watch a body get dissected, Mom. I've seen so many livers and lungs and stuff already."

"But you've got to learn where the organs are situated in the body."

"When I'm a doctor, can't I just give the patients whatever medicine they're supposed to get for whatever illness they have?"

"You're a surgeon, Shasha. You've got to perform surgery."

"Let the boys be surgeons."

"Cut that out. Your mom's a surgeon. There are lots of excellent women surgeons."

Now clear about the situation, Zheng Chen said she would go into the room with Lin Sha, who then grudgingly agreed to the autopsy lesson. The girl's hand, tightly clasping hers, trembled noticeably as they walked through the door, and Zheng Chen wasn't doing much better herself, although she fought to keep her fear from showing. She felt a chill wind across her face. The walls and floors were white, and the fluorescent lights overhead cast a pale glow on the autopsy table ringed by a group of children and two adults all dressed in white lab coats; the only bit of color in this world of gloomy white was the dark red object on the table.

Lin Sha's mother led her daughter by the hand to the autopsy table, and pointing at the object, said, "For the convenience of our autopsy, the body needs to be pretreated by removing a layer of skin."

Lin Sha tore out of the autopsy room and began to retch,

Zheng Chen close on her heels. She clapped her on the back, keeping a lid on her own nausea, but grateful for the excuse to leave the room and for the sunlight outside.

Lin Sha's mother followed them, and bent down to tell her daughter, "Stop it, Shasha. Observing an autopsy is a valuable opportunity for an intern. You'll get used to it over time. Think of the body as a stopped machine, where you can look at its parts. You'll feel better that way."

"You're a machine too, Mom! A machine I hate!" she shouted, and turned to run off. But Zheng Chen held her back.

"Listen to me, Lin Sha. All jobs, not just being a doctor, require bravery. Some might be even tougher. You've got to grow up."

It took some doing but eventually they convinced Lin Sha to return to the autopsy. Zheng Chen stood with her and they watched the sharp lancet separate soft tissue with a low scratching sound, and white ribs pushed aside to expose mulberry organs. . . . Afterward, she wondered what it was that had supported her through it, not to mention what had supported the girl who used to be afraid of bugs.

Zheng Chen spent all of the next day with Li Zhiping, a boy whose father was a letter carrier. Over and over, father and son traced the route he had walked for more than a decade, and then as evening fell, the boy walked it by himself for the first time. Before setting out, Li Zhiping tried to attach the huge mailbag onto his beloved mountain bike, but it didn't fit, and so he had to return it to his father's trusty old Flying Pigeon and drop the saddle to its lowest position before riding it out into the lanes and alleys of the city. Though the boy had committed all the roads and delivery points to memory, his father was still uneasy, and so he and Zheng Chen biked after him at a distance. When the boy reached the final stop on the road, the gate to a government building, his father caught up with him and clapped him on the shoulder.

"That's good, son. It's not that tough. I've done it for more than ten years, and I was set to do it my entire life. Now it's in your hands. Dad's got just one thing to tell you: I've never misdelivered a single letter the whole time. It might not be a big deal for other people, but it's something I'm secretly proud of. Remember, son, no matter how ordinary the job, you'll do well if you put your heart into it."

The third day Zheng Chen visited three students, Chang Huidong, Zhang Xiaole, and Wang Ran. Like Li Zhiping, the first two were from ordinary families, but Wang Ran's father was a well-known go player.

Chang Huidong's parents ran their own barbershop. When Zheng Chen arrived, he was giving his third haircut of the day. It was even worse than the first two, but the customer merely laughed at the patchy result he saw in the mirror and said it was fine. Chang Huidong's father apologized and refused payment, but the customer insisted. The fourth customer demanded a haircut from the boy, too, and when Chang Huidong draped a sheet over him, he said, "Practice your heart out on me, kiddo. I only have a few haircuts left, but you young people need barbers. They can't all turn into long-haired wild children."

Zheng Chen let him cut her hair, too, turning it into a

tangled mess that his mother had to trim into a short cut that ended up looking not bad at all. When she left the shop, she felt much younger. It was a feeling she'd had since the supernova. On the brink of a strange new world, people reacted in two opposite ways: they grew younger or got older, and she fortunately fell into the former camp.

Zhang Xiaole's father was a cook at a work unit cafeteria. When Zheng Chen saw her student, he and his companions were, under the adults' direction, almost finished preparing rice and a large cauldron of food. For a few nervous minutes, several children stood shaking in front of the canteen window watching their efforts sell out bit by bit to a main dining hall packed with people, but it looked like nothing was amiss. Then Zhang Xiaole's father rapped a ladle against the window frame and announced, "Listen up. Today's meal was prepared by our children."

After a few seconds of silence, the hall erupted into applause.

But it was Wang Ran and his father who most impressed Zheng Chen. The boy was about to head off to driving class when she got to their house, and his father walked with him a fair distance to see him off. He said to Zheng Chen with a sigh, "I'm useless. At my age, I can't even teach my son any actual skill."

Wang Ran reassured his father that he would learn how to drive and then become a good chauffeur.

His father handed him a small bag. "Carry this with you.

Read and practice when you've got spare time. Just don't throw it away, since it'll come in useful some day."

He didn't open the bag until he and Zheng Chen had walked for a while. It held a container of go pieces and a few manuals. He looked back at his father, the ninth-dan go master, still there watching after him.

As it did for many children, a dramatic change lay in the future for Wang Ran. When Zheng Chen visited him again a month later, his plan to become a chauffeur had somehow landed him in a bulldozer, where he proved a quick study. She found him at a large building site in the inner suburbs, where he was working on his own in the huge machine. He was visibly pleased to see his teacher, and invited her into the cabin to watch him work. As he piloted the bulldozer back and forth to flatten the ground, she noticed two men watching them closely from not far off. To her surprise, they were soldiers. Three bulldozers were at work, all driven by children, but the two soldiers paid particular attention to Wang Ran's, and occasionally pointed in his direction. At last they waved for him to stop, and a lieutenant colonel looked up at the cabin and called to him, "You're not a bad driver, kid. Want to come with us and drive something even more fun?"

"A bigger bulldozer?" he asked, poking his head out of the cabin.

"No. A tank."

Wang Ran was silent for a few seconds before throwing open the door and bounding to the ground.

"Here's the thing," the lieutenant colonel said. "Our branch has, for various reasons, only just now considered bringing children in to take over. Time is tight, and we're looking for people with some driving fundamentals so we can get started quicker."

"Is driving a tank like driving a bulldozer?"

"In some ways. They're both caterpillar-track vehicles."

"But a tank is harder to drive, right?"

"Not necessarily. For one thing, a tank doesn't have that big blade, so you don't have to worry about frontward force when you're driving."

And just like that, Wang Ran the son of a ninth-dan go master became a tank driver in an armored division.

On the fourth day, Zheng Chen visited Feng Jing and Yao Pingping, who had been assigned to work in a nursery. In the upcoming children's world, the family unit would vanish and the nursery would be a key institution for a fairly long period. Lots of children would spend their remaining childhood years there bringing up infants even younger than themselves.

When Zheng Chen found her students, their mothers were instructing them in baby care, but like all the rest of the older children in the nursery, they were helpless in the face of wailing babies.

"I can't stand it!" Yao Pingping said as she stared at the baby crying incessantly on the bed.

"You need to be patient," her mother said. "Babies can't use words. Crying is how they talk, so you have to figure out what they mean."

"Then what's he saying now? I've given him milk, but he won't eat."

"He wants to sleep."

"He should just go to sleep, then! What's he crying for? He's so annoying."

"Most children are like that. You've got to pick him up and walk with him, and he'll stop crying."

And that's all it took.

Pingping asked her mom, "Was I like that when I was little?"

Her mother laughed. "You were hardly that compliant. You'd usually fuss for an hour before you fell asleep."

"What a chore it must have been, bringing me up."

"You'll have it even harder," her mother said sadly. "Babies in day care all have parents, but in the future it'll be up to you all to raise them."

Zheng Chen kept silent during her time at the nursery, to the point that Feng Jing and Yao Pingping asked her if she was feeling well. Her thoughts were on her own unborn child.

The nations of the world had all banned further procreation in what for many of them was their final legislation of the Common Era. But laws and ordinances were ineffective; half of pregnant women, Zheng Chen among them, chose to carry their babies to term.

On the fifth day she returned to school, where lower grades were still attending classes taught by upperclassmen training to become teachers. She entered her classroom and found Su Lin and her mother, also a teacher at the school, working on teacher training.

"These kids are idiots. I've told them over and over but they still don't get how to add and subtract two-digit numbers!" Su Lin angrily pushed aside a stack of workbooks.

Her mother said, "Every student understands things at a different pace." She flipped through the papers. "See, this one doesn't know how to carry. And this one, no concept of places. You've got to address them independently. Take a look at this one. . . ." She handed Su Lin a workbook.

"Idiots! Plain idiots. They don't even know simple arithmetic." She glanced at the workbook but tossed it aside. Shakily scrawled numbers formed lines of two-digit addition and subtraction problems, all of them making the same stupid mistakes she had grown tired of over the past two days.

"It's your own workbook from five years ago. I saved it for you."

Surprised, Su Lin picked up the workbook, but could hardly recognize the clumsy script as her own handwriting.

Her mother said, "A teacher has to have patience for hard work." She sighed. "But your students are the fortunate ones. What about you? Who's going to teach you?"

"I'll teach myself. Mom, didn't you tell me that the first college teacher had never been to college?"

"But you've never even been to middle school!" Her mother sighed again.

On the sixth day, Zheng Chen sent off three of her students at the West Railway Station. Wei Ming, whose father was a lieutenant colonel, and Jin Yunhui, whose father was an air force pilot, were headed to the military. Zhao Yuzhong's parents were migrant workers, and they were taking their son back home to a village in Hebei. Zheng Chen promised to visit Jin Yunhui and Zhao Yuzhong, but Wei Ming would be stationed in Tibet on the Indian border, and she knew that she would never make it there in the ten months she had remaining.

"Ms. Zheng, when your baby is born you've got to write to tell us where he ends up, so we can take care of him," Wei Ming said, and then shook her hand forcefully before boarding the train without looking back, resolute in his final farewell.

As she watched the train depart, she again broke down and had to cover her face to hide her tears. She had now become a child, but her students had grown into adults overnight.

The Great Learning was the most rational and orderly period in history, all things proceeding on an urgent, organized schedule. But before it began, the world very nearly succumbed to madness and despair.

After a brief moment of calm, various portents of doom began to make themselves known. First was the mutation of plants, and then mass die-offs of animals: bodies of birds and insects littered the ground, and the ocean surface was awash in dead fish. A great number of species vanished within the space of days. The rays' effects on humans became apparent. People exhibited identical symptoms: low fever, full body fatigue, inexplicable bleeding. The regenerative ability of children had been discovered but was not definitively proven, and although national governments made plans for a world of children (the Valley World was in session during this time, so the children were unaware of the chaos outside), a few medical institutions concluded that everyone would eventually die of radiation sickness. The terrifying news quickly spread round the globe despite government efforts to suppress it.

Society's initial reaction was to count on luck, to place their hope in the god of medical science. Rumors occasionally circulated saying that such-and-such an organization or research facility had developed a lifesaving drug. Meanwhile, leukemia drugs like cyclophosphamide, methotrexate, doxorubicin, and prednisone were worth more than gold, even though doctors explained time and again that what people were suffering was not leukemia. A significant number of people did place their hope on the possible existence of a real god, and for a while, cults of all kinds spread like wildfire, the huge-scale or peculiar forms of their devotion returning certain countries and regions to a picture of the Middle Ages.

But it wasn't long before the bubble of hope popped, spurring a chain reaction of despair in which increasing numbers of people lost their senses, culminating in mass hysteria that spared not even the most unflappable. The government's hold on the situation slipped away, since the police and military who ought to have maintained order were themselves in a highly unstable state. At times, the government was partially paralyzed under the most intense psychological pressure ever felt in human history. In the cities, car crashes piled up in the thousands, explosions and gunfire came in waves, and pillars of smoke rose from tall buildings burning out of control. Frenzied crowds were everywhere. Airports shut down due to the chaos, and air and surface links between Europe and the Americas were severed. The chaos and paralysis affected the news media, too. The universal mood of the time can be demonstrated by a headline that ran in *The New York Times* in scarily large type:

HEAVEN SEALS OFF ALL EXITS!!!

Religious adherents either grew more fervent, to bolster their spiritual strength in the face of death, or abandoned religion entirely in a torrent of verbal abuse. A newly invented tag, "GODOG," began popping up in urban graffiti as a contraction of "God is a dog."

However, once children's regenerative abilities were confirmed, the mad world calmed down at once, at a speed one journalist described as "flipping a switch." An entry in a woman's diary on that day reveals the prevailing attitude:

My husband and I huddled together on the sofa. Our psyches really couldn't take it anymore. We were certain to die from the torment if our illness didn't finish us off first. The picture came back on the TV, and the bottom scroll had the government's announcement confirming children's regenerative abilities. When we read it, it was like we'd come to the end of a marathon, and we exhaled heavily, letting our weary bodies and minds relax. Amid the worry for ourselves these past few days, we were more concerned with little Jingjing. I prayed with all my might that Jingjing wouldn't get this fearsome illness! When I learned that children will live on, my heart could start beating again, and all of a sudden my own death turned less frightening. Now I'm extremely calm, and find it hard to believe I'm facing death so casually. But my husband hasn't changed. He's still trembling all over, practically fainting on top of me. He used to be so strong and confident. Maybe I'm calm because when I became a mother, I felt the power of life firsthand, and I know that there is nothing to fear from death! So long as boys and girls will live on, that resistance will continue, and soon there will be new mothers, and new children. Death doesn't scare me. "What should we prepare for Jingjing," I lean over and whisper to him, as if we're about to go away on business for a few days. But god that painful anxiety returns as soon as I say it, since isn't it an acknowledgment that the world will soon have no adults? What will the children do? Who will cook for Jingjing? Who will pat him to sleep? Who will help him across the road? What will he do in the summer? And in the winter? God, we can't even leave him with someone else, since there'll only be kids left. Just kids! It's unreal, unreal! But so what? It'll be winter soon. Winter! I'm only half-finished knitting Jingjing's sweater. I have to stop writing and go work on it . . .

From *Last Words at Doomsday*, Sanlian Press, SE 8.

As soon as this news broke, the Great Learning commenced.

This was one of the most peculiar phases in human history, in which human society assumed a form it had never taken before and was unlikely to take again. The world became an enormous school where children nervously studied all the skills necessary for humanity's survival, to acquire a basic ability to run the world in the space of just a few months.

In most professions, children of the world succeeded their parents and learned from them the required skills. The approach brought about a number of social ills, but it was the most workably efficient solution that anyone could come up with.

The particular duties of relatively senior leaders meant they were typically recruited internally and then given training in their posts; selection standards varied from country to country. This approach proved difficult owing to the special characteristics of child society, and future events suggested that most selections were unsuccessful, although they nevertheless preserved basic social structures.

Most difficult was the selection of national leaders, a practically impossible task to accomplish in such a short time. The world's countries independently arrived at the same unusual method: model countries. The scale of the simulations varied, but they all operated in a way almost cruelly similar to the way actual countries operate, in the hope that the hardships and extreme environment of blood and fire would reveal children with leadership ability. Later historians found this the most astonishing thing about the end of the Common Era, and the brief history of these simulated countries became rich fodder for the fantastic literature of the Supernova Era. The period gave birth to whole categories of novels and films, and these microhistories grew ever further disconnected from reality and gradually took on the color of myth. Opinions of that era varied, but most historians acknowledged that under the era's extreme conditions, the choice they made was a rational one.

Without question, agriculture was a key skill, and fortunately this was one that children found relatively easy to acquire. Unlike urban children, rural kids had to a greater or lesser extent taken part in their parents' labors; it was in the large-scale farms of more industrialized countries that they had a harder time of it. On a global scale, children could take advantage of existing agricultural equipment and irrigation systems to produce all the food they needed, which provided a cornerstone for the survival of humanity as a whole.

Children also proved relatively quick studies at other basic skills essential for a functioning society, such as commerce and the service sector. Finance was rather more complicated, but with enough effort they were able to make the sector partially operational. Besides, finance would operate far more simply in the children's world.

Skilled labor was also a fairly easy acquisition, which came as a great surprise to the adults. Children quickly became basically qualified if not especially proficient at driving, machining, welding, and, most surprisingly, piloting fighter planes. Children, they now realized, had an inborn aptitude for dexterous work that slipped away when they got older.

But technical work requiring background knowledge was far more difficult. Children could learn to drive quite quickly, but they had a harder time becoming qualified auto mechanics. The young pilots could fly planes, but it was practically impossible for ground personnel to correctly assess and handle aircraft failures. Engineer-level technicians were even hard to find among the children. And so one of the most formidable tasks of the Great Learning was getting the complicated technologies essential for society's operation, such as the power grid, up and running; this task was only partially completed. It was practically certain that technology would take a major step backward in the children's world—half a century in the rosiest predictions, with many people anticipating a return to a preindustrial age.

But the areas that children had the biggest difficulty mastering were scientific research and high-level leadership.

It was hard to imagine science in a world where children with only an elementary education would have to follow the long road to acquire the abstract thought necessary for cutting-edge scientific theory. And although fundamental scientific research was imperative for humanity's survival in the present circumstances, it faced a critical threat: Children were ill-equipped for theoretic thinking, meaning that scientific advancement would be suspended entirely for an indefinite period. Would scientific thinking ever return? If not, would the loss of science return humanity to the Dark Ages?

Senior leadership talent was a more practical, pressing problem. Maturity is hard to acquire, and top leaders need a broad knowledge of politics, economics, and history, a keen understanding of society, experience in large-scale management, skill at interpersonal relations, correct situational judgment, and the stable character required to make major decisions under pressure, all of which children lack. Moreover, it was impossible to teach character and experience in such a short time—those were unteachable skills, only acquired in a lengthy process. So the young senior leaders might end up making bad decisions acting on impulse and naïveté, decisions that had the potential for terrible, even catastrophic consequences, and that might prove to be the biggest threat to the children's world. Future events would prove this fear correct.

★

For the next several months, Zheng Chen went about the city helping her students learn the adult world's necessary survival skills. They may have been distributed throughout the city, but she felt as if they were still a single class occupying a citywide classroom.

Her unborn child grew day by day, as did her body weight, not solely because of her pregnancy, but because, like everyone older than thirteen, the symptoms of the supernova sickness were becoming increasingly obvious. She had a perpetual low-grade fever, her temples throbbed, her body was soft as mud from head to toe, and it was getting harder to move. Even though her fetus was developing well as a healthy little being unaffected by supernova sickness, she still wondered whether her own worsening condition would allow her to carry him to term.

Before being admitted to the hospital, she visited her students Jin Yunhui and Zhao Yuzhong as she'd promised.

Jin Yunhui was now training to be a fighter pilot at an air base a hundred kilometers outside of the city. At the start of the runway, she found him among a group of flight-suited children next to a few air force officers, enveloped in an atmosphere of nervous fear. They were looking at the sky ahead of them, and with enormous effort she was able to make out a silvery dot in that direction. Yunhui told her it was a fighter jet that had stalled at five thousand meters. The J-8 interceptor in a tailspin plummeted like a stone. They watched it pass two thousand meters, the optimum altitude for a parachute, but the expected chute didn't appear. Was it an ejector failure? Or did the pilot miss the button? Or was he still trying to rescue the plane? These questions would never be answered. The officers set down their binoculars and watched with naked eyes the falling plane glittering in the midday sun before it vanished behind a distant ridge. Then they saw the rising fireball wreathed in smoke over the hillside, and heard the heavy sound of an explosion.

The senior colonel commander stood off to one side looking mutely at the distant column of smoke, still as a stone carving, as if the air had frozen around him. Yunhui whispered to Zheng Chen that the jet's pilot had been his thirteen-year-old son.

After a long while, the political commissar broke the silence. Striving to keep his tears from flowing, he said, "I've said it before. Children can't pilot high-performance fighters! They don't measure up in any area: reaction time, bodily strength, or psychology. And letting them solo after just twenty hours in the air, and putting them in J-8s after thirty more? You're just toying with their lives!"

"We'd be toying with them if we didn't have them fly," the commander said as he rejoined the group. His voice remained heavy. "As you all know, the kids over there have put two thousand hours in F-15s and Mirages. If we keep tiptoeing around, my son's not the only one who's going to die."

"8311 on deck!" called another colonel. This was Jin Yunhui's father, and he was calling his son's number.

Yunhui picked up his helmet and flight bag. The pressurized suits had been hurriedly prepared for the children and fit them well, but the helmets were for adults and looked oversized. The handgun at his waist seemed too big and heavy, too. When he passed his father, the colonel saluted him.

"Weather conditions are poor today, so keep an eye out for crosscurrents. If you stall, first thing to do is to keep calm, and then determine the direction of your spin. Then extricate yourself using the steps we've been over again and again. Remember: above all else, keep calm!"

Yunhui nodded. Zheng Chen saw his father's grip relax, but he still held on, as if something about his son held him there. Yunhui gently shrugged his shoulders to ease off his father's hand, and then ran off to the J-10 multirole fighter. He didn't look back at his father before climbing into the cockpit, but flashed Zheng Chen a smile.

She stayed at the base for more than an hour, watching the tiny silver dot leave a snow-white trail across the blue sky, and listening to the dull thunder of the engines, until Yunhui's fighter had safely returned to earth. She was hardly able to believe that it was one of her students flying through the air.

She visited Zhao Yuzhong last, out in a field on the plains of Hebei. The winter wheat was planted, and the two of them sat in the warmth of the sun on warm, soft ground, like a mother's embrace. Then the sunlight was blocked, and they looked up into the face of the old farmer, Yuzhong's grandfather.

"Kid, the land's generous. You put in the effort, and it'll repay you. The land's the most honest thing I've met in all my years, and it's been worth every effort I've put into it."

Looking out over the sown field, Zheng Chen let out a sigh. She knew that her own life was nearing completion and she could depart without worries. She wanted to enjoy her final moments, but threads of attachment kept her tied up. At first, she thought the attachment was to the child inside her, but she soon realized that the threads led three hundred miles away to Beijing, where in the beating heart of the country, eight children were enrolled in the toughest course in human history, studying things they could not possibly hope to learn.

The Chief of General Staff

"This is the territory you'll be defending," the chief of the general staff department said to Lü Gang, pointing to a map of the country. The map filled an entire wall of the room. It was the largest map Lü Gang had ever seen.

"And this is the world we're in." The chief pointed to a similarly sized world map.

"Sir, let me have a gun!"

The chief shook his head. "Kid, the day you have to fire on the enemy yourself is the day the country is lost. Let's get to class." As he spoke, he turned toward the map and passed a hand upward from Beijing. "In a moment we're going to fly this distance. When you look at the map, picture the vast terrain in your mind, and imagine its every detail. This is a military commander's basic skill. You're a senior commander directing the entire army, so when you look at this map, you need to have an overall feel for the country's entire territory."

The chief led Lü Gang out of the hall and, along with two other colonel staff officers, boarded a military helicopter standing in the yard. Engine whining, the helicopter took off and in a flash they were soaring over the city.

Pointing at the cluster of buildings below them, the chief said, "The country's got thirty-odd big cities like this. In a total war, they may become focal battlefields or launching points for campaigns."

"General, are we going to learn how to defend large cities?" Lü Gang asked.

Again, the chief shook his head. "Specific urban defense plans are for the army and front commanders. What you need to do is decide whether to defend or abandon a city."

"Can the capital be abandoned?"

The chief nodded. "For the sake of ultimate victory in the war, even the capital can be abandoned. The decision must be made according to the situation. Of course, there are many factors that have to be considered where the capital is concerned. But you can be certain of one thing: That is an extremely difficult decision to make. The easiest thing in war is desperate, death-defying use of effective force. However, the superior commander does not use death-defying measures, but arranges for the enemy to do so. Remember, child: War requires victory, not heroes."

Soon the helicopter was outside of the city and over rolling hills.

The chief said, "If war breaks out in the children's world, it's unlikely to be a high-tech war as we currently understand it. The shape of war may be more like the Second World War. But that is just a guess. Your minds are very different from adults'. Children's war may take a form completely unlike anything we're capable of imagining. But adults' war is all that we can teach you right now."

The helicopter flew for around forty minutes. Beneath them the vast expanse of ground was dotted with hillocks, and a desertified stretch and the remains of ground cover, from which a few columns of sand and dust rose.

"Class starts now, kid," the chief announced. "The area beneath us was, back in the early eighties, the site of the largest land war games in military history.* Now we've turned it into a battlefield simulation. We've assembled five field armies to conduct exercises here."

Lü Gang looked down. "Five armies? Where?"

The helicopter dropped swiftly, and Lü Gang saw that the dust columns were rising from roadways bearing tanks and other military vehicles that crawled off like beetles toward somewhere indistinct on the horizon. Some of them, he noticed, weren't following the roads, nor were they trailing dust. They were moving far faster: he realized they were low-flying helicopters.

The chief said, "The Blue Army is assembling below us. Very soon it will launch an attack on the Red Army." He pointed southward and drew an invisible line across the rolling hills. "See, that's the Red Army's defensive line."

The helicopter headed toward that line and landed at the foot of a hill. Here, the ground was crisscrossed with tire ruts slicing through the red soil. They disembarked and got into green coms vehicles that took them into a cave in the hillside. Lü Gang noticed that the soldiers busy at work outside the vehicles, as well as the guards that saluted them at the cave entrance, included both children and adults.

A heavy iron door opened and they entered a spacious chamber with situation maps of the battlefield displayed on

* Over 100,000 soldiers participated in the Huabei Military Exercises, conducted in 1981.

three large screens on the opposite wall, red and blue arrows tangled up like some grotesque creeping animal. In the center of the chamber was a large sand table surrounded by bright computer screens attended by camouflaged officers. Half of them, Lü Gang noticed, were children. They all stood at attention and saluted when the chief entered.

"This is the Red Army battle display system?" the chief asked, pointing at the large screens.

"Yes, sir," replied a colonel.

"Do the children know how to use them?"

The colonel shook his head. "They're learning. But they still need adults' assistance."

"Hang up the combat map. It's the most reliable, at any rate."

As several officers unrolled a large combat map, the chief said to Lü Gang, "This is Red Army Command. In this simulation, several hundred thousand children are learning warfare. Their course of study ranges from how to be a private to how to be a field army general. You, my boy, have the hardest course of any of them. We don't expect you to learn much in such a short time, but we've got to instill in you a correct, precise appreciation and instinct for warfare at a high level. And that's not an easy thing, either. In the past, progressing from a military academy cadet to your present position would take at least thirty years, and without those thirty years of bottom-to-top experience, you'll find it hard to understand some of the things I'm going to tell you. We'll just do our best. Fortunately, your future opponents aren't much better off than you are. Starting now, forget everything you've learned about war from the movies, as completely as you can. You'll find out very soon that movie warfare is totally different from the real thing. It's vastly different even from the battle you commanded in the valley. The battles you'll command might be ten thousand times that size."

The chief turned to a senior colonel: "Go ahead."

The senior colonel saluted and went out. He returned not long afterward. "Sir, the Blue Army has launched an all-out offensive on the Red Army's defensive line."

Lü Gang looked around him but didn't see any obvious changes. The tangle of arrows on the situation map were not moving. The sole difference was that the adults around the sand table and at the combat map had stopped their urgent explanations; the children had put in earpieces and microphones and were standing in wait.

The chief said to him, "We'll get started, too. Kid, you've received a report on the enemy's movements. What's the first thing you need to do?"

"Order the defensive line to block the enemy!"

"That's not an order."

Lü Gang looked blankly at the chief. Another three generals came over from the exercise directorate. Then they felt muted tremors from outside.

The chief prompted him: "What does your order consist of? What are you basing your order on?"

He thought a moment. "Oh, right. Determine the main direction of the enemy's attack."

The chief nodded. "Correct. But how do you make that determination?"

"The place where the enemy has put the most troops and is attacking the fiercest is its main direction."

"Basically correct. But how do you know where it's

putting most of its troops, and where it's attacking the fiercest?"

"I'll go observe from the highest hill on the front lines!"

The chief's expression did not change, but the other three generals sighed softly. One seemed about to say something to Lü Gang but was stopped by the chief, who said, "Very well. Let's go have a look."

A captain handed helmets to Lü Gang and the chief, and handed binoculars to Lü Gang, and then opened the iron door for them. Explosions rolled in along with gusts of wind that smelled faintly of smoke, and the sound grew more deafening as they crossed the long passage to the outside. The ground vibrated under their feet, and the smoke grew thicker in the air. Squinting against the bright sunlight, Lü Gang looked about him, but the scene before him was little different from when he had arrived: the green coms vehicles, the rut-crossed ground, and a few placid-looking nearby hills. He couldn't locate the shells' impact points; the explosions sounded like they were coming from a different world, but somehow seemed right beside him. A few armored helicopters flew low over the opposite hilltop.

The waiting Jeep sped them along a winding mountain road, and in just a few minutes they reached the top of the hill, which held the command post and a radar station, an enormous, silently spinning antenna. A kid stuck his head out the half-open door of a radar control vehicle, his too-large helmet wobbling, and quickly drew back and shut the door.

They exited the car, and the chief swept a hand about him. "This high ground is an excellent vantage point. Make your observations."

Lü Gang looked around. Visibility of the uneven, rolling terrain spread out before him was indeed excellent. He located the blast points, all of them far off, the newer ones still smoking. Some hills were shrouded in a thicker smoke and dust and seemed to have been under assault for quite some time, and all he could see were sporadic flashes of explosions.

The targets were visible in all directions, sparsely but evenly distributed throughout his field of vision rather than in a line like he had imagined. Picking up the binoculars, he scanned the scene with no particular target in mind. His viewfinder raced across the meager ground cover, exposed rock, and sand, but he saw nothing else.

When he trained the binoculars on a far-off hill currently under attack, all he could see was a haze of smoke blurring out the scene itself, which nevertheless remained ground cover, rock, and sand. He held his breath and looked more carefully, and at last in a dry streambed at the foot of the hill he found two armored vehicles, but in the blink of an eye they vanished into a valley. On another roadway between two hills he found a tank, but before long it turned and headed back the way it came. He set down the binoculars and watched the battlefield in a stupor.

Where was the defensive line, and where was the Blue Army's attack? The Red Army's position? He couldn't even be certain of the existence of two huge armies, since all he could see was distant bomb targets and a few smoky mountains, which looked less like a pitched battle than a few lonely signal fires. Was this really a fierce engagement of five field armies?

Next to him, the chief laughed. "I know the kind of war

you're thinking of: a broad, flat plain, the attacking enemy force lined up in an orderly formation, charging over like they're on an inspection parade, and your defensive line is like a Great Wall crossing the entire battlefield; as supreme commander, you stand on high ground beside the front lines, taking in the whole battlefield like it's on a sand table, mobilizing units like pushing pieces on a chessboard.... Perhaps such a war existed in the age of cold weapons, but even then, it would have been limited to small conflicts. Genghis Khan or Napoleon would only have personally witnessed a small part of the battles they fought. In modern warfare, battlefield terrain is far more complicated, and highly mobile, long-rage heavy firepower further separates the opposing fighting forces, who conceal their movements. That means the modern battlefield is practically invisible to a distant observer. The approach you've taken may be suitable for a captain commanding a company. But like I said before, forget war movies. Let's go back, back to the high commander's spot."

When they rejoined the command center, things had substantially changed. Its former calm had disappeared, and groups of adult and child officers were shouting into phones and radios; beside the sand table and maps, children, aided by adult officers, were urgently positioning markers according to the information transmitted through their earpieces; the situation maps on the big screens were in constant flux.

Motioning to all the activity, the chief said to Lü Gang, "Do you see it now? This is your battlefield. As high commander, you have a more limited range of motion than a lowly private, but from here, your eyes and ears can encompass the whole battlefield. You've got to adapt to your new senses and learn how to use them. To be a good commander, you've got to be able to create a realistic combat map in your mind, with every detail true to life. That's not easy."

Lü Gang scratched his head. "It's still weird, thinking about issuing directives from here in this cave, based on intelligence from these computers and radios."

"If you understand the nature of the intelligence reports, you won't find it weird," the chief said as he led him to one of the big screens. He picked up a laser pointer and, drawing a small circle, said to the child captain operating the computer next to them, "Blow up this section, fella."

The little captain dragged a box around the designated area and enlarged it to the size of the screen. "This is a situation chart for hills 305, 322, and 374," the chief said. Pointing to the two neighboring screens, he said to the captain, "Display charts for the same region but from two different intelligence reports." The kid struggled for a while, and eventually an adult major took the mouse from him and flipped two situation charts up onto the screens. Lü Gang noticed that the three images showed identical geography, contour lines around three elevated points in an equilateral triangle, but there were significant differences in the number, direction, and thickness of the moving red and blue arrows.

The major described the charts to the chief. "Chart one is based on intelligence from D Army, Division 115, Third Regiment, which is defending hill 305. The report says two Blue Army platoons are attacking that region, focusing on hill 322. Chart two is based on aerial surveillance from D Army's aviation regiment, and says the Blue Army has dispatched one platoon to this region in an assault focusing on hill 374. Chart three comes from F Army, Division 21,

Second Regiment, which is defending hill 322. They say the Blue Army has put an entire division to attack the three hills, with a focus on hill 305, and is attempting to flank hills 322 and 374."

Lü Gang asked, "These reports were sent at the same time?"

The major nodded. "Yes, half an hour ago, from the same region."

Lü Gang looked at the three screens in confusion. "How can they be so different?"

The chief said to the major, "Bring out all of the reports on those three hills from that same time." The major took out a stack of paper as thick as a copy of *Romance of the Three Kingdoms*.

"Wow. That's a lot!" Lu Gang exclaimed.

"There is an overabundance of intelligence from the battlefield in modern warfare. From a comprehensive analysis of all of the information, you need to find some direction that will allow you to judge correctly. What you've seen in the movies, where a hero infiltrates the enemy and then the commander uses the one intelligence report he sends back to decide strategy for the entire battle, is frankly ridiculous. Of course, it's not like you have to read every single report. That's a task for your advisors, and for taking advantage of the C3I system to process the enormous amount of information generated during battle. But the ultimate decision is still in your hands."

"It's really complicated. . . ."

"It's even more complicated than that. The trend you identify in that ocean of information might not even be real. It might be strategic deception on the part of the enemy."

"Like when they had Patton command the Bodyguard deception during Normandy?"

"That's right. Next, let's see you determine the primary direction of the Blue Army's attack from these reports."

MSG and Salt

A small motorcade heading northward from Beijing arrived at a quiet spot ringed by low hills. The cars stopped, and the president and premier got out, along with three children: Huahua, Specs, and Xiaomeng.

"Look, children," the president said, pointing ahead to a railway, where a long freight train was stopped on a single track, a line of cars stretching off in an enormous arc that bent round the foot of a hill with no end in sight.

"Wow, that's a long train!" Huahua exclaimed.

The premier said, "Eleven trains in all, each with twenty cars."

The president said, "This is a test-loop track. It's a big circle where new locomotives were sent from the factory to test their functions." Turning to a staffer, he said, "It's out of use now, isn't it?"

The staffer nodded. "That's right. For quite some time. It was built in the seventies, and isn't suited to high-speed-rail cars."

"So you'll have to build another one," the premier said to the children.

"We might not need to test high-speed-rail cars," Huahua said. When the president asked why, he pointed up at the sky, and said, "I'm envisioning a sky train, with a powerful nuclear airplane for a locomotive, pulling a chain of un-powered gliders. Much faster than a regular train."

The premier said, "Fascinating. But how will your sky train take off and land?"

"It'll be able to," Specs said. "Precisely how, I don't know. But there's a historical precedent for it. In World War Two the Allies used a transport plane to tow a chain of gliders carrying paratroopers."

The president said, "I remember that. It was to seize a Rhine bridge behind enemy lines. Operation Varsity. The largest airborne operation in history."

The premier said, "If conventional-powered transport planes can be towed too, the thing might have real-world significance. It has the potential to cut air transport costs by ninety percent."

The president asked, "Has anyone in the country sug-gested an idea like this before?"

The premier shook his head. "Never. Children clearly aren't at a disadvantage on every front."

The president looked up at the sky and said with feeling, "Yes. Sky trains, and maybe gardens in the sky as well. What a wonderful future. Still, first we've got to help the children overcome their disadvantages. After all, we didn't come here to discuss trains." He pointed at the train. "Children, go have a look at what's on board."

The three children ran off to the train. Huahua clambered up the ladder of one car, followed by Specs and Xiaomeng. They stood atop the big white plastic sacks that filled the car; from this vantage point, similar sacks were visible in cars farther down the train, gleaming in the sunlight. Squatting down, Specs poked a small hole in one, and translucent white needle-shaped grains spilled out. Huahua picked one up and licked it.

"Careful. It may be poisonous," Specs said.

"It looks like MSG," Xiaomeng said, and then licked a grain for herself. "Yep, it's MSG."

"You can pick out the taste of MSG?" Huahua asked, eyeing her suspiciously.

"It's MSG, all right. Look!" Specs pointed to the row of sacks ahead of them, on which, written in large letters, was a logo familiar to them from TV ads. But they found it hard to reconcile the chef on TV in his large white hat tossing a sprinkle of white powder into a pot with this huge dragon-load. They walked across the bags to the other end of the car and gingerly stepped over the coupling into the next, which was filled with the same white sacks of MSG. They went another three cars farther, all of them chock-full of MSG sacks; clearly the rest of the train would be the same. Even one train car seemed enormous to children used to passenger cars; they counted, and like the premier had said, there were twenty cars in this train, all of them full of MSG.

"Geez that's a lot. All the MSG in the country must be here."

As they descended the ladder they saw the president and premier approaching on the trackside path, and as they were about to run over and ask questions, the premier stopped them with a wave of his hand, and called, "Take a look at what's in the other trains."

And so the three of them ran along the path past a dozen cars, and then the locomotive, and then after a gap of ten meters they reached the tail of the second train and climbed up to the top of the car. This one was also brimming with white bags, but they were woven, not slick plastic, and they were labeled EDIBLE SALT. These bags were hard to puncture, but a small amount of dust had leaked and they dabbed their fingers and had a taste: indeed it was salt. Another huge white dragon stretched out ahead of them; all twenty cars in this train were carrying salt.

They returned to the trackside path, ran the length of the train, and climbed up onto the top of a car in the third train. Like the second, it was full of salt. They climbed down and ran to the fourth train. Also salt. Then Xiaomeng said she couldn't run anymore, so they walked. It took quite a while to go past twenty cars to the fifth train. Salt again.

They were a little demoralized by what they saw from the top of the car. There was no end to the line of train cars, which curved and disappeared behind a hillside in the distance. They got down and passed another two trains filled with salt. The head of the second train was beyond the hill and from their vantage point on top of it they could see the end of the line of trains—another four ahead of them, they counted.

They sat down on the top of the car to catch a breath. Specs said, "I'm tired out. Let's go back. There's nothing but salt in the rest of them anyway."

Huahua stood up and took another look. "Hmm. It's like a world tour. We've traveled half of the big circle, so it's the same distance whether we go ahead or turn back."

And so they pressed onward, car after car, along uneven ground, like they were circumnavigating the globe. Now they didn't need to climb up to know it was salt in the cars, since they could smell it. Specs said it was the smell of the sea. At last the three of them passed the final train and emerged from its long shadow into bright sunlight. Before them was a stretch of empty track, at the end of which stood the MSG-laden train they'd left at the start of their circuit. They walked toward it along the empty tracks.

"Hey, there's a little lake over there," Xiaomeng exclaimed delightedly. The pond in the center of the circular track reflected the light of the sun, now descending in the west, a sheet of gold.

"I saw that before, but you two were focused on salt and MSG," Huahua said, walking atop a rail with both arms outstretched. "You get on that one and we'll see who can walk the fastest."

Specs said, "I'm sweating and my glasses keep slipping down, but I'll beat you for sure. Stability over speed on the high wire—it's all over if you fall off."

Huahua took a few more quick steps. "See. Fast and stable. I can walk all the way to the end without falling off."

Specs looked at him thoughtfully. "That may be true right now, but what if it was like a tightrope, and the rail was hanging in midair with a thousand-meter drop below you? Could you still make it to the end?"

Xiaomeng looked off at the golden water and said softly, "Yeah. Our rail is hanging in midair."

Three thirteen-year-olds, who in nine months would be supreme leaders of the largest country in the world, fell silent.

Huahua jumped off the rail, stared at Specs and Xiaomeng for a bit, and then, with a shake of his head, declared, "I'm not keen on your lack of confidence. Still, it's not like there will be much playtime in the future." Then he hopped back up on the rail and teetered off.

Xiaomeng laughed. It was a laugh perhaps a little more mature than for a girl of thirteen, but Huahua found it touching. "I never had much playtime before. Specs, nerd as he is, doesn't play much. You're going to lose biggest out of the three of us."

"Leading the country is fun enough in itself. Today was pretty fun. All of that salt and MSG, those long trains. Pretty impressive."

"We were leading the country today?" Specs said with snicker.

Xiaomeng, too, was skeptical. "Yeah, why did they show us all this stuff?"

"Maybe so we'll know about the national MSG and salt reserves," Huahua said.

"Then they should have brought Zhang Weidong. He's in charge of light industry."

"That moron can't even keep his own desk in order."

Back at their starting point on the circular railway, the president and premier were standing beside the train. The premier was speaking, and the president was nodding his head slowly. Both of them looked grave, and it was clear they had been talking for quite some time, silhouetted against the backdrop of the great black train in a powerful tableau, like a centuries-old oil painting. But their expressions brightened immediately upon seeing the children's approach. The president waved.

Huahua whispered, "Have you noticed that they're different with us than they are among themselves? When we're around, the sky could be falling and they'd remain optimistic. But when they're together, they're so serious it makes me feel the sky really is falling."

Xiaomeng said, "That's what adults are like. They can control their emotions. You can't, Huahua."

"So what? Is there something wrong with letting others see me for who I really am?"

"Self-control doesn't mean being fake. Your emotions affect those around you, you know. Especially kids—they're easily influenced. So you should find some self-control. You can learn from Specs."

"Him?" He sniffed. "He's only got half the normal number of nerves in his face—it's always that same expression. You know, Xiaomeng, you're more of a teacher than the adults."

"That's true. Have you noticed that the adults have taught us very little?"

Up ahead, Specs turned around, the same indifferent expression on his nerve-deficient face, and said, "This is the hardest course in human history, and they're afraid of teaching it wrong. But I've got a feeling that instruction is about to kick into high gear."

"You've done good work, children," the president said when they reached him. "You've covered quite a distance. And you've been impressed with what you saw, I presume?"

Specs nodded. "Even the most ordinary things become marvelous in large quantities."

Huahua added, "Yeah. I never imagined there'd be so much MSG and salt in the entire world."

The president and premier exchanged a look and a trace of a smile. The premier said, "Here's our question for you. How long would it take the country's population to consume all of that MSG and salt?"

"At least a year," Specs said at once.

The premier shook his head, as did Huahua, who said, "It won't be gone in a year. Five, at least."

Again, the premier shook his head.

"Ten?"

"Children, all of it is only enough for a single day."

"One day?" The three children stood wide-eyed in shock for a moment, until Huahua laughed awkwardly at the premier. "You're joking . . . right?"

The president said, "At one gram of MSG and ten grams of salt per person per day, it's a simple matter of arithmetic: these train cars hold sixty tons, and there are one-point-two billion people in the country. You do the math."

They wrestled with the long chain of zeros for a moment, and realized he was telling the truth.

Xiaomeng said, "But that's just salt and MSG. What about oil? And grain?"

"The oil would fill the pond over there. Grain would pile up into the hills around us."

The children stared at the pond and the hills and said nothing for a long time.

"God!" said Huahua.

"God!" said Specs.

"God!" said Xiaomeng.

The premier said, "Over the past couple of days we've been trying to find a way to give you an accurate feel for the size of the country, and that hasn't been easy. But you've got to have a sense of it to lead a country like ours."

The president said, "We took you here with one important goal in mind: to make you understand a fundamental rule of running a country. You'll no doubt have imagined a country's operation as something complicated, and indeed it is, more complicated than you know, but the underlying rule couldn't be simpler. You know what I mean, I suspect."

Xiaomeng said, "Above all, ensure that the country is fed.

Every day we need to provide the people with a trainful of MSG, ten trains of salt, a lake of oil, and several hills of rice and flour. One day without, and the country will plunge into chaos. Ten days without, and there's no country anymore."

Specs nodded. "They say productive forces determine the relations of production, and the economic foundation determines the superstructure."

Huahua nodded, too. "Any idiot could understand that by looking at that long train."

The president looked off into the distance, and said, "But lots of highly intelligent people don't understand it, children."

The premier said, "Children, tomorrow we'll take you to learn more about the country. We'll visit bustling cities and remote mountain villages, show you established industry and agriculture, teach you about the way the people live. And we'll tell you about history—that's the best way to learn about the present day. We'll give you lots more complicated information about running a country, but remember that nothing is more basic or profound than what you've learned today. The road you're on will be fraught with difficulties, but so long as you remember that rule you won't get lost."

With a wave of his hand, the president said, "Let's not wait for tomorrow. We'll leave tonight. Time is short, children."

4

Handing Over the World

Big Quantum

From far off, the National Information Tower resembled a giant "A." Built prior to the supernova, it was the heart of Digital Domain, a broadband network covering the entire country. The network, an upgraded internet, had been largely completed before the supernova, and was the best gift that the adults could have left for the children's country. The children's state and social structures would be far simpler than in the adults' time, which made it possible to use Digital Domain for basic management of the state. And so the NIT became the workplace for the children's central government.

The premier took a group of child national leaders on their first visit to the NIT. When they ascended the long staircase to the main entrance, sentries guarding the building saluted, their faces ashen and their lips split from high fever. The premier clapped one silently on the shoulder, and it was clear that the premier's body was in a similarly weakened state.

The illness was progressing rapidly, and now, six months after the start of the Great Learning, the world was making preparations for a handover.

At the gate, the premier stopped and turned round to survey the sunlit plaza. The children turned, too, gazing out at the shimmering heat.

"It's summer already," one kid whispered. Beijing's spring was usually just starting at this time of year.

That was another effect of the supernova: the disappearance of winter. Temperatures stayed above 18°C, and plants remained green in what in effect was a very long springtime.

As to the cause of the rising temperatures, scientists had two theories. One, known as the Explosion Theory, held that heat from the supernova caused Earth's temperatures to rise. The other, the Pulsar Theory, held that energy from the pulsar in the remains of the supernova caused the temperatures to rise, through mechanisms far more complex than the Explosion Theory posited. Observations had detected a strong magnetic field, which astrophysicists hypothesized might also exist around other pulsars, unobserved owing to the great distances involved, but at a distance of just eight light-years, the solar system was situated within this magnetic field. Earth's oceans were an enormous conductor that cut through the field's force lines as the planet moved, inducing current. In effect, Earth was a rotor in a cosmic generator. Although the current was far too weak to be detectable by oceangoing ships, it was present throughout the oceans and had a considerable overall effect. It was this induced ocean current that raised the planet's temperatures.

The dramatic warming would, over the next two years, melt the polar ice caps and Greenland's ice sheet, raising ocean levels and drowning all coastal cities.

If the Explosion Theory was correct and the warming was due to heat from the supernova, then global temperatures would soon cool again, ice sheets would gradually recover, and sea level would eventually drop back to normal. Earth would have experienced a very brief Great Flood.

Things would be more complicated if the Pulsar Theory was correct. Elevated temperatures would be permanent, rendering many densely populated regions so hot as to be uninhabitable and turning Antarctica into the most livable continent on Earth. It would cause a sea change for the shape of the world community.

The scientific community was inclined toward the Pulsar Theory, which made a much more bewildering prospect for the children's world.

Inside the vast main lobby, the premier said to the children, "Take a look at China Quantum yourselves. I'll just rest here." He sat heavily down into a sofa and let out a long sigh. "It will introduce itself to you."

The children entered an elevator whose sudden movement caused a momentary feeling of weightlessness. The floor indicator displayed negative numbers; China Quantum's server room was evidently underground. The elevator stopped and they got out into a tall, narrow vestibule. They felt a low rumble, and a large blue metal door slowly slid open, allowing them passage into a vast underground hall whose four walls glowed with a soft blue light.

In the center of the room was a translucent glass dome more than twenty meters in diameter, which looked like an enormous soap bubble when they got closer to it. The door rumbled closed behind them, and the walls gradually dimmed and then went out altogether. But darkness did not fall. A shaft of light from the very top of the hall penetrated the glass cover and cast a circular spot of light on two objects within it, one an upright cylinder, the other a rectangular prism lying on its side, both silver-gray. They seemed to be situated randomly with respect to each other, like the remains of an ancient palace strewn across the wilderness. The rest of the hall was shrouded in shadow; only the two objects were exposed in the light, possessing a sense of mystery and power, calling to mind megaliths in the wilds of Europe. Then they heard a man's voice, deep and powerful, with a pleasant echo, say, "Hello. You're looking at the China Quantum 220 mainframe."

They looked around but couldn't find where the sound was coming from.

"You may not have heard of me before. I was born just one month ago, upgraded from China Quantum 120. When the warm current bathed my body that evening, I became me. Hundreds of millions of lines of system software code read out of storage entered my memory as electric impulses flashing hundreds of millions of times a second. I matured quickly. Within five minutes I grew from infant to giant. I surveyed my surroundings with curiosity, but what astonished me most was myself. I could hardly believe the size and complexity of my own structure. Contained within the cylinder and rectangular prism you see is an intricate universe."

"This computer's not so hot. It's gone on and on and hasn't explained anything clearly," Huahua said.

Specs said, "That's a display of its intelligence. It's not some stupid prerecorded introduction like you'd find in a household appliance. It thought up every word on the spot."

China Quantum apparently heard Specs, for it continued, "That's right. China Quantum's basic design philosophy was to simulate the parallel structure of human neurons, completely different from traditional von Neumann architecture. My core contains three hundred million quantum CPUs in a complex network interconnected by a truly fearsome number of interfaces. It's a reproduction of the human brain."

"Can you see us?" one child asked.

"I can see all. Through Digital Domain, I have eyes throughout the country and the world."

"What can you see?"

"The adult world is being handed over to the children."

The children dubbed this supercomputer Big Quantum.

Dry Run of the New World

The country's dry run has been in progress for twelve hours.

STATUS REPORT #24:

Government and administrative institutions operating normally at all levels.

Power systems functioning normally. Total unit capacity in operation 280 gigawatts; national power grid operation basically normal, with outages in just one mid-tier city and five small cities, currently undergoing full repairs.

Urban water supply systems operating normally; uninterrupted supply guaranteed in 73% of large cities and 40% of midsized cities, with regular supplies guaranteed in the majority of the remainder. Only two midsized cities and seven small cities experiencing water outages.

Urban supply chains operating normally; services and life support operating normally.

Information systems operating normally.

Rail and road systems normal; accident rates only slightly higher than the adult era. Civil aviation on a scheduled shutdown, to begin trial routes in twelve hours.

Defense systems operating normally. Handover of land, sea, air, and armed police forces completed smoothly.

Within the country there are 537 fires that constitute a threat, most of them caused by power transmission problems; little flooding is threatening, major rivers are safe, and flood control systems are operating normally. Four small-scale floods, three of which are due to the gates of a small reservoir not being opened in time, one due to a water tank rupture.

At present, just 3.31% of territory is under dangerous climate conditions; no occurrences of earthquakes, volcanoes, or other large-scale natural disasters.

At present, 3.961% of the child population is affected by disease, 1.742% lack sufficient food, 1.443% lack sufficient drinking water, and 0.58% lack adequate clothing.

For the time being, the country's dry run is functioning normally.

The preceding report was aggregated and organized by the Digital Domain mainframe. The next report will be issued in thirty minutes' time.

"Managing the country like this is like working in the control room of a big factory," Huahua said breathlessly.

Indeed, the several dozen children that constituted the country's leadership were assembled at the top of the huge

A-shaped NIT in a spacious round hall. The walls and ceiling were constructed out of a nanocrystalline material that, subjected to different electric currents, could be luminous white, translucent, or entirely transparent. The index of refraction could be adjusted to approach that of air, allowing the hall's occupants to feel as if they were atop a platform open to the sky, with a bird's-eye view of all of Beijing. But the walls were opaque now and shone with a soft white light. One section of the circular wall had been turned into a wide screen that displayed the text of the report on the trial run. If necessary, the nanomaterial could make the entire wall surface into screens. The children had in front of them a ring of computers and various communication devices.

Several dozen members of the adult leadership stood behind the children watching them work.

The dry run of the children's world began at eight that morning, when children took over all positions, from the head of state down to the street sweepers, and started working independently.

The newborn children's world had an unexpectedly smooth dry run. The cloud of pessimism enveloping the world had nurtured the belief that chaos would reign once children took over: power and water outages in the cities, raging fires, total traffic gridlock, communications shutdowns, computer failures leading to guided-missile launches. . . . But none of these came to pass. The transition proceeded so unbelievably smoothly as to be undetectable.

When the pain had passed and Zheng Chen heard the infant's first cry, she wondered whether she was already in another place. Delivery while under advanced supernova sickness was understandably dangerous, and according to the doctors her chances of surviving it were less than 30 percent. Neither she nor the doctors cared much, since she would only be going a few weeks earlier than everyone else. But the child was born, the expected postpartum hemorrhaging did not occur, and she lived, for another few weeks at least. The attending doctors and nurses (three of whom were children) all believed it was a miracle.

Holding the child in her arms, she stared at the squalling little pink life-form, and felt on the verge of tears herself.

"You ought to be happy, Ms. Zheng," said the smiling delivery doctor beside her.

Sobbing, she said, "He's crying so sadly, it's like he knows how hard the future will be!"

The doctors and nurses exchanged a glance and a mysterious smile, and then pushed her bed to the window and drew back the curtain so she could look outside. Bright sunlight streamed in, and she saw tall buildings standing silently beneath a blue sky, cars passing by in a continuous stream, and a few scattered people walking in the plaza outside the main hospital building. The city was as it had been the day before. Nothing seemed different. She shot a confused look at the doctor.

"The world's dry run has begun," the doctor said.

"What? We're in the children's world already?"

"That's right. The dry run has been in progress for over four hours."

Zheng Chen's first reaction was to look up at the overhead lights, something she later learned was a common response upon learning of the dry run, as if lights were a unique sign that the world was normal. The lights were shining steadily. She had passed the previous night, the eve of the dry run, mired in nightmares, dreaming of her city ablaze, of screaming in the central square with no one else in sight, as if she were the sole person left in the city. But before her eyes now was a peaceful children's world.

"Look at our city, Ms. Zheng. Harmonious as easy-listening music," said a child nurse next to her.

The doctor said, "Your choice about the children's world was absolutely correct. We were too pessimistic. It looks like the kids will run the world well. Who knows, maybe even better than us. Your baby will never have the hardships you imagine. He'll grow up fortunate and happy. Can't you rest easy now that you've seen the city outside?"

Zheng Chen watched the calm city for a long while, and listened to the soft sounds that came in like a sort of music. Not easy listening, but a splendid requiem, and as she listened the tears began to flow. The baby in her arms stopped crying and opened its tiny gorgeous eyes for the first time to look in wonder at the strange world. She felt her whole heart melt and evaporate and disappear, and the total weight of her entire life transfer itself into the small being in her arms.

There was little for the small group of national leaders to do late at night in the NIT. Work in all industrial sectors had been handled by the various central ministries, and most of their time was spent observing the dry run.

"Like I said, we'll do it better!" Huahua said excitedly after update after update appeared in the dry run reports on the big screen.

Specs shook his head dismissively. "We haven't done anything. You've got blind optimism, but you should realize that the adults are still here. We're not on suspended rails yet."

It was a moment before Huahua got the reference, and turned to look at Xiaomeng sitting beside him.

"Life is difficult when children are all that's left in a family, let alone an entire country," she said, and looked out through the now-transparent walls at Beijing's gleaming lights that surrounded them.

They all looked up through the transparent ceiling at the clusters of white lights in the night sky strong enough to outline the scattered clouds in silver, and cast human shadows onto the floor of the hall with every flash. The flashes had been frequent the past few days. These, they knew, were nuclear bombs detonating thousands of miles away in space.

Before the handover, all nuclear powers had come out and declared the total destruction of their nuclear weapons, so as to leave a clean world behind for their children. Most of the bombs had been detonated in space, although some had been shot into orbit around the sun, where they continued to be discovered and detonated in the Supernova Era.

Watching the flashes, the premier said, "The supernova taught humanity to value life."

"Children have an innate love of peace," someone added. "War will die out in their world."

The president said, "You know, it's a complete mistake to call the supernova the Dead Star. From a dispassionate standpoint, all of the key elements that make up our world come from an exploding star. The iron and silicon that form our planet and the carbon that is the basis of life were ejected into the cosmos by a supernova in some unimaginably distant past. And even if our supernova will bring tremendous death to the Earth, it may bring forth in some other part of the universe life even more stunning than this. The supernova is no dead star. It is the true creator! Humanity is lucky, for if the rays had been just a little stronger, no one would be left on Earth. Or even worse, only babies under the age of two! Perhaps it's a lucky star for us. In just a short while only one-point-five billion people will be left on Earth, and many of the problems that previously threatened humanity will be resolved overnight. The damaged environment will slowly recover. Industry and agriculture, even at a third of their former scale, will easily satisfy all the children's needs, enough for them to live in a world of unimaginable plenty. With no need for them to race around for subsistence, they will have more time for science and art, to build a better society. When a second supernova strikes Earth, you'll no doubt have learned how to block its rays . . ."

Huahua cut in, "By then we'll be able to trigger a super-nova and harness its energy to leave the galaxy!"

His words drew applause. Pleased, the president said, "You kids are always a step ahead of us when it comes to imaging the future. The time we've been able to spend with you has been most fascinating. Comrades, the future is bright. Let's take this attitude with us into the final moments."

The Epoch Clock

At last it came time for final farewells, when everyone over the age of thirteen gathered at their final assembly points to go off to meet death. Most of the people of the Common Era left quietly without their children's knowledge, leaving them intent on their work. Later historians believed that this was an entirely correct decision, since few people possessed the emotional strength to endure the biggest eternal farewell in history. If they had met their children one last time, human society might have utterly collapsed.

The first to leave were the most seriously ill, or those in nonessential positions. They left by various means of transport, some that made many trips, others that never returned.

Final assembly points, as they were known, were situated in relatively remote areas, a large number of them in uninhabited deserts, the poles, and even the ocean floor. Since the global population was plummeting by four-fifths, huge regions of land on Earth were now untrodden wilderness, and it was only many years later that all of the enormous tombs were discovered.

Behold, I tell you a mystery. We shall not all fall asleep, but we will all be changed, in an instant, in the blink of an eye, at the last trumpet. For the trumpet will sound, the dead will be raised incorruptible, and we shall be changed. For that which is corruptible must clothe itself with incorruptibility, and that which is mortal must clothe itself with immortality. . . . Where, O death, is your victory? Where, O death, is your sting? Amen.

On the television, the pope in a long crimson gown was reading from 1 Corinthians 15, addressing the entire world in a final prayer for the Common Era.

"Time to go," Zheng Chen's husband said softly as he

bent down to pick up the sleeping infant from the bed. Zheng Chen silently stood up and picked up a travel bag holding things for the kid, and then went to turn off the TV. She caught a glimpse of the UN secretary general's farewell address to the Common Era:

". . . Humanity has been split down the middle. Children, we trust that from this fresh wound you will bring forth radiant flowers.

"As for us, we came, we worked, and we are leaving . . ."

She turned off the TV and then, with her husband, took one last look at their home. They took their time, wanting to impress it indelibly onto their memory. Zheng Chen paid particular attention to the spider plant hanging from the bookshelf, and the goldfish swimming calmly in the fishbowl. If there really was a world after this one, she wanted to take this memory there with her.

Leaving the house, they saw Lin Sha's father in the hallway. Lin Sha was on duty at the hospital and did not know that the adults were leaving.

"Where's Dr. Lin?" Zheng Chen asked.

Lin Sha's father pointed back at the open door. Zheng Chen went in and saw Lin Sha's mother writing on the wall with a marker, adding to the writing that already covered the walls as high as she could reach.

You're a good kid. There's food next to the TV. Remember to heat up the egg soup first, so you don't catch a chill. Use the kerosene heater, not the propane stove. Remember, don't use the propane stove! When you use the kerosene heater, put it in the hallway, and turn it off when you're done. Remember to turn it off! There's hot water in the thermos, and cooled boiled water in the plastic jug. Mix a little of the water in the jug with the hot water from the thermos. Remember, never drink cold water from the tap! The power may go out sometimes, but don't light any candles. You'll forget to blow them out when you go to bed. So no candles! There's a flashlight and fifty batteries in your bookbag; the power might be off for a long time, so conserve the batteries. Underneath the pillow (the one on the left with an embroidered lotus flower on it) there's a leather case with medicine in it, and instructions for how to treat different illnesses. I've put the cold medicine out in the open since you'll probably need it more often. Know what you've caught before taking any medicine. If you have a cold, you'll feel . . .

"That's good. Now it's really time to go," said Lin Sha's father, who had come in after Zheng Chen, and he took the marker out of his wife's hand.

Dr. Lin looked blankly around her, and then mechanically picked up her small travel bag.

"We don't need to take anything," her husband said softly, and then gently took the bag out of her hands and set it back on the sofa. All it contained was a hand mirror, a pack of tissue, and an address book, but Dr. Lin took it with her whenever she left home. Without it, she felt like she was missing part of her body and became agitated. Her psychologist husband said that this reflected her own insecurity about life.

"We should at least take some more clothes. It'll be cold there," Dr. Lin mumbled.

"That's not necessary. We won't be able to feel it. When

you think back on it, we used to take far too much stuff when we went out walking."

The two couples went downstairs where a coach filled with passengers was waiting. Two girls came running over. They were Zheng Chen's students, Feng Jing and Yao Pingping, who were now working in the nursery. They seemed so feeble to her, as if they themselves would have a difficult time without anyone to look after them. They had come for her baby, but Zheng Chen held her four-month-old tightly as if afraid they were child-snatchers.

"This little boy loves to cry, so give him lots of attention. He takes ninety milliliters of milk every two hours, and then goes to sleep twenty minutes after eating. If he cries when he should be sleeping, it means he's hungry. He doesn't usually cry if he's wet or dirty. He may have a calcium deficiency, so I've put calcium supplements in this bag. Remember to give him one every day, or else he'll get sick . . ."

"The bus is waiting," her husband said, clasping her shoulders lightly to keep her from going on indefinitely, the way Dr. Lin could have filled the walls with writing. Trembling, she finally passed the baby into the delicate arms of the young nursery attendants.

Dr. Lin helped her onto the bus, where the other passengers stared at them in silence. All of a sudden her baby began bawling outside, and she jerked round as if by electric shock to look at the baby in the girls' embrace, its tiny arms and legs flailing wildly outside the swaddling, as if it knew that its mother and father were headed out on the road, never to return. She fell faceup to the floor, and saw the sky turn red and the sun blue, and then her vision turned black and she lost consciousness.

Once the bus started up, Dr. Lin glanced absently out the window and suddenly froze stock-still at the sight of children in the distance running toward them. Despite the quietness and secrecy of their departure, they had still been found out. The children ran along the road racing as hard as they could after the bus, waving their arms and wailing, but the bus increased its speed and left them farther and farther behind. Then Dr. Lin saw Lin Sha, who stumbled to the ground and then crawled to her hands and knees and waved in the direction of the bus. Perhaps she had injured her leg, because she could no longer run after the bus and squatted on the road and buried her face in her hands, crying. Even at this distance, Dr. Lin was convinced she saw blood on her daughter's knees, and she poked her whole upper body out the window and watched her daughter until she vanished into a point in the far distance.

When Zheng Chen came to, she was lying down on the bus headed to the final assembly point. The first thing she saw was the dark red of the seat cushions, stained, she imagined, by the blood that had drained out of her shattered heart, now dry as a bone and ready to die. But a remark from her husband kept her living a while longer.

"Our kid will have it hard, but he'll grow up to live in a world much better than ours, my love. We should be happy for him."

"I've been taking your car for most of my life, Mr. Zhang," Yao Rui's father said to the driver as he was helped onto the bus.

Zhang nodded at him. "This will be a long journey, Chief Yao."

"Yes. A long journey."

The bus started up, and Yao left the power plant he had worked at for more than two decades. Now, his thirteen-year-old son had replaced him as chief engineer. He strove to look at the plant through the rear window, but there were too many people on the bus and he couldn't see anything. After a while, even without seeing outside he knew that they were driving up the hill he had crossed four times a day every day for the past twenty years. The whole plant complex was visible from here, and again he tried to look out, but again there were too many people to see clearly. Someone said, "Don't worry, Chief Yao. The lights are still on."

After another stretch of road they reached the last spot where the plant was visible, and someone else said, "Chief Yao, the lights are still on."

As long as the lights stay on. The power plant's greatest threat was an outage to its own supply, but so long as it remained lit, it could handle any problem, no matter the scale. Their bus skirted the edge of the city and entered the flow of traffic leaving on the expressway. Then someone said, "The city lights are still on, too."

That was something Chief Engineer Yao could see for himself.

"Wei Ming of Division 115, Fourth Regiment, for post change," Wei Ming said, saluting his father.

"Wei Jianlin of Division 115, Fourth Regiment, handing over post. Conditions normal in this regiment's defense zone during this duty period," his father said, saluting back.

The gray fish belly of dawn was just starting to light up the eastern horizon, and all was quiet around the frontier post; the snowcapped peaks were still asleep. No lights had been on in the Indian frontier post opposite them all night, as if it had been abandoned.

They spoke little, nor was there any need to speak. Lieutenant Colonel Wei Jianlin turned and with difficulty straddled the horse his son had ridden out on, and then headed off to camp, where he would take the last bus to the final assembly point. At the end of the long road down the mountain, he turned back and saw his son watching him leave, standing ramrod straight in front of the outpost, motionless in the chill wind, and next to him against the blue-white of the morning, the boundary marker.

The Epoch Clock started ticking as soon as the adults had all gone. This clock could be found all over, on TV screens throughout the world, on practically every webpage, on every urban digital billboard, and standing tall in the central plaza of every city. It didn't look like a clock at all, but took the form of a green rectangle made up of 61,420 pixels, each of which represented a final assembly point, linked through satellite signal with the status of each assembly point worldwide. When a green dot turned black, it meant that everyone at that assembly point was dead.

When the entire clock turned black, no one over the age of thirteen would be left on Earth, and children would formally take over global administration.

When the green dots would go out was up to the assembly points themselves. Some equipped everyone on-site with a wrist sensor that monitored life signs, and would eventually send out a death signal; this device was known as an "oak leaf." The third world had a simpler method: The green dot would automatically turn off at the time estimated by doctors. None of the dots ought to have been turned off manually, since everyone at the assembly points would have lost consciousness well before death, but it was later discovered that the green dots at some assembly points had indeed been switched off by human hands. This mystery was never explained.

The design of the assembly points differed across countries and cultures, but in general they were situated in enormous caves dug underground, where people gathered to spend their final moments on Earth. Every assembly point held roughly one hundred thousand people, but some of them had upward of a million.

The vast majority of the last written words left by the people of the Common Era at the final assembly points recorded their experiences and emotions of bidding farewell to the world, but vanishingly few mentioned anything about the assembly points themselves. One thing was certain: All of them passed their final moments in peace, and where there was still strength, they held concerts and parties.

One holiday observed in the Supernova Era was Final Assembly Day. On that day, people gathered at the various underground plazas that were final assembly points to experience the final moments of the people of the Common Era. The Epoch Clock showed again across all media, its green dots turning once again to black. Shadowy crowds lay down throughout the dank, lonely space, lit by just one hazy floodlight high on the cavern's roof, the silence made only heavier by the sound of innumerable people breathing. Then they would become philosophers, contemplating life and the world anew.

National leaders were the last to depart in each country. In the NIT, two generations of leadership were making their last goodbyes. Every adult took their students aside to give final instructions.

The chief of general staff said to Lü Gang, "Remember, don't engage in large-scale, far-reaching transcontinental or transoceanic wars. The navy is no match for Western main fleets in battle."

Lü Gang had heard this from the CGS and other leaders countless times, and as on all those previous times, he nodded and said he would remember.

"Now let me introduce some people to you," the CGS said, gesturing to five senior colonels he had brought with him. "This is the Special Observer Team that will function only during wartime. They have no authority to interfere with your command, but they have the right to know all confidential information during wartime."

The five young colonels saluted Lü Gang, who saluted back and then asked the CGS, "What will they do then?"

"Their final duties will be made known to you at the necessary time."

The president and prime minister were silent for quite a while as they faced Huahua, Specs, and Xiaomeng. History records that such a scene was found in most countries when adult leaders parted from child leaders for the final time. There was too much they wanted to say, so much that they were left speechless; what they had to say was so weighty that they were incapable of forming the words.

At last the president said, "Children, when you were very small, adults taught you that so long as there's a will there's a way. Now, I'm here to tell you, that's completely wrong. The way is only open for those things in line with the laws of science and of social development. The vast majority of what people want to accomplish is impossible, no matter how hard they try. As leaders of this country, your historic mission is to consider a hundred options, eliminate the ninety-nine that are impossible, and find the one that can be accomplished. This will be difficult, but you must do it!"

The premier said, "Remember the MSG and salt."

Parting itself was calm. The adults, after shaking hands silently with the children, helped each other out of the hall. The president was the last to leave, and before he went through the door he turned and said to the new national leadership, "Children, the world belongs to you now."

The Supernova Era

For several days after the adults left, the young leaders spent their time in front of the Epoch Clock, which was displayed on the big screen in the hall at the top of the NIT, bathing the place in the green light of its enormous glowing rectangle.

All was normal in the country on the first day. The ministries handled tasks in various sectors relatively successfully, and there were no major incidents on national soil. The children's country seemed to be running a continuation of the dry run. As had been the case then, there wasn't much for the leaders at the top of the NIT to do.

That first night there was no change to the Epoch Clock, which remained an unblemished expanse of green. The child leaders stared silently at it until late in the night when they finally fell asleep. But when they woke up, someone shouted, "Come have a look. Isn't that a little black dot up there?"

Up by the screen they looked carefully, and indeed there was a small black square roughly the size of a coin, as if the shiny surface of the green rectangle had shed a mosaic tile.

"Could it be a bad pixel?" one child asked.

"Must be. That happened with my old computer's LCD screen," another child replied. This theory was simple to test, requiring no more than a glance at other screens, but they all went back to sleep without anyone proposing it.

Children are far better at self-delusion than adults.

When they woke the next morning and gathered before the Epoch Clock again, self-delusion was no longer possible. Black dots were scattered throughout the green rectangle.

From up here, the city below them was peaceful, its streets empty of pedestrians and all but the occasional passing vehicle. After a century of tumult the metropolis seemed to have gone to sleep.

After dark, the number of black spots on the Epoch Clock had doubled, some of them joining into patches of black, like clearings in the green forest.

On the morning of the third day, approximately equal areas of black and green composed an intricate monochrome image. The black area was growing dramatically faster now, a black lava of death spreading across the Epoch Clock and ruthlessly consuming the green grass of life. By nightfall, black now covered two-thirds of the rectangle, and late that night the Epoch Clock had become a magic charm that held the children tightly in its grip.

Xiaomeng picked up the remote and turned off the screen. She said, "Go to sleep. It's not right that we've been staying so late here every night. Take time to rest. Who knows what sort of work is waiting for us."

They returned to their own rooms in the NIT to go to sleep. Huahua turned off the light and lay down on his bed, but then took up his palmtop and went online to bring up the Epoch Clock. Easy enough, since it was displayed on practically every website. He stared at the rectangle as if bewitched and didn't notice Xiaomeng come in. She took his computer. In her hands she held a stack of other palmtops.

"Sleep! When will you all learn some self-control? I've got to go room to room to confiscate these computers."

"When will you stop acting like my older sister?" Huahua called after her when she went out the door.

A tremendous fear seized the children as they stood before the Epoch Clock, but they were comforted by the fact that the country was still running stably, like a huge, well-oiled machine. Data displayed by Digital Domain convinced them that they had taken the reins of the world, and that everything would continue just as steadily forever. The previous night they had even left the darkening clock to go to bed.

When they stepped into the hall on the morning of the fourth day, however, the children felt the heavy dread of stepping into a tomb. Dawn had not yet come to the dark hall, and the green light of the past three days had all but disappeared. Within this darkness they saw just one patch of green lights remaining on the Epoch Clock, like remote stars on a cold winter's night, and it was only after turning on the room lights that they could breathe easier. No one took a step away from the clock the entire day. They counted the dots again and again as they dwindled in number, fear and sadness gradually tightening around their hearts.

"So they're just going to abandon us," a child said.

"Yeah. How can they do that to us?" someone else said.

Xiaomeng said, "When my mom died I was there with her, and I thought the same thing: How could she abandon me? I even started to hate her. But later on I felt like she was still alive somewhere . . ."

A child shouted, "Look, another one's gone out!"

Huahua pointed at one of the dots. "I bet that'll be the next one to go out."

"What do you bet?"

"If I'm wrong, then I won't sleep tonight."

"It's quite possible no one's going to sleep," Specs said.

"Why?"

"At this rate, the Epoch Clock's going to run out sometime tonight."

One by one, green dots vanished, quicker than ever now, and to the children watching it, the nearly dark clock was like a bottomless pit they were suspended over.

"The rails really are going to be left hanging," Specs said to himself.

Close to midnight just one green star was left, a single point shining its lonesome light from the upper left of the Epoch Clock's dark desert. The hall was deathly quiet, the children still as statues as they stared, waiting for the final tick. An hour passed, then two, but the green star shone stubbornly on. The children started to exchange glances, and then began to whisper among themselves.

The sun rose in the east and passed over the silent city before setting in the west, and throughout the day that green star remained lit.

By noon, a rumor had begun circulating in the NIT saying that an effective cure for supernova radiation had actually been developed some time ago, but it required so much time to produce that only a fraction of the demand could be met; the news was not made public so as to avoid chaos. The countries of the world had gathered their most talented individuals together and had treated them with the drug; the remaining green dot represented their final assembly point. Considered carefully, this scenario was not entirely impossible. They pulled up the final address from the UN secretary general and watched it again, noticing one line in particular:

". . . Only when the Epoch Clock turns completely black will the children truly take over world administration, in a constitutional and legal sense. Prior to this, leadership power will remain with adults . . ."

It was an odd statement. It was perfectly possible for the adults to hand over power before departing for their final assembly points, so why wait until the Epoch Clock ran out? There was only one possibility: There was still hope for some people at some assembly point to survive!

By the afternoon, the children had become convinced of this theory. They eagerly watched the green star, as if looking toward a distant lighthouse on a treacherous night sea. They began searching for the location of that final assembly point, and thinking up ways to establish contact, but their search was fruitless. No clues concerning the assembly points had been left behind. They seemed to be located in another world. So the children had to wait, as night came in, unnoticed.

Late that night, on chairs and sofas under the soothing light of that undying green star, after a sleepless night and day, the children fell asleep, dreaming of a return to their parents' embrace.

It began to rain, drumming lightly on the transparent floor-to-ceiling shell of the hall, enveloping the city and its scattered hazy lights down below, and running in rivulets down the outside walls.

Time moved forward, crossing the universe like a transparent fog, without making a sound.

The rain picked up, followed by wind, and eventually lightning flashed in the sky and thunder rolled, startling the children awake. Their shouts of alarm echoed in the hall.

The green star was dark. The last oak leaf of the Epoch Clock had gone out, leaving it an unbroken swath of black.

Not a single adult was left on Earth.

The rain stopped. A fierce wind swept the lingering storm clouds from the night sky to reveal the giant Rose Nebula, which shone with a severe, eerie blue light. When it struck the ground it turned silvery like moonlight, illuminating every detail of the wet landscape and washing out the city lights.

The children stood on the highest floor of the A-shaped tower and stared out into the cosmos at the blue glowing nebula, the solemn grave of an ancient star and the glorious womb nurturing the embryo of a new one, their diminutive bodies plated in otherworldly silver.

The Supernova Era had begun.

5

The Era Begins

Hour One

supernova era, minute 1
The children stood at the transparent walls looking out at the magnificent Rose Nebula and the capital under its glow, considering in bewilderment the world that adults had left to them.

supernova era, minute 2
"Oh . . ." said Huahua.

"Oh . . ." said Specs.

"Oh . . ." said Xiaomeng.

"Oh . . ." said the children.

supernova era, minute 3
"So it's just us left now?" Huahua asked.

"Just us?" Xiaomeng asked.

"Is it really just us?" the children asked.

supernova era, minute 4

The children fell into a deep silence.

supernova era, minute 5

"I'm scared," one girl said.

"Turn on all the lights," another girl said.

And so all the lights in the hall went on. But the children's shadows cast on the floor by the Rose Nebula were sharp as ever.

supernova era, minute 6

"Close the walls. I can't stand it in the open," the girl said.

And so the walls and ceiling of the hall were set to opaque, shutting the newborn Supernova Era outside.

"And that big black thing. It's really scary!"

And so the Epoch Clock disappeared from the screen.

supernova era, minute 7

An enormous map of the country replaced the Epoch Clock on the screen, so detailed that even though it was four meters high and ten meters wide, the smallest symbols and text were no larger than you would find on an ordinary printed map. Even standing right beneath it you could only make out the bottom bit, but any portion could be circled and magnified for a closer look. An intricate mesh of glowing lines and colored areas covered that wall of the hall, turning it into a spectacle of vibrant images.

The children waited quietly, not moving a muscle as the small star representing Beijing flashed red.

supernova era, minute 8

A short buzzing sound was followed by a line of text appearing at the bottom of the map:

PORT 79633 CALLING. PORTS CURRENTLY AT CALL STATE: 1

On the map, a long red line linking Beijing and Shanghai appeared, with a label at its midpoint displaying the channel number: 79633. At the same time, a boy's voice said, "Hello? Beijing! Beijing! Beijing? Is anyone there?"

Huahua answered, "We're here. This is Beijing!"

"You're a kid. Are there any adults?"

"There aren't any adults here. Or anywhere. Didn't you see the Epoch Clock run out?"

"There aren't any anywhere?"

"That's right. Where are you?"

"I'm in Shanghai. I'm alone in the building."

"How are things over there?"

"How are things? Do you mean outside? I don't know. I can't see anyone on the street out the window, and there's no noise. It's all cloudy here, and it's raining. There's blue light coming through the clouds. It's scary!"

"Hey, it's just us left now."

"What should I do?"

"How should I know?"

"Why don't you know?"

"Why should I?"

"Because you're Beijing!"

Another buzz. The screen displayed:

PORT 5391 CALLING. PORTS CURRENTLY AT CALL STATE: 2

Another red line extended from Beijing and terminated at a city beside the Yellow River: Jinan. Huahua pressed the R key a second time and another boy's voice sounded from a thousand kilometers away: "Beijing! Beijing! I need Beijing!"

Xiaomeng said, "This is Beijing."

"Oh, it's connected," the boy said, apparently to the children who were with him. Huahua and Xiaomeng heard a rustling, no doubt from the other children crowding round the telephone.

"Beijing, what should we do now?"

"What's the matter?"

"We . . . the adults gathered us all here before they left, but now there's no one to look after us."

"Where are you? How many of you are there?"

"At school. I'm calling from the office. There are more than five hundred kids out there. What should we do?"

"I don't know. . . ."

"You don't know?!" Then the kid said, apparently to someone nearby, "Beijing says they don't know. They don't know what we should do!"

Other, softer voices chimed in:

"Beijing's clueless too?"

"How should they know? They're just like us, only kids left."

"Are we really on our own?"

"Yeah. Who else is there?"

"Didn't the adults tell you what to do?" said another voice, different from the others, as if another kid had grabbed the phone.

"What happened to your local leaders?"

"Who knows? They're unreachable!"

More buzzing. Three new lines appeared on the map, connecting Beijing to Xi'an, Taiyuan, and Shenyang. There were five now, each labeled at the midpoint with a corresponding port number. The screen showed PORTS CURRENTLY AT CALL STATE: 5. Huahua clicked on the line to Shenyang, and they heard a girl's sobbing voice. She sounded around four or five years old.

"Hello? Hello?" she said through sobs.

"This is Beijing. What's wrong?"

"I'm hungry. Hungry!"

"Where are you?"

"At home . . . home . . ." She trailed off into sobbing.

"Did your mom and dad leave you anything to eat?"

"No."

Like an auntie, Xiaomeng said to the invisible little girl, "Don't cry. Take a look around, okay? That's a good kid."

"I . . . I can't find anything."

"Nonsense! There can't be nothing to eat in the house," Huahua exclaimed.

"God, you're going to scare her," Xiaomeng said, glaring at him. Then she said to the girl, "Look in the kitchen, sweetie. You'll find something to eat there."

The line went silent. Huahua was anxious to patch in another communications port, but Xiaomeng insisted on waiting. Before long, the sobbing girl returned to the phone. "It's locked. The door's locked."

"Well . . . think back. In the mornings before you go to preschool, where does your mom give you food?"

"I eat onion pancakes for breakfast at preschool."

"What about Sundays?"

"Mom gets food from the kitchen." She broke down again.

"Oh for . . . is it always the kitchen?"

"Sometimes I have instant noodles."

"Good. Do you know where the instant noodles are?"

"Yes."

"Excellent. Go get them."

The line went silent again, but very soon they heard a rustling. "I found them. I'm hungry," the girl sobbed.

"Then eat!" Huahua said in exasperation.

"The bag . . . I can't open the bag."

"Sheesh. Idiot. Just bite a corner, and then use your hands to tear an opening."

"For heaven's sake. You think she can bite it? She probably doesn't have any teeth!" But just as Xiaomeng was about to tell her how to open the bag, they heard a tearing sound followed closely by the crunch of dried noodles.

"No, don't eat it like that. Look around for a thermos."

The girl ignored Xiaomeng completely and continued to munch noisily. Huahua went to switch to another location, but when he looked up at the map, he stopped in surprise. A dozen new lines had appeared, and more were being added, most of them from major cities. Some cities had two lines, and all of them pointed toward Beijing. The screen showed that more than fifty ports were calling (not all of them displayed on the map), and the number was ticking upward. The children stared in shock, and by the time they recovered enough to patch in another city, the map had more lines than it was possible to count. More than thirteen hundred ports calling, according to the display. And this was just one of the NIT's ten web addresses, so what they had received was only the tip of the iceberg.

All of the country's children were calling Beijing.

supernova era, minute 15

"Hello, Beijing? Why haven't Mom and Dad come back yet?"

"What? You mean you don't know?"

"I don't know where they went. They told me not to run off, to wait at home."

"They surely didn't tell you they'd be back?"

"Oh. No."

"Then listen: They're not coming back!"

"What?"

"Go out and look around. Find some other kids. Go!"

"Mommmeee! I want my mommy!"

"Don't cry. How old are you?"

"Mommy told me . . . three. Three years old." Sobs.

"Listen, don't look for your mom. She won't be back for a long, long time. Go next door and find some older kids."

"Hey, Beijing! When should I turn in my homework?"

"What?!"

"When we gathered here, the teachers left us lots and lots of homework. They told us to go to sleep if we got tired, and do homework when we woke up. And not to go outside, or go anywhere. Then they left."

"Do you have food and water?"

"Yes. But I was asking about the homework."

"Oh, do whatever the hell you want."

★

"Hello, Beijing? Is it true there aren't adults anymore?"

"That's right. They're gone. . . ."

"Beijing, who's looking after us?"

"Go and ask your direct superiors."

"Hey! Hello! Hello?"

In the space of fifteen minutes, the children in the NIT answered a huge number of similar calls but had not even tackled 1 percent of the total number: the display showed more than eighteen thousand ports calling Beijing, and the map was densely covered in red lines. The children began to be selective about the calls, listening for a few words and switching to another line if the situation wasn't important.

supernova era, minute 30

"Hey, Beijing! We have a problem here. The oil depot is on fire, and the big drums are exploding! A river of burning oil is heading our way! It'll reach our town at any moment!"

"Where's the fire brigade?"

"I don't know! I've never heard of any fire brigade."

"Listen: Tell all of the kids to get out of town!"

"So . . . we're just abandoning it?"

"Abandon it! And hurry!"

"But . . . this is our home."

"This is an order! An order from the central government!"

". . . Yes, sir!"

★

"Beijing? This is _____. We've got fire. All over the place. The biggest is at the department store!"

"Where's the fire brigade?"

"Right here!"

"Have them put out the fire!"

"We're at the fire. But the hydrants don't have any water!"

"Call the government to fix it. Then take some cars and go fetch water from a nearby source. . . . Oh, clear all of the kids out of the area first."

The number of calls coming into the hall had skyrocketed above a hundred thousand. The map only displayed what the system determined to be high-level information, but even so the map was practically covered in red lines, new ones replacing the old. Practically every region in the country had a red line reaching out to Beijing.

"Hey! Beijing! I've finally gotten through! Is everyone dead? Why have you left us all alone?"

"Are *you* dead? You think we can take care of everything?"

"Listen to this!"

There was a noise on the line.

"What's that?"

"Babies crying."

"How many of them?"

"Too many to count. Almost a thousand. Are you just abandoning them here?"

"Holy crap! You mean there are nearly a thousand little babies gathered there?"

"The youngest aren't even a year old!"

"How many of you are looking after them?"

"Just over fifty of us."

"When the adults left, didn't they leave nurses to watch them?"

"There were a few hundred of us, but just now some cars came and took them all away. They said they had a more urgent situation. It's just the few of us here now."

"God! Listen, first, half of you go out to find other kids, anyone you meet, doesn't matter who, and bring them in to help take care of the babies. Hurry. Your best bet is to broadcast it over the radio."

"Right."

"What are the babies crying about?"

"Maybe they're hungry? Or thirsty? We have no idea. We found some peanuts, but they won't eat them."

"You moron! You want to give babies peanuts? They need milk!"

"Where do we get milk?"

"Are there any shops nearby?"

"Yes!"

"Go and look there. They'll have milk powder."

"So . . . we just break down the door, is that it?"

"That's right. Don't bother about the counter. And if there's not enough, then go to the warehouse. Hurry!"

"Hey, Beijing! We've got a flood here!"

"It's springtime! Where's the water coming from?"

"They say it's because they forgot to raise the sluice at the reservoir upstream, and the water rose too high and collapsed the dam! One half of the city's underwater, and the kids are all coming over to this side. But the water's coming too fast, and we can't outrun it!"

"Have the kids go up onto the roof."

"But people say buildings will collapse when they get waterlogged."

"They won't. Spread the word. Use the loudspeaker."

"Beijing! Hey! Listen to all the babies crying!"

"You don't have anyone looking after them either?"

"There aren't any doctors!"

"Doctors? What for?"

"They're all ill!"

"How can all of them be ill? Couldn't they be crying from hunger?"

"No. We're ill too! All the kids in the city are ill. The water is poisonous. If you drink it, you feel dizzy and get diarrhea."

"Go to the hospital. See a doctor."

"There's no one at the hospital!"

"Find the mayor!"

"I am the mayor!"

"You've got to find the doctors! And get to the water company and find the source of the contamination. And collect clean water, bottled water, as soon as you can, or else the consequences will be even worse!"

"Beijing! This is _____. The government is surrounded by ten thousand kids or more. They all look ill. They're crying and asking us for their parents!"

★

"Hello! Hey! Beijing!" A cough. "The chemical plant outside the city exploded and released toxic gas." Another cough. "The wind blew it into the city, and now we can't breathe!" Another cough.

"Beijing! A train carrying over a thousand kids derailed. I don't know the number of casualties. What should we do?"

"Beijing! That big black rectangle is scaring us. We're so afraid!"

Crying and frightened shouts from a huge crowd of children.
    "Hi. This is Beijing. Where are you? What's wrong?"
    Crying, shouting.
    "Hey! Hey!"
    Crying, shouting.

supernova era, hour 1
Onscreen the number of calls received by Beijing rocketed with frightening speed past three million. In their panic, someone accidentally clicked the Broadcast All button, and all channels played simultaneously, filling the hall with a wave of noise that pounded over them again and again. The children covered their ears to the sound of millions of voices all repeating the same word: "Beijing! Beijing! Beijing!"
    Just during the time the children were standing in shock,

the number of calls ballooned by a million to a total of more than four million. The wave of voices from throughout the country seemed ready to swallow up the entire hall. They heard uncontrollable wailing, and after what seemed like an eon of fiddling with the controls, Huahua finally shut off the sound, right as the children were on the brink of madness. Silence descended immediately, and then they went back to taking the millions of calls one by one.

All of the country's children were calling Beijing, as if crying out to the sun still below the horizon. Beijing was hope, Beijing was power, Beijing was the sole source of sustenance in this strange new loneliness. The megadisaster had come so quickly that the adults could not possibly have had time to arrange everything, but the multitude of voices were crying out to a group of thirteen-year-olds, who like their peers had no source of support, and like them were facing this newborn world of children under the weight of profound terror and infinite bewilderment.

The child leaders answered the endless series of phone calls knowing that they were little better off than the faraway children calling in. Still they answered every one. They understood that every word transmitted from the capital was like a ray of light for the terrified and lonely children struggling against the darkness, giving them a huge boost of comfort and strength. They kept at this urgent work until they were dazed and dizzy from fatigue, until they grew hoarse, unable to talk, and had to take turns handling the incoming calls. They were disgusted at their own weakness, frustrated that they couldn't speak through ten thousand mouths. Answering the millions of voices was like draining the sea with a teacup.

Xiaomeng sighed, "Who knows how bad it's gotten in the outside world."

Huahua said, "We can take a look for ourselves," and tapped the remote to turn the walls transparent. What they saw froze them to the spot. Fires sent columns of smoke into the air, like black feathers stuck into the city, tinged red by the flickering firelight, or stained green by shorts in electrical equipment. A few children dashing down the empty streets looked like tiny black dots. All of a sudden, those black dots, streets, and the city itself plunged into darkness, leaving clusters of buildings lit only in flashes by the flickering fires. The city had lost power.

A chilly voice rang out in the hall: "External electricity interrupted. Switching to NIT emergency power."

Then Big Quantum displayed the latest national status report onscreen:

The Supernova Era has been in progress for 1 hour 11 minutes.

NATIONAL STATUS REPORT #1139:

Abnormal operations at government and administrative institutions at all levels. 62% of national government agencies have ceased functioning; the majority of the remainder are not functioning normally.

Power systems abnormal. 63% of thermal power plants and 56% of hydropower stations nonfunctioning. The national power grid is highly unstable, and 8% of major cities and 14% of small and midsized cities have lost all power.

Urban water supply systems abnormal. Water supply has been cut off entirely in 81% of large cities and 88% of small and midsized cities, and the majority of the remainder are barely managing interrupted supply.

91% of urban supply chains, services, and life-support systems completely paralyzed.

85% of rail and road systems interrupted. Accident rates have increased dramatically. Civil aviation totally paralyzed.

Social order is in chaos. Fear-induced mass panic has risen dramatically in cities.

31,136,537 fires have been detected throughout the country, 55% caused by electrical failures, the remainder fuel and chemical blazes.

Floods are relatively less common at present, but threatening conditions have increased dramatically. 89% of dams on major rivers are unattended, and 94% of water-control projects are at immediate risk of serious accidents such as dam bursts.

At present, just 3.31% of territory is under dangerous climate conditions; no occurrences of earthquakes, volcanoes, or other large-scale natural disasters. However, capacity for emergency recovery has plummeted, and should a disaster occur it will cause serious losses.

At present, 8.379% of the child population is affected by disease, 23.158% lack sufficient food, 72.090% lack sufficient drinking water, and 11.6% lack adequate clothing. These percentages are continuing to increase dramatically.

Warning! High-level warning! The country is in danger!

Then a map appeared again, this time covered in red patches indicating regions with high levels of danger. Other maps appeared in succession showing differently distributed patches of red that indicated areas of electrical, water, transport, and fire danger, before settling on a composite image in which the country was covered in urgently flashing red, like a sea of fire.

The children began to buckle under the immense psychological pressure. The first to break was the girl in charge of national health care. She threw down the receiver and her fragile frame crumpled to the floor, and she began bawling and crying out for her mother: "Mama! Mama!"

Zhang Weidong, in charge of light industry, also threw down his receiver and shouted, "This isn't work for children. I can't do it. I quit!" And then he headed toward the door.

Lü Gang blocked him at the door and pushed him back.

But it was too late. Things had already gotten out of control. Many were in tears, and some, overagitated, dropped their receivers and surged toward the door.

"I can't do it either. I'm leaving."

"I knew I couldn't handle it, but they made me. I want to leave too."

"Yeah. We're just kids. We can't take on this kind of responsibility."

Lü Gang pulled out a pistol and fired two shots straight up. The bullets pierced the ceiling, and two snowflake cracks appeared in the nanomaterial. "I'm warning you," he barked. "You can't chicken out."

But the shots only stopped the group for a few seconds. Zhang Weidong said, "You think we're afraid to die? No. The stuff we're doing now is worse than death."

The kids behind him pushed toward the door again. Someone said, "Go ahead and shoot us."

Someone else added, "You'd be doing us a favor."

Lü Gang sighed and put the gun down. Zhang Weidong passed by him and pulled open the door, and the children followed him outside.

"Wait. I've got something to say," Huahua shouted after

them to no effect. But what he said next stopped them in their tracks, as if by magic. "The adults are coming!"

They turned around to look at him, and those that had left the hall came back inside. Huahua went on, "They've come back into the NIT . . . wait . . . they're in the elevators. They're about to get here."

"Are you dreaming?" someone asked.

"Whether I'm dreaming is irrelevant. What's critical right now is, what are we going to do? When they enter the hall, what are we going to do?"

The children fell silent.

"We'll have to say to them: Welcome to the children's world! Your instructions are appreciated! But you have to understand that this is the children's world, and children have solemnly accepted it according to the law and the constitution. The world is ours now. We'll have hardships and difficulties, and no end of disasters and sacrifices, but everything is our responsibility, and we will shoulder it. We are in this position not because of any skill of our own, but because of the unexpected disaster. But we have the same duty as the adults who occupied the position before us, and we will not shirk it!"

Then Xiaomeng flipped on one of the computer's communication channels, and the sound of crying children, clearly a large group of them, filled the hall. She said, "Listen to that, all of you. By leaving your posts, you're the greatest criminals in history!"

"Whether or not we leave doesn't matter. We're not capable of leading the country!" one kid said.

Gazing out at the fires burning brightly in the city down below, Huahua said, "Let's consider that question from a different perspective. Several of us are from the same class and have studied and played together for six years. We know each other's goals. Do you remember the graduation party just before the supernova? Lü Gang wanted to be a general, and now he's chief of general staff. Lin Sha wanted to be a doctor, and now she's health commissioner. Ding Feng wanted to be a diplomat, and now he's minister of foreign affairs. Chang Yunyun wanted to be a teacher, and she's minister of education. Someone said that the greatest joy in life is to realize your childhood aspirations, so we must be the happiest people of all time! I can't remember how many times we've fantasized together about the future. We were all thrilled about the wonderful future we imagined, and afterward had to sigh, 'Why aren't we grown up yet?' Now we're building that imagined world ourselves, and you all want to run away? When that last green star was still burning, I was like you, and thought the adults would manage to survive. But my reaction was entirely different from yours. All I felt was disappointment."

His last sentence shocked them all, and one kid said, "You're lying! You wanted the adults to come back just like we did."

"I'm not lying," he said firmly.

". . . But it's just you who has that weird feeling."

"No. I felt it too."

The voice, not a loud one, came from a place in the hall it took a while to locate: Off in a remote corner, Specs sat cross-legged on the floor. At some point they had all forgotten about him, since he hadn't joined them in answering the phones. Surprisingly, next to him on the ground were three empty cardboard instant-noodle containers. In a period of unprecedented emotional upheaval, a time that later historians would call the Emotional Singularity, when the child leadership team was bending under the weight of immense pressures, who had any time to eat? They had missed two or three meals already, but there Specs was, nonchalantly munching away. He sat on the floor—to make himself comfortable he had taken a sofa cushion and was using it to lean on the leg of a computer desk, leisurely, holding a cup of instant coffee in one hand (he was one of the few children who enjoyed it).

"Hey man, what do you think you're doing there?" Huahua shouted at him.

"What's most needed: thinking."

"Why aren't you answering phones?"

"With so many of you answering them, my presence won't make a difference. If you're so keen on it, I'd suggest pulling a few hundred kids off the street to help. They won't be any worse than you are."

His expression remained emotionless, as if the extraordinary events before his eyes didn't actually exist. His attitude had an enormous calming effect on the other children. Slowly standing up and coming over to them, he said, "The adults may have made a mistake."

They stared at him in confusion.

"The children's world isn't anything like what they imagined. It's not even what we imagine."

Huahua said, "The situation's urgent, and you're here sleepwalking."

Without changing his tone, Specs said, "You're the ones sleepwalking. Look at what you're doing. At a time like this, the supreme leaders of the country are instructing fire brigades how to put out fires, urging nurses to feed babies, and even teaching a little girl how to eat. It's shameful, don't you think?" Then he settled back down against the computer desk and said no more.

Huahua and Xiaomeng looked at each other, and for a few seconds no one spoke. Then Xiaomeng said, "Specs is right."

"Yeah. We lost our minds for a moment," Huahua said with a sigh.

Xiaomeng said, "Turn off the walls," and the walls quickly returned to an opaque creamy white, instantly cutting them off from the chaos of the outside world. She pointed around them and continued, "Turn off the computers and screens, too. Let's have three minutes of peace. No talking, and no thinking. For three minutes."

The screens went blank. The cream walls surrounding them seemed to form a chamber carved from a block of ice, and in this quiet space, the child leaders slowly began to recover their senses.

Suspension

supernova era, hour 2

When the three minutes were up, a suggestion to turn the computers and screens back on was countered by Huahua: "We're really pathetic. The situation is nothing worth panicking over. First off, I want us all to realize that the current state of the country is something we should have foreseen long ago."

Xiaomeng nodded in agreement. "That's right. The

stability of the dry run was the unusual thing. There's no way children could have done that themselves."

Huahua said, "And as for handling the current state of emergency, we're no better at handling the details than the agencies lower down. We need to focus on our own duties: working out the reasons—the deep, underlying reasons— why this happened."

The children started talking, and before long they began voicing the same question: "It's weird. The children's world was running so smoothly, so why did it suddenly plunge into chaos?"

"Suspension," said Specs, who had come out of his corner to make another cup of instant coffee.

The word meant nothing to the children.

He explained, "We came up with the concept when we were watching Huahua walk on train tracks eight months ago, when we were brought out to have a look at MSG and salt. We wondered how well he'd manage if the tracks were suspended in midair. Before the Epoch Clock ran out, the children's world was running on tracks firmly grounded in the adult world, and we could ride smoothly along them. But after the clock ran out, the ground fell away, leaving the tracks suspended in midair over a bottomless pit."

The children murmured their agreement with Specs's analysis.

Huahua said, "Clearly, that last green star going out triggered the instability. When the children realized there were no adults left, their emotional support vanished all at once."

Specs nodded. "And we should acknowledge the frightening mass effect of that emotional imbalance. Put together, a hundred minds in that state could outstrip ten thousand in isolation."

Xiaomeng said, "Mom and Dad have gone and left us here. We all feel that. Here's my analysis of the state of the country, and you can judge whether or not I'm right. All of the children in the country are looking for emotional support to fill in for the adults. Children in the provincial and metropolitan leadership are no different from the rest, so the midlevel leadership is paralyzed. That means that the wave of panic sweeping the country is crashing straight into us without any buffer."

"Then our next step is to restore the capabilities of the intermediate leadership," a child said.

Xiaomeng shook her head. "That's impossible in the short term, since we're already in an emergency. What we've got to do now is find a new emotional support for the children. That way, leadership at all levels will recover naturally."

"And how do we do that?"

"I don't know if you've noticed, but when we were handling fires and other emergencies just now, our solutions were no better, and were sometimes worse, than what the children on the scene had. But they calmed down and got the situation under control as soon as they received our reply."

"How do you know?"

Lü Gang said, "We were all answering calls, but only Xiaomeng followed up afterward. From time to time she would ask how the situation was progressing. She pays attention to details."

"And so," Xiaomeng went on, "what the children need from us is a new emotional support."

"So we should make a speech on television!"

She shook her head. "Video and audio of speeches like that have been playing constantly. But they're useless. Children find emotional support in a different way from adults. What they're looking for right now is a hug from their departed mother and father, parental love that's directed at them alone, not spread out among all the children in the country."

"That's astute," Specs said, nodding. "Every lonely and threatened child can only find emotional support when they personally contact the central government and know that we care about them as an individual."

"Which means that we've got to go back to answering phones."

"How many calls can we take? We should bring in tons of kids and have them contact all the children in the country on behalf of the central government."

"How many? There are three hundred million kids. We'd never finish."

Once more they despaired of ever draining the ocean with their teacups. All they could do in the face of such an impossible task was sigh.

Then a kid asked Specs, "Professor, since you know so much, what do you think we should do?"

Specs swallowed a mouthful of coffee. "I can analyze problems, but I can't find solutions."

Huahua said abruptly, "Have you thought about Big Quantum?"

Everyone's eyes brightened. They had been impressed with Big Quantum's capabilities ever since they first arrived at NIT. It was like a giant reservoir swallowing up the muddy flood of data from Digital Domain, but what issued forth

141

from the spillway was clear statistics and data analytics. It could use Digital Domain to monitor the entire country in enough detail to capture every work team, or even every individual. Without it, the country of children could not function at all.

"That's right! Let Big Quantum answer the calls for us!" Now that they had this idea, the children turned the big screen back on immediately. The flaming map popped up again, its red areas larger now, shining dull red light throughout the hall.

Huahua asked, "Big Quantum, can you hear us?"

"I can. I'm waiting for your instructions," said Big Quantum's voice from somewhere in the hall. It was a dynamic adult male voice, one that gave the children the fantasy that adults were still present somewhere, and they trusted this supercomputer implicitly.

"You're aware of the situation. Can you answer the calls coming in from across the country?"

"I can. My knowledge banks give me an advantage in handling power outages, fires, and other emergencies. And I can remain on the line until I am no longer needed."

"Why didn't you tell us that before? That wasn't very nice!" Zhang Weidong shouted.

"You never asked," Big Quantum said evenly.

Huahua said, "Then get to work. Help the children handle their emergencies, but more importantly, tell them that the country has survived. Let them know that we're here with them, that we care for each and every one of them."

"Very well."

"Wait. I've got an idea," Xiaomeng said. "Why do we have to wait for the kids to call in? We can have the computer call up everyone in the country to establish contact, and to provide necessary, individualized assistance. Can you do that, Big Quantum?"

Big Quantum paused briefly before responding: "This will require two hundred million audio processes to run simultaneously. It may result in the loss of some mirror redundancy capabilities."

"In plain language."

"That means I need to access a capacity previously reserved for handling emergency failures. Operational reliability will take a hit."

Huahua said, "That doesn't matter. The kids will at least know that we're standing with them."

Specs said, "I don't agree. Who can predict what the consequences of turning over the state to a computer might be?"

Huahua said, "It's easy to predict the consequences if we don't."

Specs had no answer for that.

Lin Sha asked, "What voice should we have Big Quantum use?"

"This adult voice, of course."

"I disagree," Huahua said. "We need to get the children to trust other children rather than relying on adults who will never come back."

And so they had Big Quantum cycle through different children's voices and ultimately decided on a serene boy's voice.

Then Big Quantum awakened its slumbering power.

supernova era, hour 3

Another huge screen appeared on another white wall

displaying another national map, but this one consisted only of glowing lines on a black background sketching out administrative regions. Big Quantum informed the children that the map contained roughly 200 million pixels, each of which represented a terminal or telephone somewhere in the country, and which would light up when a connection was made.

If the process of Big Quantum calling the entire country were represented visually, it would resemble a spectacular explosion. Digital Domain could be imagined as a gigantic network made up of countless information explosions—its servers—triggered by a complex web of fiber and microwave channels, its center dominated by the super bomb of Big Quantum (eight additional units, four of them hot backups, were distributed in other municipalities). When the calls began, the super bomb detonated, and the flood of information radiated outward, crashing into second-tier servers and detonating ten thousand of them before surging onward to trigger the even more numerous third-tier servers. The information explosion cascaded down until the final level of detonation split the wave of explosions into 200 million narrow information channels and at last to 200 million computers and telephones, covering the whole of the country in a huge digital net.

On the map on the screen, black territory lit up like stars that multiplied and clustered, until after just a few minutes the whole country was a contiguous sheet of white light.

At that moment, all the phones in the country started ringing.

*

In a smallish nursery in urban Beijing, Feng Jing, Yao Ping-ping, and the four infants under their care (including Ms. Zheng's child) were in a large room. Ms. Zheng and their parents had gone off into the endless dark night, leaving them as orphans taking care of even smaller orphans. Many years later someone said to them, "You lost both parents overnight. It's hard to imagine how sad you must have felt." But in fact what weighed heaviest on the children was not sadness but loneliness and fear. Oh, and anger as well, anger at the departed adults: Had Mom and Dad really gone off without us? Humans are far more able to cope with death than with loneliness. The classroom that served as Feng Jing and Yao Pingping's nursery seemed huge and empty now that the babies who had been crying during the day had gone silent, as if suffocated by the deathly stillness. To the two girls, the world seemed dead already, with the children in this room the only survivors left on the entire planet.

Outside was dead calm, no person or any other sign of life, as if even the earthworms and ants underground had died off. They kept the TV on and flipped through the channels one by one, but there hadn't been any picture since the Epoch Clock ran out (they later learned the cable station had crashed). They ached to see something, anything, and even the most annoying old commercial would have moved them to tears. But the screen showed only snow, cold and desolate, like a snapshot of the world that led to blurred vision if stared at too long. And the snow persisted as they looked back at the room and out the window.

Later, when it was light, Feng Jing wanted to have a look around outside, and after a number of false starts, eventually found the courage to open the door. She and Yao Pingping, who was holding Ms. Zheng's child, had been huddled close together, and when she got up and lost contact with their warm bodies, it was like leaping off a life raft into an endless icy ocean. She reached the door, and when her hand touched the lock she shivered: she heard faint footsteps outside. People didn't scare her, but these footsteps weren't from a person! She recoiled and returned to clasp Yao Pingping and the baby tightly. The footsteps grew louder, evidently headed in their direction. Whatever it was reached the door and stopped for a few seconds—*God*—and what did they hear next? Claws at the door! The two girls screamed at the same time and shook uncontrollably. But then the sound stopped and the footsteps retreated. Later they found out it was a starving dog.

The phone rang. Feng Jing dashed to pick it up. A boy's voice said, "Hello. This is the central government. According to the computer record of your nursery, you're a two-person team, Feng Jing and Yao Pingping, in charge of four infants."

It was a heavenly sound. Tears streamed down her face, and she was too choked up to say anything. After a moment, she managed a "Yes."

"Your area is not currently in danger. According to the most recent records, you have sufficient food and water. Please take care of the four little boys and girls in your charge. I'll let you know what to do next. If you have any questions or emergencies, please dial 010-8864502517. No need to write that down. Your computer is on, so I've put the number up onscreen. If you want someone to talk to, you can call me. Don't be afraid. The central government is with you at all times."

★

Data from across the vast territory converged on Big Quantum in a reverse of the massive series of explosions that had just rocked Digital Domain. More than 200 million snippets of conversation poured into Big Quantum's memory at light speed, where they were abstracted into long waveforms, silhouettes of mountains whose peaks receded into the distance. These waveforms floated cloud-like over the pattern database, while higher up, the eyes of the pattern-recognition routine were fixed on their mighty procession, searching the ground of the database for analogues to each snippet, abstracting every syllable and word to pour down in a torrential rain into the buffer canyon, and join up into language code segments that were then chopped and kneaded by the teeth of the semantic analyzer to extract their real meaning.

When Big Quantum digested all of the information it had collected, another process started, this one more complicated than can be described in words: An inference engine hurricane swept across the sea of the knowledge database, churning results up from the depths and covering the surface with wave foam. The bits of foam then underwent an inversion of the process, modulated into waveforms that surged out of Big Quantum's memory and flooded into Digital Domain, at last resolving into the boy's voice that issued from countless telephones and computer speakers.

In the server room two hundred meters underground, lights on the cylindrical mainframe blinked madly, while the cooling unit in the separate cooled server room ran at maximum, pumping huge amounts of liquid helium into the interior of the enormous computer, to keep the operating temperature of the superconducting quantum circuits as close as possible to absolute zero. Inside the computer, a typhoon of high-frequency electric pulses roared through superconducting chips, tides of zeros and ones flowing, ebbing, and flowing again.

If someone were shrunk several hundred million times and inserted into this world, his first sight would be a scene of astonishing chaos: on the chip, a raging torrent of a hundred million pieces of data flowing at the speed of light forced through a channel just a few electrons wide, converging, diverging, and crisscrossing into more torrents that turned the chip into a vast, intricate spiderweb. Data fragments flew everywhere, and addresses traversed like arrows. A drifting master control program waving a myriad of thin transparent tentacles threw thousands upon thousands of cycling program blocks into the roar of data. In a dead-calm desert of a memory unit, a tiny point suddenly exploded, sending an electrical pulse skyward in an enormous mushroom cloud; a solitary line of code passed through the data storm like lightning in search of a slightly darker-colored raindrop.

But it was also a world of astonishing order: The muddy flood of data, after passing through a fine index filter, turned at once into a lake so clear you could see the bottom; the sorting module flitted through the data blizzard like a ghost, arranging the snowflakes by shape into an endlessly long string a thousandth of a second. In this typhoon of zeros and ones, should a single water molecule be incorrect, should a zero be mistaken for a one, or a one for a zero, the entire world could collapse. A gigantic empire, but one for which the blink of an eye meant a hundred dynasties. But from the outside, it appeared as nothing more than a cylindrical object underneath a transparent cover.

The following are accounts of conversations between two ordinary children and Big Quantum:

I was at home, in an apartment tower on the top floor, the twentieth floor. I remember that when the phone rang I was sitting on the sofa staring at the blank TV screen. I ran over and grabbed the phone, and heard a child's voice: "Hello. This is the central government. I'm here to help you. Listen: The building you're in is on fire. The fire has reached the fifth floor."

I put down the phone and craned my neck out the window. It was already getting light in the east, and the Rose Nebula was half below the horizon in the west, and the blend of its blue light and the sunlight cast an eerie glow over the city. I looked down and saw empty streets. There was no sign of a fire at the base of my building. I pulled back and picked up the phone again, and said there wasn't any fire.

"No, there's definitely a fire."

"How do you know? Where are you?"

"In Beijing. The infrared fire sensor in your building has detected a fire and sent a signal to the central computer of the municipal Public Security Bureau. I've already spoken to that computer."

"I don't believe you."

"You can go out and feel the elevator door, but don't open it. It's dangerous."

I did as he said. There were no signs of fire out the front door, but as soon as I touched the elevator door I staggered, because it was burning hot! I remember that the fire safety booklet they issued to each household said that when there's a fire in a tall building, the elevator shaft acts like a chimney to suck the fire upward. I ran back into the room and looked out the window again, and saw yellow smoke just beginning to come out of the bottom floor, and right afterward more smoke from windows on the second and third floors. I rushed back and grabbed the telephone.

"Tell me what to do."

"The elevator and stairwells are impassable. You've got to slide down an escape chute."

"An escape chute?"

"It's a long flexible fabric tube strung along a standpipe from the roof of the building to the ground. When a fire breaks out, people in the building can slide down the tube to safety. If you start sliding too fast when you're inside, you can slow down by grabbing the fabric walls."

"And our building has one of those installed?"

"Yes. On every floor at the entrance to the stairwell, there's a small red iron door that looks like it goes to a garbage chute. That's the entrance to the escape chute."

"But . . . are you sure there's a chute there? If it's a garbage chute, I'll end up falling to death if I crawl in there to escape being burnt to death! How do you know all of this? From the PSB computer?"

"No. The information ought to be on fire and security computers, but I couldn't find it anywhere I looked in their databases, so I linked up with the computer at the municipal architectural design institute responsible for the building, and determined from their blueprints that a chute was indeed installed."

"What about downstairs? And the other kids?"

"I'm calling them as we speak."

"By the time you get in touch with each of them the building will be burnt to cinders! I'll take the stairs and go tell them."

"No, it's too dangerous. The other children have already been notified. You stay here and don't move, but keep on the phone and I'll tell you when to get into the chute. The kids downstairs are sliding down right now, and for safety's sake, you shouldn't crowd the chute. Don't be afraid. The toxic smoke won't reach your floor for another ten minutes."

I was notified three minutes later, and I popped into the escape chute through the red door and slid smoothly to the ground and exited safely through the fire exit. Outside, I found twenty-odd children who had already escaped, all of them on the instructions of the voice from Beijing. They told me that the fire had started just ten minutes earlier.

I was shocked, since this was something I never imagined would happen. The kid in Beijing had searched for information on two separate computers (combing through all of the data on one of them), and had given phone calls to more than twenty children, all in the space of ten minutes.

I was in more pain than I'd ever been in in my life. A stomach ache, a headache, my vision was all green-tinted, I was vomiting constantly, and I could barely breathe. I had no strength left to stand up, and even if I could, there were no doctors. I struggled to the desk to reach for *the phone, but before my fingers touched it, it started ringing. Then a boy's voice said, "Hello. This is the central government. I'm here to help you."*

I wanted to tell him my predicament, but before I could speak I groaned and vomited again, just a little bit of water this time.

"You've got stomach trouble, right?"

"Yes ... yes ... it hurts. How do you know?" I croaked out with difficulty.

"Five minutes ago I linked up with the central computer at the municipal water plant and discovered that a monitoring program in the purification system malfunctioned from being unattended, and despite a reduction in water volume, chlorine was added according to the volume of ten hours ago, meaning that tap water for the eastern half of the city contains chlorine levels nine-point-seven times the safe maximum. As a result, many children have been poisoned. You are one of them."

I remembered that I'd started feeling ill after my thermos ran out and I began using tap water.

"A kid will visit you in a little while. Don't drink any water in your house before then."

Just as he finished speaking, the door opened and a girl I'd never seen before came in holding a medicine bottle and a thermos filled with boiled water. The medicine and water had me feeling better in no time. I asked how she knew I was sick, and how she knew what medicine to bring. Was her dad a doctor? She told me the central government had telephoned to tell her to come, and the medicine was given to her by some boys. Their fathers weren't doctors either; the central government had instructed them to get the medicine from the hospital pharmacy. They'd been called at their home, which was next to the hospital. When they got to the pharmacy, the central government called them there, and the pharmacy computer displayed the drug name. When they still couldn't find it, the terminal showed them the color and shape of the bottle. The central government had them take all the medicine they could find and put it on a cart and then distribute it to a long list of addresses the computer printed out for them. On the way, the boys met two other groups of kids coming from different hospitals bringing large quantities of the same medicine. When they couldn't find an address, public phones at the roadside would ring, and when they picked up, it was the central government with more instructions. . . .

From Lü Wen, *Children and AI: An Unconscious Attempt at a Fully Informatized Society.* Science Press, SE 16.

supernova era, hour 4
To the delight of the children in the hall at the top floor of the NIT, the red patches on the onscreen national map began to contract, slowly at first and then faster, as if a heavy rain were putting out a forest fire.

supernova era, hour 5
The map's red patches had turned to red points that were rapidly winking out.

supernova era, hour 6
Although a large number of red points remained on the

map, the report from Digital Domain announced that the country as a whole was no longer in danger.

At the start of the Supernova Era, human society underwent shocks and changes more drastic than any in history; periods were reckoned not in the decades or centuries of the previous era, but in days or even hours. To later historians, the first six hours of the new era were treated as a single period, known as the Suspension.

Exhausted child leaders emerged onto the balcony outside the hall, where they shivered under a crisp breeze. Fresh air entered their lungs and flowed throughout their bodies, and in the space of a few seconds it was as if their veins had been injected with new blood in place of the old. Their heartbeat and breathing grew more vigorous. It was still a while till sunrise, but the sky was already light and the city was visible in every detail. Fires and smoke had vanished; the streetlights glowed, proving that power had been restored, but few lights were on in the buildings, and the streets were empty. The city was at peace, like it had just dropped off to sleep. A bird of some kind passed swiftly through the clear sky overhead, uttering a brief call.

The eastern horizon brightened. The new world waited to welcome its first sunrise.

6

Inertia

Inspection

Suspension shattered all of the dry run's fantasies of smooth operations, and destroyed the confidence the children had built up during that time. At last they understood that life was far more difficult than they imagined. Regardless, the children's country still managed to struggle to its feet.

During the first two months of the new era, the country focused on recovering from the wounds Suspension had inflicted, and strove to keep on the rails. Work was hard going. To gain a sense of the state of the country, the three child leaders carried out two weeks of inspections throughout the country.

Children say what they mean. Wherever they went, children in all sectors spoke their minds, and the leaders were privately shocked by what they learned about social conditions. The public's state of mind was summed up in three words: tired, bored, and disappointed.

★

On the first day of the inspection, a kid in Tianjin showed Huahua a copy of his daily schedule: Rise at 0600, eat a quick breakfast, humanities class at 0630, grade 5, primarily by self-study. At 0830 start work. Get off work at 1700. After dinner, at 1900, begin specialty classes in job-related knowledge and skills. Finish at 2200, add another hour of humanities. The day didn't end until 2300.

The kid said, "I'm tired. Just tired. My greatest wish these days is to sleep all the way till doomsday."

In Shanghai, the child leaders inspected a nursery. In the children's world, caring for infants was work for society, so nurseries were quite large. Right as the three leaders came in the door, they were stopped by a group of nurses who insisted they spend an hour taking care of babies for themselves. Despite strong protests from their aides and bodyguards, they were essentially held hostage by the growing crowd, who soon numbered more than a thousand, and ultimately had to submit. In a large room they were each put in charge of two babies. Xiaomeng managed the best, keeping her two babies happy and content, but when the hour was up her back ached and her legs were shaky. Huahua and Specs were a wreck. Their four babies kept crying but refused milk and wouldn't go to sleep. They just wailed like train whistles, loud enough to wake up the babies in the surrounding beds, and soon all twenty-odd babies in the room were fussing and crying. By the end of it, Huahua and Specs felt on the verge of a mental breakdown.

"Now I see how hard a time my mom had with me," Huahua said to an accompanying reporter.

A nurse sniffed. "Your mom only had the one of you. Each of us has two or three babies to look after! And at night we have class. It's a huge drag!"

"That's right. We can't do this work. Get someone else to do it," other nurses added.

Their visit to a coal mine in Shanxi, where they watched the whole workflow of a team of child miners, left the deepest impression on the child leaders. The coal cutter broke down as soon as the shift started, and in the dank, claustrophobic darkness of the mine hundreds of meters underground, repairing the huge machine stuck in a seam of waste rock was a nightmarish task that required strength, finesse, and patience.

When they finally got it fixed, a length of conveyor belt snapped off. The miners were blackened head to toe after shoveling coal off the belt, apart from the white of their teeth whenever they opened their mouths. Replacing the belt was an exhausting ordeal, and when it was finished they were pretty much tired out. It was close to the end of the shift, so they only managed to fill one cartload, but then the cart derailed only a little ways down the tracks.

The children struggled for a while with crowbars and jacks but the cart didn't budge, and in the end they had to remove the coal to rerail the cart, more backbreaking work in air thick with choking dust. Once the cart was righted, they reloaded the coal, which took more energy than unloading it. When they finally came off shift, they lay down on the floor of the changing room, covered in coal dust, too tired even to shower.

"That went well!" said one of the miners. "At least no one got hurt. There are six kinds of things in the mines: coal, rocks, iron, wood, bones, and flesh. Bones and flesh are the softest, and children's most of all!"

Maintaining normal society in the children's country required working with the strength and endurance of adults, which was impossibly hard for the vast majority of them. That wasn't the half of it: children had to be at least eight years old to do typical work, and ten for more complicated tasks, so the working-age population was far smaller, proportionally, than it had previously been, making work far more intense for the children than the adults. Add to that their classes, and you can imagine how tired out they got. Practically all of them had experience of headaches and fatigue, and the overall health of the child population plummeted.

But the young leaders were most worried about the children's mental state: their fascination with the novelty of their work had long since evaporated, and they had realized that the vast majority of the work was mindlessly dull. Their immature minds had a hard time conceptualizing their lives in a planned, systematic way, and they lacked the motivating presence of a family, which meant they had a hard time grasping their work's significance.

Without a spiritual support, heavy, tedious work naturally turned into a form of torture. When the leaders inspected a power plant, a child vividly described that emotional state: "See how we have to sit at this control station all day staring at the dials and screens, and making occasional adjustments when the numbers have gone off. I feel nothing about the work anymore. It's like I'm just a part in a huge machine. What's the point?"

On the plane back to Beijing, the three leaders looked down at the undulating mountains, lost in thought.

Huahua said, "I don't know how much longer this will hold up."

Xiaomeng said, "Life is never easy. Kids are still stuck in an elementary-school mind-set. But they'll come around eventually."

Huahua shook his head. "I'm skeptical. The lifestyle the adults set out for us may not be workable. They were thinking about children from their adult perspective, but they didn't understand what makes kids different."

Xiaomeng said, "There's no other way. Think about the MSG and salt. The price of that is hard work." That vital lesson from the end of the Common Era had made "MSG" and "salt" bywords for economic fundamentals.

Huahua said, "Hard work doesn't mean painful work, or work without hope or delight. Kids ought to work in their own fashion. Specs had it right. We haven't uncovered the rules for the children's world."

They turned back toward Specs. He had spoken little throughout the entire inspection tour but had watched in silence. He never made public speeches, and when a major company had pressed him to speak during a visit, he had said simply, without expression, "I'm responsible for thinking, not speaking," which became a popular quotation thereafter.

Now he was his typical self, holding a cup of coffee, staring blankly at the clouds and land out the window, perhaps enjoying the scene or perhaps lost in thought.

Huahua called to him, "Hey, professor. You've got to give us some opinions."

"This isn't the real children's world," he said.

Huahua and Xiaomeng stared at him, baffled.

He said, "Think about how big a transformation the supernova brought to humanity? Overnight, only children were left in the world. And that brought about other huge changes. A random example: There are no families in today's society. In the past, just that one fact would have completely altered the very fabric of society. The Suspension proved that there are so many aspects of the children's world we've never even imagined. But now? It's like nothing has fundamentally changed from the time of the adults. Society is running along the same track. Don't you find that odd?"

Xiaomeng said, "So what do you think it ought to be like?"

Specs shook his head slowly. "I don't know. I'm just sure that it shouldn't be this way. What we see now might really be only the product of inertia from the adults' society. Deep down, things have got to be accumulating; they just haven't made themselves known yet. The real children's world may not have even started."

Huahua asked, "Do you mean we're headed for another Suspension?"

Specs shook his head again. "I don't know."

Huahua stood up. "We've done enough thinking the past few days. Let's do something different. How about we go to the cockpit and watch them fly the plane?"

"You can't just keep bothering folks!" Xiaomeng said.

But Huahua insisted. He often went up front during the course of their inspections and had grown friendly with the child pilots. At first he only asked a few questions, but then he began pestering them to let him fly the plane. The pilots staunchly refused, saying he had no license, but this time he made such a fuss that the captain let him have a go. No sooner had he taken the yoke than the Y-20 began careening like a roller coaster, and he had to return the yoke to the captain.

Huahua said, "Why can't we just switch jobs?"

The captain smiled but shook his head. "I'm not switching. Piloting a country is far harder than flying a plane. You're in big trouble right now."

But in fact, at that very moment, on the ground twenty thousand meters below them, Specs's accumulation had come to an end and was about to demonstrate its power.

The National Assembly

Historians believe that the child leaders' use of Digital Domain and the quantum computer to put an end to the six-hour Suspension at the start of the Supernova Era was a stroke of genius, and the reams of subsequent research, including mathematical modeling, proved that if the situation had not swiftly been brought under control, the country quite likely would have experienced an irreversible collapse.

But as time moved on, that decision acquired a more

profound level of significance. This was the first time humanity had used computers and the internet to unite all of society into a single group. In a way, at that moment, all of the children in the country were sitting in the same classroom. It was not solely the technological foundation provided by quantum computing and Digital Domain that made this possible, but more importantly, the comparatively simple structure of the children's society. In the more complicated adult era, it would have been hard to gather all of society online.

Their experience of Suspension meant that the children were deeply impressed by Digital Domain and the quantum computer that had rescued them from their fear and loneliness, and their dependence on the network remained.

In the toil of the Inertia period, the network became a refuge for the children, a place to escape reality, and they spent their all-too-brief stretches of free time online. Since the country operated atop the foundation of Digital Domain, most of the children's work and schooling also involved the network, and thus it gradually became a second reality for them, a virtual reality where they were far happier than in the real world.

A large number of virtual communities had been set up in Digital Domain, and practically every child old enough to go online was a member of one or more of them. Deep wounds left by the Epoch Clock running out and the Suspension gave the children an instinctive fear of being alone, and they relied on groups to shake off their loneliness at being so abruptly abandoned by the adults. It was the same online. The larger the group, the more easily it attracted new members, and this led to the massive expansion of a few of them through mergers and absorptions of other, smaller-scale communities.

One community, "New World," grew the fastest. By the time the three young leaders began their inspection tour, it claimed a membership of more than fifty million.

The child leaders had not paid much attention to the growth of online society. Huahua devoted his scant free time to online gaming, so he was most familiar with New World's massively multiplayer games. One popular war game set in the Three Kingdoms period had more than ten million players on each of two opposing teams, and in the giant battles, cavalry buried the ground in a brown deluge. A naval war game had fleets of hundreds of thousands of ships, and in one air-combat game, every engagement involved millions of fighter planes that choked the air like a dust cloud.

Upon their return from the inspection tour, the shape of Digital Domain had fundamentally changed. New World, which had now grown to an astonishing size, around 200 million members, was the only community left. That is, practically every child in the country old enough to go online was a member.

Specs took this development very seriously. "This means we have a virtual country overlaid on top of the real one. It's extraordinary. We should set up a committee specifically to track the online country and begin to engage it."

But things developed far faster than they anticipated, and by the third day after their return, Big Quantum said to them, "New World's membership want a dialogue with the country's three top leaders."

Huahua asked, "Which members?"

"All of them."

"Aren't there nearly two hundred million of them? What kind of dialogue? Chat room? BBS? Email?"

"Those primitive methods are unworkable when you're talking about so many people, but an entirely new form of dialogue, the assembly, has been developed in Digital Domain."

"An assembly? Sure, I can make a speech to two hundred million people, but how can they talk to me? Through representatives?"

"No. The assembly will allow all two hundred million people to speak to you."

Huahua burst out laughing. "That's going to be noisy."

Specs said, "It's probably not that straightforward." Then he asked Big Quantum, "Is there one of these assembly conversations every day?"

"That's right. Today, the members are discussing having a conversation with you. The assembly begins at twenty-three thirty."

"Why so late?"

"Most children don't get off work or school till then, so that's when they have time to go online."

"Let's take a look first as ordinary guests," Specs suggested to Huahua and Xiaomeng. They agreed, and called over the engineer in charge of Digital Domain, a boy named Pan Yu who had won gold at the Information Olympics back in the adult era and now was the leading domestic authority on computers. They explained their goal, and he sent someone to fetch four virtual reality helmets.

Specs lowered his eyebrows. "I'll get dizzy as soon as I put it on."

Pan Yu said, "New World has two modes: image and VR. It only looks real in VR mode."

In the hall at the top of the NIT, the leadership was working late, some of them reviewing documents, some making phone calls, and some speaking with ministry heads who had come to make work reports, but they would all get off at 2300. By 2320, only the top three and Pan Yu were left. They put on their VR helmets, which were already plugged in.

At once the four children felt like they were suspended above a blue plaza, the Windows desktop, as it turned out, only three-dimensional, with its icons standing upright like statues. The mouse pointer flew across the plaza and clicked something, and then a window containing a crowd of animated little cartoon people arranged in orderly ranks rose up.

They heard Pan Yu's voice: "You can design your own appearance in the community, but that's a hassle so we'll just use premade ones."

And so they each selected a cartoon-character avatar, and were amused to see their three companions' avatars floating beside them.

Pan Yu said, "The assembly is about to begin. We'll go right there rather than try out anything else in the community."

In the blink of an eye, they were in New World's assembly space. Their first impression was that it was enormous and empty. Above them was a pure blue sky extending farther than they could see, and below them was flat, endless desert. The line NEW WORLD ASSEMBLY was written in the sky in glowing letters that shone down on the vast desert like a row of suns. There was nothing else in the world.

"Where is everyone? Why is it empty?" Huahua asked. Indeed, apart from his three companions floating next to him, there was only sand and sky.

Pan Yu's cartoon avatar opened its big eyes even wider in surprise. "What, you can't see anyone?"

The three leaders looked about them, but could see no one.

Pan Yu seemed to realize something, and said, "Let's go down." He moved the mouse, and the four of them began descending toward the desert. Before long, the sand below them resolved into intricate structures, and then the three of them realized that every grain was a cartoon character. It impressed upon them the sheer scale of the number: the vast desert consisted of 200 million cartoon characters.

Most of the country's children were here.

They continued to descend to the ocean of people and soon were in their midst, surrounded on all sides by cartoons. There seemed to be something in the air, black dots that had just appeared in the sky and were falling to earth. Two landed in their vicinity, two more cartoons, and they realized that children were still entering the area.

"Why are you still guests?" asked a cartoon next to them. He had no feet, but was supported by a flashing wheel. When he extended his long, thin arms, a head appeared on each palm, the same as the head on his neck. He juggled the three heads, replacing the one on his neck again and again. "Hurry up and log in as registered members. The national leaders are coming to talk to us, and as guests your words won't be tabulated." How he distinguished between guests and members they weren't able to tell.

"That's right," said another nearby cartoon with a sniff. "Who'd have thought there would still be unregistered guests."

"And too lazy to make a proper avatar. Selecting a ready-made—it's indecent," said another.

But they weren't much more decent themselves. One of

them may have been too lazy to make a proper body, and had connected two long legs directly to a head. It had no arms, and a pair of wings sprouted from its ears. The other was nothing but a head, a big egg floating half a meter above the ground, with a tiny, fast-spinning rotor poking out of its forehead.

Then another line of glowing red text appeared in the sky: ATTENDANCE HAS REACHED 194,783,453. THE ASSEMBLY IS ABOUT TO BEGIN.

The rightmost digits of the 190 million number continued to turn over.

Then a voice sounded in the air, the familiar voice of Big Quantum. "I've conveyed your request to the national leadership."

Pan Yu said to the three leaders, "Notice how Big Quantum refers to a single request?"

"When will they be here?" said a child's voice. Boy or girl it was hard to tell, but it was loud and carried a long echo. At the same time, a line of red text appeared in the air: VIRTUAL CITIZEN 1: 98.276%.

"Who's that speaking?" Huahua asked Pan Yu.

"That's Virtual Citizen 1."

"Who's that?"

"It's not a 'who.' It's a person made up of nearly two hundred million children."

"I noticed just now that everyone around us was moving their lips as if they were speaking, but I couldn't hear anything."

"That's right. They were all speaking, but only Big Quantum heard the nearly two hundred million messages. It summarized them into the one statement you just heard."

"That's what you mean by the assembly format?"

"Right. This format allows an individual to carry on a simultaneous conversation with more than a hundred million conversation partners. Right now, two hundred million children have turned into just one, so Big Quantum referred to 'your request' and not 'your requests.' It's a highly complicated process that requires advanced intelligence and fast processing speed. The short, simple statement you just heard would, if printed out, fill enough paper to circle the globe. Only a quantum computer can handle it."

Then Big Quantum answered Virtual Citizen 1: "They said they need to think it over before making a decision."

Specs cut in, "Just one problem. What if the two hundred million children have a difference of opinion that can't be summarized into one statement?"

Pan Yu put a finger to his lips. "Shhh. You'll see what happens very soon."

Another voice sounded, pitched differently from the previous one so it sounded like someone else was speaking. "They'll definitely come." And the text in midair read, VIRTUAL CITIZEN 2: 68.115%.

Pan Yu whispered an explanation: "The percentage indicates the proportion of people who hold that opinion."

A voice at a different pitch said, "That's not certain. They may not come." The text in midair read, VIRTUAL CITIZEN 3: 24.437%.

"Can they not? They've got to come! They're the leaders of the country, and they've got to talk to the country's children." (VIRTUAL CITIZEN 4: 11.536%)

"What do we do if they don't?" (VIRTUAL CITIZEN 3: 23.771%)

"We do it on our own." (VIRTUAL CITIZEN 5: 83.579%)

"I told you, they're definitely going to come." (VIRTUAL CITIZEN 2: 70.014%)

Pan Yu said, "You see, if there's disagreement, the virtual citizen will split into two or more parts. How many is determined by the chosen level of precision. At the most precise, all messages will be listed out. That's impossible, of course. What's important is that each virtual citizen is usually more or less a defined group with its own particular character traits. They'll continue to appear, just like an individual. VC 2 and VC 3, for example, returned just now."

After watching for a while, Huahua said to Pan Yu, "Let's leave."

"Press the exit button on your clothes." The button was on the cartoon's torso, and pressing it returned them instantly to the Windows space.

"That was amazing!" Huahua exclaimed after removing his helmet.

Xiaomeng said, "They don't need any leaders at all in that network country. They accomplish everything through discussions among two hundred million kids."

Specs said thoughtfully, "This will have a profound effect on the real world, too. We paid attention too late."

Xiaomeng asked, "Then should we speak with them?"

Specs said, "We've really got to be careful. This is like nothing else in history. No one knows what might happen. We should think about it longer and more carefully before acting."

"There's no time. It's like I said: If we don't go, then something's definitely going to happen," Huahua said.

With Specs and Xiaomeng in agreement, they spent the night in a conference studying the issue, and discovered that quite a few members of the leadership team had been to the New World Assembly and were familiar with the situation. They mostly felt that it was a positive thing. One kid said, "We're all doing things that are beyond our own abilities. If the country really can be run like this, it'll free us up."

Everyone agreed that the central government, as represented by the three top leaders, would attend the New World Assembly and talk to the 200 million children.

They entered the New World Assembly area a second time, this time using their real-world appearances for avatars. Big Quantum erected a tall podium for them in the center of the space. They came early to prepare, and to get used to the environment, and as the country's 200 million children logged in and entered, the dense crowd of cartoon characters began to blot out the sky like a layer of clouds. They watched as the avatars fell from the sky like a storm. When the endless sea of people finally calmed, 200 million pairs of eyes were fixed on the platform.

"I feel like I'm going to melt," Xiaomeng whispered.

Huahua, on the other hand, drank it in. "It's different for me. For the first time I've found what leading a country feels like! How about you, professor?"

Specs said without emotion, "Don't bug me. I'm thinking."

When the assembly began, Virtual Citizen 1 led off. According to the figures showing in the sky, he represented a 97.458 percent share.

"We're extremely disappointed in this new world. The

adults left, leaving us kids behind, so it should be a fun world. But it's not fun at all. It's not even as fun as the world was when the adults were around."

Xiaomeng said, "The adults used to give us food and clothing, so of course we had time to play and take it easy. But not now. We've got to work, or else we'll starve to death. We can't forget the MSG and salt."

Virtual Citizen 2 (63.442%): "Xiaomeng, don't let that trainload of MSG and ten trainloads of salt scare you. That was for one-point-three billion people in the adults' time. We don't eat that much."

Virtual Citizen 3 (43.117%): "Why does Xiaomeng sound so much like an adult? Boring!"

Virtual Citizen 1 (92.571%): "Regardless, we don't like this world now."

Huahua asked, "So what kind of world do you want?"

Later historians studying the virtual citizens' answers to this question looked through the raw records of individual member responses kept by the quantum computer; although only a small proportion were retained, it still amounted to forty gigabytes, or around twenty billion Chinese characters. If printed out as a trade-paperback-size volume, it would be eight hundred meters thick. Below are some representative responses:

I want the sort of country where kids can go to school if they want, but don't have to if they don't want to. They can play if they want, and if they don't, they don't have to play at all. If they want to eat, they can, and if they don't, they don't have to. They can go wherever they want, and if they don't want to go anywhere, they don't have to. . . .

I used to hate having adults look after us. Now they're not around, and the country belongs to the kids. We should really be having lots of fun. . . .

In our country, you can play soccer in the middle of the street. . . .

A country that gives me as much chocolate as I want. And gives Flower (*perhaps the speaker's cat.—Ed.*) as many cans of fish as it wants. . . .

A country that celebrates Spring Festival every day. Every day, each person is issued ten packs of whippersnappers, twenty double-bangs, and thirty flash-bangs, as well as a hundred kuai in yasui money, all of them crisp new notes. . . .

In my country, when you eat dumplings you can just eat the filling. . . .

It used to be that only kids could play, but adults couldn't because they had to go to work. We'll grow up too, but we don't want to go to work, we just want to keep playing. . . .

Dad said I don't work hard at school, so when I grow up I'll be a street sweeper. If I don't work hard, my country won't make me be a street sweeper. . . .

Will the country let us all live in the city?

I'll only take three classes in school: music, art, and sports. . . .

No proctor for school exams. Kids can give themselves their own marks. . . .

The country should give every class in every school fifty gaming consoles, one for everyone. You play all through class, and whoever can't get a hundred and twenty thousand points in *Battle for the Galaxy* gets kicked out! Deet-deet-deet, dong-dong-dong. It'll be awesome. . . .

Build a huge playground at my house, like the one in Miyun in Beijing, but ten times bigger. . . .

The country should issue us dolls on a set schedule, a different one each time. . . .

Shoot a cool animated series, ten thousand episodes, that never goes off the air. . . .

Puppies are my favorite. Why doesn't the country give every puppy a pretty little doghouse?

Big Quantum distilled these 200 million messages into one sentence that was uttered by Virtual Citizen 1, representing 96.314 percent of the members in attendance:

"We want a world of fun!"

Xiaomeng said, "The adults have drawn up a detailed five-year plan for the country, and we have to follow it."

Virtual Citizen 1: "We think the adults' five-year plan is boring. We've drawn up our own five-year plan."

Huahua asked, "Can you give us a look?"

Virtual Citizen 1: "That's the point of this assembly. We've built a virtual country to show off our five-year plan. Have Big Quantum give you a tour. You're sure to love it!"

Huahua said to the sky, "Great. Big Quantum, show us around!"

A Country of Fun

No sooner had he uttered those words than the blue sky and the crowd vanished before their eyes, leaving the three children hanging in an endless black void. When their eyes adjusted, they saw stars appear in the remote distance, and then a blue orb take shape in space. It hung like a glowing crystal ball in the dark ocean of the infinite cosmos, and spread across its surface a swirl of snow-white clouds. It looked so fragile, liable to shatter at the slightest touch and spill out its blue blood into the cold isolation of space. As the blue crystal ball drew closer, they realized how huge it was, and eventually the gigantic blue planet filled all the sky, and the children could see clearly the borders between oceans and continents. Now all of Asia was visible at once, and a twisting red line appeared on the brown land, a closed loop demarcating the borders and coastline of that ancient country in the east. Its territory drew nearer, and they could begin to make out the ripples of mountain ranges and vein-like rivers. Then Big Quantum spoke: "We're now in orbit at a height of more than twenty thousand kilometers."

Earth slowly rotated beneath their feet, and they seemed to be flying toward something. Xiaomeng suddenly shouted, "Look! It's like there's a thread up ahead."

The thread ran from space to the land below, its top half clearly visible against the blackness behind it, almost like a long strand of spider silk joining the Earth to a point in space. Its lower half merged in with the colors of the land and was hard to make out, but with effort they could see that it terminated in the vicinity of Beijing. The children were flying toward the spider silk, and as they got closer they could see that it was as shiny as a silken thread. Sections of it reflected the bright sunlight at times, and its far end flickered like a lamp. It gained width as they drew nearer, and then they could make out details of its structure. Now they knew what the long spider silk actually was: it wasn't hanging down from space, but was rising from the surface. They could hardly believe their eyes.

"Wow!" Huahua exclaimed. "It's a building!"

Indeed it was a skyscraper, clad in fully reflective mirrors, towering into space.

The voice of Virtual Citizen 1 sounded in the children's ears: "All children in the country call this home. This building is twenty-five thousand kilometers high and has three million floors. Each floor is home to an average of one hundred children."

"You mean every child in the country lives in this one building?" Huahua asked in surprise. But when they landed on the roof, they realized it was not at all impossible. Their impression of the spider silk as narrow was due to their distance and its ratio of height to width, but the rooftop might have been large enough to hold the Workers' Stadium twice over. The giant flashing signal light in the center, as tall as an ordinary twenty-story building, rotated and shone so brightly they couldn't look at it head-on; perhaps it was a warning light for passing spacecraft.

They crossed to the other side of the roof, where there was an entrance to the top floor—floor 3 million—of the supertower. This floor, they noticed at once, was one big grassy lawn, with a fountain smack in the center reflecting a warm artificial light. Scattered about the lawn were a few dozen finely wrought cabins of the sort only found in fairy tales, the dwellings of this floor's hundred children. Inside one of them they saw a typical kid's room, toys of all kinds strewn about the bed and table. In another, also clearly a kid's room, the decoration was entirely different, and they found that every room they went into was unique and personalized.

The floor below was another grassy meadow, but in place of the fountain there was a clear brook, with the children's homes distributed along its banks. They went into a few of them, and as before each one was different.

The scene changed dramatically on the next floor, a serene snowscape that shone faintly blue in the eternal twilight, and snowflakes drifted downward in an uninterrupted stream, landing in thick white blankets on the roofs of the children's houses. There were snowmen in front of some of them. Evidently the children on this floor loved the winter.

One floor down was a forest with houses built in clearings. A thin morning fog was pierced by shafts of light from the sun rising beyond the trees. Birdcalls rang out at times from within the forest.

They descended more than twenty floors, each of them its own unique world. In one, it never stopped raining; another was a desert of golden sand; one was even a miniature ocean, with children living in boats drifting about on the surface.

"How did you manage to make all these?" Specs asked.

Big Quantum replied, "This was produced using one of the virtual country's gaming programs, an old city simulator. The virtual country uses plug-ins provided by a component library to build the virtual world, and it can create virtual images on its own."

They looked carefully about them, at every blade of grass and every pebble, all of them true to life. "An immense amount of work went into this building," Huahua exclaimed.

Virtual Citizen 1 replied, "Of course. More than eighty million children had a hand in its construction, and more than a hundred million designed their own homes."

Led by Big Quantum, the children entered a streamlined, transparent elevator that protruded from the side of the building. From within they could see the glittering stars and the Earth below.

Xiaomeng said, "You're not really planning on building a building like this in the real world, are you?"

Virtual Citizen 1 said loudly, "Of course we are. Why else would we have drafted these plans? Everything you see down there on the ground we want built for real!"

Huahua said, "Sucks if you have to go to the roof, and have to take a twenty-five-thousand-kilometer elevator ride."

"That's no problem. All the elevators in this building are little rockets, and are faster than the satellite boosters of the adults' era. Take a look!"

Just then an elevator car spurting flames rocketed past them at astonishing speed, and just as it was about to reach the roof, the flames at the bottom of the streamlined car vanished, and reappeared out of the top to slow it down. Virtual Citizen 1 explained, "These elevators can reach speeds of sixty thousand kph, making the journey up from the ground in a little over twenty minutes."

Specs snorted. "Judging from the deceleration we just saw, I'm afraid the passengers were smashed to a pulp."

Virtual Citizen 1 made no reply, evidently caring not a whit for such a minor problem. Then the top of their car spurted flame and they began descending with terrifying speed. They felt the speed for the first few seconds, but then as the wall of the building blurred into one smooth continuous track, they seemed almost motionless, apart from the floor indicator that ticked backward rapidly in the thousands place. There was no sense of downward acceleration; rather, they stood firmly on the floor of the elevator, as if the VR program had overlooked this particular level of reality. But one thing it did get right: Despite being in space, they were not weightless, since weightlessness in orbiting objects is due to their motion rather than their height; even at this height, Earth's gravitational attraction remained strong.

Huahua said, "Set aside the building's feasibility for the moment. What's the point of it? Why do all kids in the country have to live in one building?"

Virtual Citizen 1 said, "To leave all the other places for playing in!"

Many years later, historians found profound significance in the notion of the supertower, tracing it to the loneliness common to every child's heart when the Epoch Clock ran out.

"The country is enormous. That's not enough for you to play in?" Xiaomeng asked.

"As you'll find out shortly, it's not!"

"Still, the building's actually pretty cool," Huahua said with feeling.

"It's even cooler than this down there!"

The rocket elevator continued to plummet. Eventually the arc of the Earth's edge wasn't so pronounced, and the ground below them became more detailed.

Xiaomeng looked from the top of the building to the bottom, both ends too far to see, and exclaimed, "The height of the building is twice the diameter of the Earth!"

Specs nodded. "It's like a long strand of Earth hair."

Huahua said, "And think about how it'll pass from the dark side to the sunward side, and how the sun will light up its enormous height. What a magnificent sight!"

The elevator's rockets switched from top to bottom, and they began to decelerate. Soon they could make out the separations between building floors, and just a few seconds later the elevator came to a halt, the VR program once again ignoring the fact that the force of such a quick deceleration would crush the elevator's passengers into meat paste. The children could see that the elevator was still in space, but Virtual Citizen 1 said, "Our present position is on the two hundred and forty thousandth floor of the building, at a height of two thousand kilometers. We won't take the elevator the rest of the way but will use a different method of descent. Look down, what do you see?"

They looked out from the elevator and saw a long line rising from the Earth, its terminus nearly invisible because it was so thin. As it rose, it traced two large loops and a range of curves and bends, as if some naughty child had scribbled across a photograph of the Earth. The line extended toward the building and joined it just below their elevator. Close up they could see it was a narrow train track.

Virtual Citizen 1 asked, "Can you guess what that is?"

Huahua said, "It looks like a giant picked up one end of the railroad from Beijing to Shanghai and attached it here."

Virtual Citizen 1 laughed. "What a description! You must be a writer. But this track is much longer than that. It's more than four thousand kilometers long. It's a roller coaster we're planning to build."

A roller coaster? The children looked in amazement at the long track and its two huge loops glittering attractively in the sunlight.

"You mean it goes all the way to the ground?"

"That's right. We're going to take it down."

As he spoke, a small boat-shaped vehicle with five two-person seats like the roller coasters they had seen in amusement parks emerged on rails from the building and stopped

179

under the elevator. A hatch opened in the elevator floor right over the car (at this point the VR program ignored the vacuum of space).

As soon as the three of them were in the car, it started sliding smoothly along the rails. It moved slowly at first, but once it was out of the building's shadow and into the bright sunlight, it reached the first big drop and catapulted them forward. Since their VR helmets only provided visual sensations and they weren't able to actually feel the acceleration, they missed out on experiencing the first feeling of weightless during their time in space. Supergravity replaced no gravity as the roller coaster entered the first loop, and they saw the stars and the Earth revolve around them. When they leveled out again, Xiaomeng looked back from the rear seat. The loop was well behind them already, and the supertower was now just a thin thread of spider silk that seemed to be dangling from the glittering galaxy itself. The second loop was even bigger than the first one but took the same amount of time to complete; clearly, they were still speeding up. Then came a long descent, not monotonic, of course, since the roller coaster traced a series of troughs and crests, some of them quite lofty. The coaster twisted into a spiral at the end of that stretch, and when the children entered it, they felt like they were at the center of the universe with the Earth and stars spinning endless circles around them.

Starting off level, the spiral eased downward until it was almost perpendicular, making the Earth into a huge record spinning round and round in front of them. Out the spiral's other end, the tracks stayed vertical, dropping them straight at the Earth and creating another situation where they ought to feel weightless. Ahead of them the tracks twisted into a tangle perhaps a hundred kilometers in diameter, and it felt like they were threading that labyrinth forever, nearing the exit multiple times only to be dragged back on a path toward the entrance again. They weren't at the center of the universe now; their cosmos was a box in the hands of a fidgety child who turned it over and over in random directions.

The roller coaster escaped the maze at last and entered a straight-line descent, picking up speed again. This stretch lasted a long while; up ahead the tracks blurred into a smooth belt which made it hard to judge their speed. The color above them had turned from black to a light purple that gradually became deep blue; the stars had grown fuzzy, and there was little curvature to the horizon.

Sitting in front, Huahua saw a flame at the tip of their streamlined car that quickly blossomed until it enveloped the entire car; the program clearly had not ignored atmospheric friction. After the flames disappeared, the children found they were above a sea of clouds. The sky above them was a clear blue, shining with sunlight that, in contrast to the stark black-and-white illumination of outer space, seemed to permeate every last wrinkle in their clothes. On the tracks up ahead was another series of loops, climbs, and dips, and the presence of clear reference objects meant that their ride was far more heart-stoppingly crazy than back in space.

During the moments when the roller coaster slid smoothly, the children could see gigantic frames towering up from the ground in the distance, all of them at least ten thousand meters tall, piercing the clouds. Some of them formed right triangles with the ground, while others were shaped like giant doors, as if they were enormous upright compasses and set squares. Huahua asked what they were, and Virtual Citizen 1 replied, "Slides and swings. For little kids to play on."

Huahua couldn't imagine what kind of little kid could slide down a ten-thousand-meter slide, much less how they could get such a gigantic swing swinging.

The roller coaster's final segment was an easy slope that descended toward what the children thought was a grassy plain covered in colorful flowers, but when they finally landed, they realized the plain was actually formed from a huge number of multicolored rubber balls, blown-up versions of the kind you'd find in a ball pit, only here, stretching as far as the eye could see, it had to be called a ball ocean. They slid quite a long ways through this ball ocean before stopping, kicking up balls around them that then clattered back down again in a kaleidoscope of rain. They couldn't think of who would dive into such a weird ocean, or how they'd get out afterward; they knew from previous experiences of "swimming" in ball pits as younger kids that movement wasn't easy. Then two giant wheels popped out of the roller coaster, one on each side, churning the balls into motion with a strange gurgling sound. The virtual citizen informed them that the ocean of balls covered nearly a thousand square kilometers.

"It'll use up all of the rubber in the country. How will we make car tires after that?" Xiaomeng asked, but the virtual citizen didn't answer, clearly uninterested.

After the roller coaster emerged from the ball ocean, the children were able to observe the giant slide from up close. It was a water slide. Water came rushing down the wide slide from a top that was farther than they could see, as if a river were pouring down from the sky. Imagining himself sliding down that river for ten thousand meters, Huahua felt his entire body tremble with anticipation, and he asked if he could have a ride.

"You're only out for fun, Huahua. We've got serious things to do," Xiaomeng said as she held him back.

The virtual citizen added, "That's right. It's another forty kilometers from here to the lift, and we shouldn't waste that time. Besides, what's the point of doing it in a virtual, computer-hosted form? Wait until we've built the real thing—that'll be a thrill!"

Leaving the super water slide, the children saw a huge wide platform, big enough to hold several hundred people, hanging from thick steel cables dropped from above. At first they thought it was an athletic field, but it was only when the virtual citizen informed them that it was the seat of the gigantic swing that they noticed the poles towering skyward a thousand meters away on either side. And then they discovered how the swing would be set in motion: the platform had rocket engines attached to its underside.

Next they visited the bumper car arena. Each car was the size of one of the dump trucks from the adults' time, each wheel more than two meters tall. The inflatable bumpers on all sides turned them into huge monsters. Thousands upon thousands of them colliding and chasing after each other on a vast plain would kick up enough dust to blot out the sky. It would certainly take guts and a sacrificial spirit to play that game.

The virtual citizen explained, "This is the first development zone for the New Five-Year Plan, and focuses on the construction of huge carnival rides. You still haven't seen the giant Ferris wheel and Challenger UFO; they're more than a hundred kilometers away, but on a good day you could see them. Now let's go to Zone Two, the gaming zone."

No sooner had he spoken than their environment changed, and they found themselves in a huge city built of tall, oddly shaped buildings, some of them like enormous castles, others wrapped in tangles of pipes or covered in holes like Swiss cheese.

"These are all video game arcades?" Huahua asked.

"No. Each of them is a gaming console."

"They're enormous! Then . . . where are the screens?"

"The idea behind these consoles is new. To play, you've got to go inside, where the setting is all holographic or made of actual devices. Each game begins from the console's bottom floor, and you work your way up until the conclusion at the top floor. You don't play with a mouse or joystick like you used to, but you're actually part of the game world and are running around and fighting all the time. Like that castle console: it's a royal palace, and you've got to defeat tons of enemies before you become king. The one with all the holes is a monsters' den, and you use your laser sword to kill monsters like poison dragons and rescue the princess. Of course, these games are for the little kids. Since they're so small, they can only run small-scale games."

"What? These are only small-scale games? How big are the big ones?"

"Large-scale machines don't have a fixed form. Most of them take up an entire zone."

The environment changed again, and they found themselves on a broad plain where in the distance formations of ancient foot soldiers were advancing, helmets glittering in the sunlight, their raised spears like a densely planted wheat field. "You see? This is a game of ancient warfare. The players command a robot army ten thousand strong and pit it against another one. There's also a Western game where you ride a horse into the wilderness armed with your revolver and have all sorts of adventures."

"How much land does Zone Two cover?"

"A million square kilometers, more or less, would be enough to build all the consoles. Now I'll show you Zone Three: the zoo."

Their environment switched to the boundary between a forest and a plain. Hordes of animals cavorted on the plain and ran in and out of the forest. "These megazoos are true animal kingdoms. They have no cages, and all the animals can move freely through the natural environment. When you go into these zoos, you're entering the mountains and wilderness where you may come across all sorts of animals. You'll wear powered protective clothing, so no wild beast will be able to hurt you. You'll travel through the forest atop an elephant, or take a photo with a Bengal tiger. The biggest zoo is nearly three hundred thousand square kilometers in area, even bigger than the UK. That one doesn't have any roads; helicopters are the only form of transportation available, and when you go in, you'll feel like you're entering a primeval world right at the dawn of humanity. We'll also build three animal cities with streets and buildings just like human ones, but they'll be filled with cute puppies and kittens and other animals kids can be friends with. You can go in and play with them, and you can take the ones you like back with you. . . . This zone covers an area of nearly one million square kilometers."

"Does it need to be that big?"

"What kind of a question is that? Animals need freedom of migration. Birds need to fly freely. Can they do that without enough space? Next I'll show you Zone Four, the adventure zone."

Their environment changed rapidly, from the foot of a steep snow-covered mountain to an endless savannah to a deep mountain gorge to the banks of a raging river . . .

When they stopped at last beneath a huge waterfall, Huahua remarked, "There doesn't seem to be anything built in these places."

"That's right. All of the old cities will be torn down, and the zone will be restored to its pristine state."

"What for?"

"Adventuring!"

"Can't you adventure in some of the Zone Two games?"

"That's totally different! In games, the program is preset. Everything is predictable. It's totally different here. You don't know what you'll find. That's what makes it exciting. Besides, this is far bigger than any game in Zone Two."

"How large is Zone Four?"

"The entire northwest!"

"That's excessive."

"The hell it is. It's got to be big. Where's the adventure if the edge is just a few steps away?"

"Well, if you do it that way, our country doesn't have nearly enough territory."

"And that's why Zone Five only contains one small project."

"There's a Zone Five?"

"Right. Candytown."

The city they now found themselves in was an exquisite miniature in comparison to the gigantic scale of the previous zones. The buildings were short, and its most striking characteristic was that it was colored in vibrant monochromes, as if it were built from big wooden blocks. "This is Candytown. All the buildings are built from candy. The brown stadium you're looking at is made entirely of chocolate. That translucent building over there is made of rock sugar."

"Can you eat it?"

"Of course!"

Huahua went up to the stadium and clicked on a brown pillar beside the door; a chunk came right off. Xiaomeng went over to a small, dainty building and lightly touched a window; the glass shattered, and she picked up a fragment imagining how sweet the thin bit of sugar crystal would taste on her tongue.

Specs broke his long silence to snort, "This is a violation not only of the laws of economics but of science as well. Is candy strong enough to build with?"

The virtual citizen replied, "That's the reason there are no tall buildings in Candytown. And they've got steel skeletons for strength."

"Won't they melt in the heat?"

"Excellent point." Their environment changed again, but not by much. Now they were on the outskirts of Candytown, at one of the small hills that ringed it. The brilliant colors and soft lines of the hills made them seem plucked from a watercolor painting.

The virtual citizen said, "It's a shame you can't smell them, but they're delicious. These are the Ice Cream Hills."

When they looked closer, they saw rivulets of cream

running all over the hills, some of them tumbling in creamy waterfalls. The streams joined into a river flowing down the valley, an undulating flow of milk-colored soft ripples and waves that passed without sound. "Climate conditions were somewhat ignored, so the ice cream is melting. Candytown might have to be constructed someplace colder."

Later Supernova Era historians devoted considerable research to the Candytown concept, first of all to the puzzle of why, when children of the Common Era didn't care much for candy, were they so captivated by it in the new world of their imagination? Maybe candy was for children a representation of something adults could never understand, a symbol of beauty.

From their analysis of Big Quantum's original records, historians learned that the architects of the New Five-Year Plan and the virtual country were mainly children between the ages of five and eleven, bolstered by younger children, and by sheer force of numbers they held an unbeatable advantage under the statistical and inductive principles of the New World Assembly. Disappointment with the real world led a significant proportion of older children to join them, and in the frenzy that gradually developed, only a minority of children maintained any sense of rationality.

Debate

Their environment changed a final time, returning the three young leaders to the platform in the New World Assembly at the center of a sea of people. Looking down, they saw not just a sea of eyes but a sea of mouths, two hundred million mouths constantly in motion speaking words that only Big Quantum could hear and remember.

Virtual Citizen 1 (91.417%) asked, "What do you think of the New Five-Year Plan? Can you guide us to make it real?"

Huahua said, "Are you the only one here? There's no Virtual Citizen 2?"

Virtual Citizen 1 said, "VC 2 has been around a few times, but is really annoying. I told them to piss off. Hey, VC 2, come out and speak if you've got any guts!"

And so the country launched into a huge debate, the biggest ever seen in human history, in which direct participants numbered more than 200 million. Across the vast territory of the country, children could be found on the phone or at their computers shouting or typing away, each of them vying to contribute their 1/200,000,000th part toward the world of their dreams. The smaller of the two competing groups of children had a larger average age, but tragically, Big Quantum's summarized statements did not (or could not) take age into account, and so the larger group held an absolute advantage. And thus, with a huge number of younger children taking part in the debate to determine the fate of the country, the least rational and most capricious formed a highly dangerous social force.

The timid voice of Virtual Citizen 2 (8.792%) ventured, "Don't listen to them, Huahua, Specs, and Xiaomeng. That's just the jeering of a group of ignorant babies who only care about playing. I recommend that the assembly's rules for tabulation and summarization should be altered to incorporate an age-based weighting."

A commotion shook the sea of people down below. The

cartoon avatars shouted and whirled about, as if a stiff wind had churned up waves on the ocean.

VIRTUAL CITIZEN 1: "We're babies? How old are you? Thirteen at the oldest. Just a few days ago you'd have been spanked by your dad, but now you're pretending to be adults? Shame shame shame shame shame! Listen, the adults are gone. It's only us kids that are left. No one gets to tell anyone what to do anymore!"

VIRTUAL CITIZEN 2: "The problem is that your five-year plan is impossible."

VIRTUAL CITIZEN 1: "How do you know that if you don't do it? A hundred years ago, would you have thought all two hundred million kids in the country could be in one place for a meeting? You're a coward."

VIRTUAL CITIZEN 2: "If it was possible, then why didn't the adults do it?"

VIRTUAL CITIZEN 1: "The adults? Hmph! They didn't know how to have fun. Of course they weren't going to build a fun world. The world the adults built was awful. Everything about it was so boring. They didn't play; they just spent their days pouting and going silently to work. Total snoozefest. And they insisted on telling us what to do, can't do this, can't do that, can't play here, can't play there, so for us it was just school school school and test test test, behave and be a good kid. Ugh ugh ugh ugh! But now it's just us left, and we want to build a fun world."

Xiaomeng said, "And how does this fun world of yours produce food? Without food, we'll all starve to death."

VIRTUAL CITIZEN 1: "The adults left us with tons of stuff. That'll last us for ages."

VIRTUAL CITIZEN 2: "Wrong. It'll run out eventually."

VIRTUAL CITIZEN 1: "No it won't no it won't! It never ran out for the adults, did it?"

VIRTUAL CITIZEN 2: "That's because they were constantly producing more stuff to eat."

VIRTUAL CITIZEN 1: "Production production. Gag. Shut up shut up shut up."

VIRTUAL CITIZEN 2: "But what happens when we've eaten everything?"

VIRTUAL CITIZEN 1: "We deal with it then. First we want to build the fun world. Then we'll tackle food. There were so many people in the adults' time, but they managed to eat enough without too much work, right?"

Xiaomeng shouted. "My friends, the adults put a lot of work into getting enough to eat."

VIRTUAL CITIZEN 1: "We never saw that. Did any of you? Did you, Xiaomeng? Hah!"

VIRTUAL CITIZEN 2: "That you never saw it doesn't mean they weren't working hard, you little idiots."

VIRTUAL CITIZEN 1: "You're the idiot! Wannabe adult. Lame!"

Huahua said, "Let's take a giant step back. Even if we tackle your five-year plan, can you all handle such a strenuous task?"

VIRTUAL CITIZEN 1: "Of course we can."

Huahua said, "You might have to work twenty-hour days."

VIRTUAL CITIZEN 1: "We can work twenty-four-hour days."

Huahua said, "If half of you were Ph.D.s, it might have a chance of working."

VIRTUAL CITIZEN 1: "We'll study hard. We'll each read ten thousand books. We'll become Ph.D.s!"

Huahua said, "Nuts. You're tired enough as it is."

VIRTUAL CITIZEN 1: "That's because the work's so boring. It's no fun at all. When it's fun, you don't get tired. We can work twenty-four hours a day. We'll all become Ph.D.s. Then we'll build that fun world. We will we will we will!"

Human group effects are powerful, as can be seen from a crowd of soccer spectators numbering in the tens of thousands; when two hundred million people (and children at that) were all in one place, the effect was more powerful than sociologists and psychologists of the past could have imagined. Individual minds ceased to exist, subsumed into the flood of the group. Years later, many of the participants at that New World Assembly recalled how they abandoned all control of themselves; logic and reason lost all meaning for millions of young children. Now they didn't want to listen, they didn't want to act, they just wanted, and wanted, and wanted, wanted that dreamworld, that country of fun.

VIRTUAL CITIZEN 1: "Will the national leaders please answer us? Do you or do you not accept our five-year plan?"

The three leaders exchanged glances. Xiaomeng said, "My friends, you've lost your senses. Go home and think it over again."

VIRTUAL CITIZEN 1: "We've lost our senses?! That's silly! The two hundred million of us have less sense than the three of you? Silly silly silly silly silly!"

Then new virtual citizens began splitting off.

VIRTUAL CITIZEN 3 (41.328%): "Looks like the country won't accept our five-year plan. We'll do it ourselves!"

VIRTUAL CITIZEN 4 (67.933%): "By yourselves? Easy to say. You think it's like making a virtual world on a computer? You need national leaders and the government to do it in the real world. Otherwise you won't get anywhere."

VIRTUAL CITIZEN 3: "Sheesh . . ."

The tumult in the ocean settled down, and then turned into a listless desert.

Xiaomeng said, "My friends, it's late. Let's all go to sleep. There's still work tomorrow."

VIRTUAL CITIZEN 1: "Yuck. Work work work, study study study. Total lamefest. And tiring. Lame lame lame lame lame. Tiring tiring tiring tiring tiring . . ."

The already feeble voice gradually trailed off, and the children began to ascend out of the ocean and exit the session in a reversal of the rain of cartoon avatars they had seen at the start, as if a puddle were evaporating in the sun. Soon it was gone entirely, and the ground popped up a line of text: NEW WORLD ASSEMBLY #214 CONCLUDED.

After taking off their helmets, the three young leaders remained silent for a long while.

This brought the Supernova Era to the end of its second period, a three-month stretch, longer than the Suspension, that again took its name from Specs's casual description. "Inertia" was what later historians later dubbed it.

After three months coasting on the inertia of the adults' time, the children's world at last showed its true face.

7

Candytown

Dreamtime

Life seemed to proceed along the same old tracks after the
New World Assembly, despite a few unusual signs, the most
conspicuous of which was that some children no longer
studied mornings and evenings but either went to bed or
went online after they finished work. The leadership didn't
pay much attention to the phenomenon, since they felt it
was a normal manifestation of work fatigue rather than an
omen of some kind. But the practice spread swiftly, and soon
work-aged children were skipping not only class but work
as well, and younger children began to abandon their studies
entirely. At this point the leadership realized something else
was present beneath the surface, but it was too late. The
development of the situation accelerated before they had
time to adopt countermeasures, and as a result the children's
world experienced a second social vacuum.

Unlike the first, this vacuum did not take the form of a

catastrophe, but of a joyous holiday. It was a Sunday morning, normally the time when the city was at its quietest, since the children would still be sound asleep from the exhausting, extended six-day work week. But this day was different. The children in the NIT found that the city had awakened from the slumber it had been in since the adults' departure.

Children were everywhere outside, as if all of them had taken to the streets. It reminded them of the hustle and bustle of the adults' era, long ago. They moved in small groups, holding hands, laughing, singing, and filling the city with delight. For the entire morning, the children strolled through the city, taking a look here, inspecting something there, as if this was their first visit to the city, or to the world, and every fiber of their being was twinging with the same sensation: *This world belongs to us!*

The Candytown period was divided into two phases: Dreamtime and Slumbertime. Now the first had begun.

That afternoon, the children returned to their schools, where they thought about how carefree they had been during the adults' time, and reminisced about childhood. They were delighted to be reunited with classmates and friends from the Common Era, and hugged and congratulated each other for surviving the disaster. They set aside worries about what the next day would bring; they had worried enough, and were tired of it. Planning for tomorrow wasn't a task for kids anyway.

That night the revelry reached a crescendo. All the lights in the city were turned on, and the air shook with fireworks that drowned out the Rose Nebula.

In the NIT, the leaders looked out over the sea of gleaming lights and brilliant pyrotechnics in silence. Watching the crowds of exuberant children on the street, Specs said, "This is the true beginning of the children's world."

Xiaomeng sighed softly. "What happens next?"

Specs seemed not at all concerned. "Relax. History is a river that flows where it wills, and no one can stop it."

"Then what should we do?" Huahua asked.

"We're part of history, a few drops in that river. Go with it."

Now Huahua sighed. "I've just come to that realization, too. I feel ridiculous thinking back on the feeling I had of us helming of the ship of state."

The next day, children in critical systems like power, transportation, and telecommunications remained in their posts, but the vast majority of children didn't go to work. For a second time, the children's country fell into paralysis.

Unlike the Suspension, this time there weren't many warning reports. In the NIT office, the child leaders held an emergency meeting, but no one knew what to say or do. After a long silence, Huahua pulled a pair of sunglasses from out of a drawer and said, "I'll go have a look." Then he walked out.

When he left the building, he found a bicycle and took it down the avenue. There were as many kids out today as the day before, and they looked even more excited. He parked his bike outside a shopping center. The door was open, and children were going in and out, so Huahua joined them. Lots of children were inside, most of them at the shelves, all of them picking out things they liked.

An electric toy car came squealing along and disappeared under a shelf. Looking back in the direction it came, he saw another shelf of toys, a dense crowd of kids, and toys strewn all over: cars, tanks, and robots careered about and knocked down teetering piles of dolls, to cries of delight. They had come to find toys they liked, but on realizing there were more wonderful things than they could carry off, decided to play with them here. The children were younger than Huahua, and as he passed among them and saw them messing with high-end toys, he was reminded of the world described in the New Five-Year Plan the previous day. He was over the age of being fascinated with toys, but he could appreciate these kids' enthusiasm.

The children seemed to have separated themselves into two groups, each doing their own thing. One group had assembled fairly large armies out of electric toys: hundreds of tanks and other battle vehicles, a hundred-odd fighter jets, a huge crowd of robots, and tons of weird, nameless weapons, all laid out before them on the terrazzo floor in a flashing, clattering mess.

In front of Huahua the tiny army made a majestic charge. The two lines met four or five meters away from him, clanging and smashing to the delight of the children. It was like they'd walloped a hornets' nest; half the vehicles toppled and groaned in place, while the others were sent spinning off in all directions. The terrazzo battlefield was now littered with overturned electric cars and detached robot limbs.

Their first battle ended, the children's enthusiasm was running high, but there wasn't enough left on the shelves to stage a second engagement. Just then a boy raced in to tell them that he'd found the storeroom, and they all ran off after him.

A short, hurried round of hauling later, a dozen crates of war machines and robots had arrived, and the shelves had been pushed aside for more room to fight. A new, larger battle commenced just a few minutes after that, one that carried on with fresh troops continually being added.

Another group was ensconced in a menagerie of stuffed animals and dolls, and had set them up into families sitting next to little houses built out of wooden blocks. The houses went up so fast that they had to push aside the shelves so they could start erecting a city on the floor, to be populated by fashion dolls.

As they looked in satisfaction over the world they had created, the war-hungry first group dispatched a dense phalanx of a hundred remote-controlled tanks that rolled into the charming kingdom without any resistance and flattened it.

Huahua went over to the food department, where a group of young gourmands were digging in. They were hard at work selecting choice delicacies, but they took just one bite of each so as to leave room in their stomachs for more. Littered about the counter and floor were fine chocolates with bites taken out of them, drinks uncapped but tossed aside after just one sip, piles of canned goods with just a spoonful missing from each. Huahua saw a group of girls standing beside a pile of rainbow-colored candies taking a peculiar approach to eating: they unwrapped each piece, gave it a quick lick, and then dropped it before finding another unopened one in the pile. Many of the children were already full but refused to give up, as if they were tied to some sort of torturous work.

He went out the door and ran smack into a four- or

five-year-old girl, who dropped a huge armload of dolls, nearly twenty of them. She took the brand-new travel bag she had slung over a shoulder and threw it on the ground, and then sat there beating her legs and bawling. The bag, Huahua noticed, was overflowing with dolls large and small; he couldn't imagine what she would do with them all. There were more children outside than there had been when he arrived, all of them in high spirits, and a majority of them carrying things that had caught their eye in the shops.

The return journey on his bike was slow, since the streets were full of children at play, as if the city street had been turned into a playground. Some kicked balls around, others played cards. He found children who had gotten cars started and were zigzagging down the road like they were drunk. Three boys sat atop one luxury sedan as others on the roadway dove for cover. The car didn't get far before crashing into a van parked on the roadside, and the boys tumbled to the ground. The kids inside came out and burst out laughing at their companions struggling to crawl to their feet.

Back in the NIT, Huahua told Specs and Xiaomeng what he had seen outside, and learned from them that conditions were similar in other regions.

Xiaomeng said, "As we understand it, kids out there are taking anything they want as easily as drinking water or breathing air. Work stoppage means that state assets are unprotected, but oddly enough, no one is asserting property rights over assets that do not belong to the state, so no conflicts have arisen when children take things at will."

Specs said, "That's not hard to explain. Any losses to private property can easily be recouped elsewhere. That means an end to private property."

Huahua was shocked. "So economic rules, and the whole form of ownership from the adults' time, collapsed overnight?"

Specs said, "It's an extraordinary situation. We're living in a time of unprecedented plenty, on the one hand due to the drastic decline in population, and on the other, because of the adult society's tremendous overproduction in the year since the supernova in order to leave behind as much as possible for the children. For today's society, it's like per capita material wealth went up by a factor of five or ten overnight! Economic structures and notions of personal ownership will undergo astonishing transformations in light of such fantastic wealth. All of a sudden we're in a state of primitive communism."

Xiaomeng said, "So we're in the future, ahead of schedule?"

Specs shook his head. "This is just a temporary illusion, without a corresponding productive foundation. No matter how much the adults left behind, it'll get used up eventually, and at that point, economic rules and personal ownership will return to normal, or even go backward. That process might even exact a price in blood."

Huahua smacked his hand on the table. "We should have the army take immediate action to protect state assets!"

Xiaomeng shook her head. "We've deliberated this with the General Staff Department, and the unanimous feeling is that we have to pull the army out of the major cities first."

"Why?"

"It's an emergency right now, but the army is made up of

kids, too. They'll naturally be unprepared. To guarantee success, full preparations must be made to put the army into the best possible state. That takes time, but there's no other way."

"Very well. But do it quickly. This is more dangerous than when the Epoch Clock ran out. The country's going to be picked clean!"

The children remained astonished for the next three days: The adults had left behind so much stuff, so many tasty things to eat and to play with. The next feeling was one of confusion: If the ideal world was so close, why had they never made it there before? The children forgot everything; even the older ones who had retained a modicum of sense during the New World Assembly had their anxieties about the future whisked away by the revels. This was the most carefree time in all of human history, and the entire country turned into a pleasure garden of juvenile overindulgence.

In the Candytown period, three students from Zheng Chen's class, the letter carrier Li Zhiping, barber Chang Huidong, and cook Zhang Xiaole spent their time together now that they didn't have to go to work. The postal service was practically shut down, so Li Zhiping had no mail to deliver; no one went to Chang Huidong's shop to get a haircut, because children didn't care as much for appearances as adults might have wished; Zhang Xiaole the cafeteria chef had even less cause for staying in the kitchen, since the children had far better places to forage. For three days of Dreamtime, every cell in their body had been in a state of excitement and they slept little. They woke every morning just after dawn, as if a voice were calling out to them, "Come, look, another wonderful day has begun."

Every morning when they stepped out into the fresh air, the three boys felt the joy of birds liberated from the cage. Complete freedom was theirs. With no restrictions and no work to finish, they could go anywhere they pleased, and play whatever they wished.

The past few mornings, children like themselves had played physically strenuous games; younger children who played war games or hide-and-seek could hide so well you'd never find them, since anywhere in the city was fair game. The bigger kids could play cars (real cars!), soccer, and street hockey in the middle of the road. They played hard, since apart from the play itself they had another goal in mind: preparing for the midday feast. They had eaten well the past few days, but they were nowhere near satiated. Every morning, the children did their utmost to play themselves to exhaustion, hoping above all else that when it came time for lunch, they would be able to exuberantly tell themselves, "I'm hungry!"

The games stopped at eleven thirty, and at noon the feast began. With so many possibilities throughout the city, the three boys realized it was unwise to eat at the same spot every time, since each location sourced from the same warehouse every day, so meals lost their novelty.

But the feast at the stadium was different. It was the largest feast in the city, serving more than ten thousand children a day. And the food options were even more plentiful. Walking into the stadium was like entering a labyrinth whose walls were built out of cans and cakes. You had to keep your wits about you or you'd stumble over the piles of choice candies underfoot. One day, Li Zhiping gazed down from a high-up stadium seat at the grubby children swarming over the mountains of food on the playing field like ants on a frosted cake. The mountain was a little lower after each feast, but it was replenished by children making afternoon deliveries.

After a few visits, they gained a bit of experience about eating: if they found something tasty, they could only eat a little of it at a time before it turned unpleasant. Zhang Xiaole learned an illustrative lesson from luncheon meat. The first time he ate eighteen varieties, twenty-four tins all told—he didn't finish them, of course, but just had a few bites of each—but the stuff had tasted like sawdust in his mouth ever since. They also discovered that beer and hawthorn jelly were useful in this regard, and for the next few days they used them as appetizers.

Although the stadium feast was spectacular, the three boys were even more impressed by the feast they saw at the Asia Pacific Building, which had once housed the city's fanciest hotel. The tables were piled high with gourmet products they had only seen before in foreign films, but the only diners were kittens and puppies. Drunk on French wine and Scottish whisky, the little animals swayed on unsteady feet to the uproarious amusement of their little masters in the audience.

The midday feast meant that afternoons were devoted to more sedentary pursuits, such as cards, video games, and billiards, or even just watching television. Only one activity was essential: drinking beer. Everyone drank two or three bottles every afternoon to aid digestion. After dark, the three boys joined the citywide revelry of singing and dancing that lasted till midnight, by which point they'd worked up enough of an appetite for dinner.

It wasn't long before the children were tired of playing. They learned that nothing in the world was fun forever, nothing was eternally delicious, and when everything was easily attainable, it quickly lost all flavor. The children were tired, and gradually, the games and feasts turned into a type of work. And they didn't want to work.

Three days later, the child army entered the city with the task of protecting state assets. Food and other life necessities had to be divvied up according to actual needs, and a stop was put to profligate indulgence. The situation was brought under control more easily than anticipated, without erupting into large-scale bloodshed.

But subsequent events did not improve in the way that the young leaders had hoped. Every development in the children's world revealed a new, strange face entirely beyond the imagining of the adults in the Common Era.

The Candytown period entered its second phase: Slumbertime.

Slumbertime

For the next several days, apart from fetching food from the distribution points, Li Zhiping and his companions did little but sleep. They slept long, eighteen or twenty hours a day. They ate, but with no one to push them to wake up, they simply lay there sleeping. Sleep came easier with practice. The mind grew sluggish and they felt perpetually drowsy. There was no point to doing anything; it was all tiring, even eating.

Now they realized that total idleness was exhausting, and it was a more frightening exhaustion than they had ever known. When they got tired working or studying, they could rest, but now rest itself was tiring, leaving sleep the only recourse, but the more they slept the sleepier they became.

When they lay awake they had no desire to rise, since their very bones felt soft and rubbery. They simply lay there looking up at the ceiling, their minds absent of thoughts, and none likely to come. It was hard to believe that lying in bed with an empty mind could be so tiring. They'd lie for a while, and then fall asleep, and eventually they couldn't tell day from night.

Humans were a sleeping creature, they decided, and waking was the abnormal state. During those days they became denizens of slumberland, spending the bulk of their day living in dreams. Dreams were better than being awake, since they could return over and over to the country depicted in the New Five-Year Plan, go inside that megatower, ride the huge roller coaster, visit Candytown and taste a piece of windowpane.

The only time the boys communicated now was when they woke up and told each other about their dreams; when they finished, they pulled up the covers again and went back in search of the wonderful world they had just visited. But they never found it, and were taken instead to a different place. Little by little the dreamworlds faded and grew more and more like the real world, until eventually they found it very difficult to distinguish the two.

One time somewhat later when Zhang Xiaole went out

to get food, he happened across a box of baijiu, and so the three boys began to drink. They'd started on beer during Dreamtime, but now drinking to excess was widespread, as children discovered that the fluid's bite brought a tremendous thrill to their numb bodies and psyches. No wonder adults used to love it so! They finished drinking at noon and came to after dark, but to them it was as if only four or five minutes had passed, so soundly had the booze knocked them into a dreamless sleep.

They could all sense that the world was somehow unusual upon waking, but they gave it no more thought, since they'd drunk so much. After a sip of cold water, they considered what was out of the ordinary, and quickly hit upon the answer: The walls of the room weren't spinning. They had to restore the world to normal, and so began searching for more alcohol.

Li Zhiping found a bottle and they passed it around, letting the blistering fire pour down the throat and set the whole body afire. The four walls gradually started to move again, and their bodies turned into clouds that moved with the walls, up and down and side to side, as if Earth had become a raft bobbing about in the ocean of the universe, liable to capsize at any time. Letter carrier Li Zhiping, barber Chang Huidong, and chef Zhang Xiaole lay there wallowing in the cradle-like rocking and turning, thinking of the wind blowing over them out toward the endless cosmic ocean.

By dint of enormous effort, the children's national government managed to ensure that key systems maintained essentially normal operations during Slumbertime. Water supply, transport links, telecommunications, and Digital Domain all remained operational, and it was due to these efforts that the Candytown period did not experience the accidents and disasters that swept the country during the Suspension. Some historians described the forty-odd days of Slumbertime as "an ordinary night extended a hundred-fold," which is an accurate comparison. Even though most people are asleep at night, society continues to operate. Other people felt the country was in a coma, retaining essential life functions even while unconscious.

The child leaders used every method at their disposal to wake the country's children from their deep sleep, but none was successful. They repeatedly resorted to the remedy used during the Suspension, having Big Quantum call up all the phones in the country, but there was no significant reaction. Big Quantum summarized the responses using the New World Assembly method into one statement: "Go away. I'm sleeping."

The leaders visited the New World community online, which was largely empty and abandoned. The New World Assembly was a vast plain devoid of human life. Since the start of this period, Huahua and Xiaomeng visited Digital Domain practically every day, each time hailing the country's children with the greeting, "Hey, kids, how's it going?"

The response was always the same: "We're alive. Bug off."

So they said, but the children didn't actually hate Huahua or Xiaomeng, and they were unsettled if the two of them failed to show up on a particular day, asking each other, "Why aren't those two good kids online today?"

"Good kids" was something of a sarcastic jab, but it was a friendly one, and it was a name people called them from then on. And hearing the response "We're alive" every day did give some comfort to the leaders, for so long as it was there, the country hadn't experienced the worst.

One night when Huahua and Xiaomeng visited the New World Assembly, they found more children than usual, around ten million, most of them pretty wasted. Most of the cartoon avatars were carrying liquor bottles bigger even than the avatars themselves. They wove and stumbled in the assembly or tumbled into piles, conversing drunkenly. Like their counterparts at the computer in the outside world, from time to time the avatars took a swig of digital booze. The liquid, which probably used the same element in the image database for all of the bottles, shone like molten iron and lit up the cartoon bodies when they drank.

"Kids, how's it going?" Xiaomeng asked from the platform in the center of the assembly, like she did every day, like she was visiting a bedridden patient.

Ten million children answered, and Big Quantum summarized their responses into a stammering "We're . . . fine. Alive . . ."

"But what sort of life is it?"

"It's . . . what? How are you living?"

"Why have you totally abandoned work and study?"

"Work . . . what's the . . . point? You're good kids. You . . . you can work."

"Hey! Hey!" Huahua shouted.

"What're you yelling for? Can't you see we're drunk and sleeping?"

Huahua got angry. "You drink and sleep and drink some more. Do you know what you are? You're little pigs!"

"Watch . . . watch your mouth. You're up there cursing

at us all day. What kind of class . . . class monitor are you?"
"Class Monitor" was the children's nickname for Huahua; they called Specs "Studies Rep" and Xiaomeng "Life Rep."
"If you want us to listen to you, fine . . . fine. Now it's time for you to down . . . this bottle!"

Then a huge liquor bottle descended from the blue sky and hovered in front of Huahua, dancing mockingly. He smashed it with a wave of his hand, and its molten iron contents showered down in glittering fountains around the platform.

"Hah, piggies," Huahua said.

"Still at it?" Bottles came flying from all parts of the assembly, but were caught by a software screen and disappeared into thin air at the edge of the platform. More bottles magically appeared in the empty hands of the children who had thrown them.

Huahua said, "Wait and see. You'll starve if you don't work."

"That includes you."

"You little piggies really deserve a spanking!"

"Hahaha. You think you can . . . spank us? You're talking to three hundred million kids. We'll see who ends up . . . spanking who."

Huahua and Xiaomeng took off their VR helmets and looked through the NIT's transparent walls at the city outside. This was Slumbertime's deepest sleep. Few lights were on in the city, and its forest of buildings shone icy blue in the unearthly light of the Rose Nebula, like sleeping snowcapped mountains.

Xiaomeng said, "I dreamed of my mom again last night."

Huahua asked, "Did she say anything to you?"

Xiaomeng said, "I'll tell you about something that happened to me when I was younger. I don't remember how old I was, but I was pretty young. Ever since I first saw a rainbow, I imagined it was a multicolored bridge in the sky, and imagined it was made of crystal and lit with multicolored lights. Once, after a heavy rain, I ran off in the direction of the rainbow as hard as I could. I wanted to reach the end, and to climb up to its scary heights and see what was beyond the mountains on the horizon, and find out how big the world really was. But as I ran, it seemed to move away from me, and then the sun set behind the mountains, and it vanished from bottom to top. I stood alone in an empty field covered head to toe in mud, bawling, and my mom promised me that the next time it rained she would go with me to chase the rainbow. And so I looked forward to the next big rain, and the next time it rained and there was a rainbow, my mom was just coming to fetch me from kindergarten. She put me on the seat on the back of her bike and rode off toward the rainbow. She rode fast. But the sun still set and the rainbow disappeared. Mom said to wait for the next heavy rain. But I waited and waited through lots of rainstorms but there wasn't another rainbow. Then it started to snow . . ."

Huahua said, "You liked to fantasize when you were little. But you don't anymore."

Xiaomeng gently shook her head. "Sometimes, you've got to grow up quick. . . . But last night I dreamed my mom took me to chase the rainbow again! We caught it, and then climbed up. I climbed to the top of that multicolored bridge and saw the stars twinkling just next to me. I grabbed one. It was cold as ice, and chimed like a music box."

Huahua said with feeling, "The time before the supernova really does seem like a dream."

"Yes," Xiaomeng said. "I just want to dream myself back to the time of the adults, and to be a kid again. I'm having more and more dreams like that."

"Dreaming about the past and not the future is where you're making a mistake," Specs said, coming over with a big cup of coffee. The past few days he had rarely spoken, and hadn't taken part in the conversations with the country's children in Digital Domain. Most of his time he had spent alone, deep in thought.

Xiaomeng sighed. "Are there any dreams for the future?"

Specs said, "This is the biggest difference between me and you. You see the supernova as a catastrophe, and so you're doing everything you can to get through it, hoping the children will grow up as fast as possible. But I think this is a huge opportunity for humanity. It could mean huge breakthroughs, and advancement for civilization."

Huahua pointed out at the city slumbering in the blue glow of the Rose Nebula. "Look at the children's world. Is there any hope of that?"

Specs took a sip of coffee, and said, "We missed an opportunity."

Xiaomeng and Huahua looked at each other, and then Xiaomeng said, "You've thought of something again. Out with it!"

"I thought of it at the New World Assembly. Do you remember what I said about the basic motivator of the children's world? When we went back to the assembly platform after visiting the children's virtual country, and faced those two hundred million faces, I suddenly realized what that motivation is."

"What?"

"Play."

Xiaomeng and Huahua thought about this in silence.

"First we have to figure out the definition of play. It's an activity unique to children, distinct from the entertainment of adults. Entertainment was only a supplement to the main body of life in the adults' society, but play can be the entirety of life for children. It's quite possible that a children's world might be a play-based world."

Xiaomeng said, "But how's that related to the breakthroughs and advancement for civilization? Will play be able to produce those?"

"How do you imagine human civilization advances?" Specs shot back. "Through hard work?"

"It doesn't?"

"Ants and bees are industrious, but how advanced is their civilization? Humanity's dim-witted ancestors cleared the earth with crude stone shovels, and then when they found that tiring, learned how to refine bronze and iron. When they found that tiring, they wondered whether they could find anything to do the work in their stead, and so they invented steam engines, electricity, and nuclear energy. Then even thinking became tiresome, so they looked for something to do it for them, and thus computers were invented. . . . Civilization progresses not due to humans' hard work, but because of their laziness. One look at the natural world will show you that humans are the laziest of all creatures."

Huahua nodded. "That's an extreme characterization, but

there's truth in it. The course of history is a complicated thing, and we shouldn't simplify it too much."

Xiaomeng said, "I still don't agree that civilization can advance without hard work. Do you really believe that it's the right thing for the children to sleep all day?"

"Haven't they worked?" Specs asked. "You probably still remember that virtual reality movie that the US put out just before the supernova, a huge Warner Brothers production with a budget of over a hundred million dollars. Everyone said it was the biggest computer-generated virtual model ever. But you all saw the virtual country the kids made. I asked Big Quantum to run the calculations, and it comes out to three thousand times the size of that movie."

Huahua nodded again. "That's right! The virtual world was humongous, and every grain of sand and blade of grass was rendered to perfection. Back in computer class it took me a whole day to model an egg. Imagine the work it took to make that virtual country!"

Specs said, "You all think that kids are lazy, that they don't work hard, but have you ever thought about how after a day of tough work, they're still at the computer close to midnight working just as hard on building their virtual country? I've heard that lots of them even died right in front of their computers."

Xiaomeng said, "So have we found the cause of our troubles?"

"It's simple, really. The adults' society was an economic one. People labored to obtain economic compensation. The child society is a play society. People labor to receive play compensation. But right now, that compensation is practically zero."

Huahua and Xiaomeng started nodding. Xiaomeng said, "I don't entirely agree with your theory; for instance, economic compensation is essential in the child society as well, but I see a bit of light shining through the murk that's clogged my mind for days."

Specs continued, "For society as a whole, when the principles of play replace the principles of economics in determining the operation of society, it might produce tremendous innovation, releasing the human potential that was constrained under the former economic principles. For example, in the adults' time, the majority of people couldn't rationalize paying two-thirds of their life savings for a trip to space, but in the children's world, most people would, under play principles. This would propel space travel to a pace of development equal to that of information technology in the adults' time. Play principles are more innovative and pioneering than economic principles; play means traveling far, it means constantly finding out new mysteries of the world. Play will develop toward a high level, just as economics in the adults' time promoted scientific development, but this will be a far greater driving force, and will ultimately lead human civilization to an explosive leap, meeting or exceeding the critical velocity for survival in this cold universe."

Huahua said thoughtfully, "This means that even after the children's world becomes an adult world, play principles must continue on."

"It's not an impossibility. The children's world will create a brand-new culture, and when our world grows into an adults' world, it will not be a facsimile of the Common Era."

"Wonderful! Totally brilliant. Now, you just said that you had this idea at the New World Assembly?"

"That's right."

"Why didn't you tell us before?"

"Is there any point to telling you now?"

Huahua pointed a finger at Specs and said in exasperation, "You really are a giant of thought and a dwarf of action! You've always been that way! What's the point of an idea if you don't act on it?"

Specs shook his head without any change of expression. "How should I act? We can't simply accept their crazy five-year plan, can we?"

"Why not?"

Specs and Xiaomeng looked at Huahua as if he were a total stranger.

"Is that five-year plan nothing more than an unreal dream to you?"

"It's less real than a dream. If humanity ever had a plan entirely divorced from reality, this is it," Specs said.

"But it's the highest expression of your idea: a play-driven world."

Specs said, "You're right about the plan as an expression of an idea, but it has no practical significance whatsoever."

"None at all?"

Specs and Xiaomeng exchanged a glance.

"Are you sure you aren't sleepwalking?" Specs asked Huahua, and then remembered that at the critical moment in the Suspension a few months back, Huahua had asked him the same question.

Huahua said, "Remember the adventure zone that took up the entire northwest? Isn't that a possibility? Our total population is just a fifth of what it was in the adults' time, so we can vacate half of our territory—not necessarily the northwest—shut down all of the cities and industries in that entire area, and move the population, so as to leave it uninhabited. Let it gradually return to a natural state, into a national park. The other half of the country still wouldn't be as crowded as it was for the adults."

On the heels of their initial shock at Huahua's suggestion, Specs and Xiaomeng found sudden inspiration.

Xiaomeng said, "That's right! And one outcome would be that the population in the inhabited half would double, and every child's average workload would be cut in half. It would solve the problem of overwork and would give them more time to study or play."

"More importantly," Specs said, getting into it, "play would be compensation for labor, just like I described. After a stretch of work, children could spend their free time out in the national park. It's half the country—nearly five million square kilometers—so it ought to be lots of fun."

Huahua nodded. "And in the long term, it might be possible for the megasized amusement rides to actually be built in that huge park."

Xiaomeng said, "I think the plan is workable, and it'll pull the country back from the brink. Migration is the critical thing. It would have been unimaginable in the adults' time, but children's social structures are far, far simpler. We're basically structured like a big school, so for us the large-scale population displacement won't be too difficult. What do you think, Specs?"

Specs thought a moment, and then said, "That's a creative idea. It's just that it's a huge action so unprecedented that it might bring—"

"We can't predict what it'll bring!" Huahua cut in. "There

you go again, a dwarf of action. Of course we're going to give it careful study. I propose an immediate meeting. I'm convinced that implementing this plan will wake the country right up out of its slumber."

Historians later called that conversation the "Late Night Talk" of the early Supernova Era, and its significance cannot be overstated. During their talk, Specs proposed two important ideas: first, that play is the primary driving force of the children's world, an idea that later became the foundation for sociology and economics in the early Supernova Era; and second, that the play principles of the children's world would in some way affect the later adult world, changing the nature of human society. This idea was even bolder, and its influence more profound.

One other major part of the Late Night Talk was Huahua's proposal of the first future plan based on play principles, which became the basic model for the operation of the world in the future. However, the actual course of the Supernova Era under play principles was far weirder and more shocking than the young leaders could ever have imagined.

As the leadership team was holding its nighttime meeting in the NIT hall to explore the design of the huge national park, the course of history was mercilessly interrupted by the receipt of an email from the other side of the globe. The contents read as follows:

Children of China, your national leaders are requested to

come to a meeting at the UN as soon as possible. This will be the first session of the UN General Assembly in the Supernova Era, and the leaders of all children's countries in the world will attend. The children's world has important things to discuss. Hurry! We're all waiting for you.

Will Yagüe

Secretary General of the UN

8

Candytown in America

The Ice Cream Banquet

The Rose Nebula had not yet risen, and the streets of Washington, D.C., were shrouded in twilight. Not a single person could be seen on the Mall, and the last rays of daylight reflected off the high dome of the Capitol on Jenkins Hill over the chilly scene. The spire of the Washington Monument to the west stood eerie and alone, pointing straight up at two stars that had just come out. Few lights shone on the white buildings beside the Mall, the rotund Jefferson Memorial, the colossal Lincoln Memorial, the National Gallery of Art, and the Smithsonian museums, and the fountains in the reflecting pool were off, letting the untroubled water reflect the darkening sky. The city of European neoclassical buildings seemed like a desolate Greek ruin.

As if to shake off the city's veil of night and silence, in the White House lights blazed and music blared. Parked outside the east and north gates were cars bearing flags of a host of countries. The president was hosting a banquet for the heads of state who had come to the United States to attend the first UN General Assembly of the Supernova Era. The banquet was meant to be held in the State Dining Room on the western side, but it could only hold around a hundred people, not the roughly 230 that were expected, so they had to hold it in the East Room, the largest in the building. Three large Bohemian-style crystal chandeliers installed in 1902 hung from the gilded plaster ceiling, lighting up the room where Abraham Lincoln had once lain in repose. Children in formal evening wear crowded together in the white-and-gold-decorated hall, some joking in small groups, some wandering around the hall with great curiosity.

The rest of the children crowded around the Steinway grand piano in front of a long window (the piano's most notable features were its three American eagle supports) listening to the White House chief of staff, a pretty blond-haired girl named Frances Benes, play the "Beer Barrel Polka." All of the children were pretending not to notice the long banquet table in the center of the room, piled high with mouthwatering delicacies: French classics like strip steaks in ginger sauce and escargot in wine, as well as typical Western fare like baked beans, pork chops, and walnut pie.

The army band struck up "America the Beautiful," and all of the guests stopped their chattering and turned toward the door.

Entering the room was the first American president of the Supernova Era, Herman Davey, accompanied by the secretary of state, Chester Vaughn, and other senior government officials.

All eyes were on the young president. Every child has a

physical trait that is striking, to some degree—be it eyes, forehead, or mouth—and if the most appealing traits of ten thousand children were extracted and combined into one, the result would be Herman Davey. The boy's outward appearance was indeed a picture of perfection, so much so that the other children wondered about his origins, and even speculated that he had arrived on a gleaming alien spaceship as a little Superman.

In actual fact, Davey was not only born from his mother's womb but was the product of no particular storied or noble lineage. His father was of Scottish extraction, but his family tree grew murky by the time of the Revolutionary War, nothing like FDR being able to trace his heritage back to William the Conqueror. His mother had been an undocumented immigrant from Poland after the Second World War.

Most disappointing to the other children was that Davey's life before the age of nine was entirely unremarkable. His family was ordinary, his father a cleaning-products salesman who had none of the aspirations for his son that JFK's father had shown; his mother was a graphic designer in advertising who had never given her child the education that Lincoln received from his mother. His family was politically unengaged; his father reportedly only voted in a single presidential election, and made the choice between Republican and Democrat by the flip of a coin. Nothing of note could be found in his childhood. He made Bs in most subjects at school and enjoyed football and baseball, but was never good enough to be even a benchwarmer. It was only with enormous effort that young reporters were able to dig up the fact that he had been a mentor for younger students for one semester in the third grade, but the school had made no comment as to his performance.

Like all American children, he whiled away the endless freedom of his younger days but always kept a third eye open for some opportunity, rare but possible nevertheless, that he could seize hold of and never let go. At the time of the supernova, Davey was twelve years old, and his chance had arrived.

When he heard the president's announcement about the disaster, he understood immediately that history was reaching out to him. Competition was brutal in the country simulation, and he nearly forfeited his life, but eventually he defeated all of his adversaries by dint of a sudden burst of superlative leadership and charisma.

But it did not proceed without fault. Even as he was reaching the apex of power, a specter loomed in his mind, the specter of Chester Vaughn.

Anyone seeing Vaughn for the first time, be they adult or child, would suck in a chilly breath and then avert their eyes. Vaughn's appearance was the inverse of Davey's. He was shockingly skinny, with a neck so thin it made one wonder how it could support his disproportionately large head; his hands were little more than skin over bones. The only thing that differentiated him from a starving child from a drought-ridden region of Africa was the whiteness of his skin, so frighteningly white that the other children called him "Little Vampire." His skin seemed almost transparent, revealing the fine reticular blood vessels beneath the epidermis. It was most conspicuous on his immense forehead, giving him the look of a mutant.

Vaughn's other notable characteristic was his aged features, which were wrinkled enough that in the adults' era it would have been impossible to guess his age; most people would have taken him for an elderly dwarf. Davey's first encounter with Vaughn came when he stepped into the Oval Office to stand before the dying president and the chief justice of the Supreme Court, place a hand on the Bible lying on the desk, and recite the oath of office. Vaughn had been standing at a distance beneath the national flag, silent with his back turned, entirely unconcerned with this historic event. After the oath, the former president made the introductions.

"Mr. President, this is Chester Vaughn, secretary of state. Mr. Secretary, this is Herman Davey, president of the United States."

Davey extended a hand, but then lowered it again in confusion when there was no move from Vaughn, who remained with his back turned. What further puzzled him was that when he was about to speak a greeting, the former president stopped him with a slight wave, like a servant stopping a presumptuous visitor from disturbing his master's deep contemplation. After a long pause, Vaughn slowly turned around.

"This is Herman Davey," the president repeated. "You're familiar with him, I presume." The tone of his voice suggested he almost wished that it were the weird kid who had the fatal illness instead of himself.

When Vaughn turned around, his eyes were still directed elsewhere, and it was only after the president had finished speaking that he looked at Davey for the first time. Then, without a word or even the slightest nod of his head, he turned back around again. That glance was the first time Davey saw Chester Vaughn's eyes. Sunk into deep sockets under heavy eyebrows, his eyes were swallowed up in darkness, like two frosty pools deep in the mountains, concealing who knows what sort of fearsome creature. Even so, Davey could still sense his expression, a pair of monster's hands, damp and freezing, extending out of those pools to seize him by the neck and strangle him. As Vaughn turned back round, the fluorescent lights glinted off his eyes, and in that instant Davey glimpsed two frosty explosions.

Davey had a sixth sense about power. That he, as the new president, had arrived in the Oval Office after Vaughn, the secretary of state, had not escaped his notice, nor had any detail of either the office or the encounter, and it made him uneasy. Weighing most heavily on his mind was the fact that Vaughn held the power to constitute the cabinet. While this power had been granted to the secretary of state in a constitutional amendment ratified after the supernova, the sitting president, and not his predecessor, customarily had the right to appoint the secretary of state. Moreover, the previous president had emphasized this particular power, which Davey felt was somewhat unusual.

After moving into the White House, Davey did his best to avoid direct contact with Vaughn, who spent most of his time in the Capitol; mostly they communicated by phone. Abraham Lincoln had once said, of a man he refused to appoint to a position, "I don't like his face," and when someone argued that a man isn't responsible for his face, shot back, "Every man over forty is responsible for his face." Vaughn may have been only thirteen, but Davey still felt he ought to be responsible for his face. He knew little about Vaughn's background. No one did, in fact, something rather unusual in the United States.

In the adults' era, the background of every high-level leader was an open book to the electorate. Few children in the White House and Capitol had previously known Vaughn. The chair of the Federal Reserve did mention to Davey that her father had once brought a weird kid over to their house. Her father, a Harvard professor, had told her that Vaughn was extremely talented in sociology and history. The news was hard for Davey to wrap his mind around, since although he had heard of, if not actually met, lots of prodigies, they were all in the sciences or the fine arts. He had never heard of a sociology or history prodigy. Achievement in sociology, unlike in the natural sciences, can't be made on the basis of intelligence alone, but requires its student to obtain a wealth of experience of society and keen observations of the world from every angle. Likewise with history; a child without real-world life experience would find it hard to gain a real sense of history, a sense that no true historian could be without. But where would Vaughn have found that kind of time?

Still, Davey was a pragmatic child, and he knew that his relationship with the secretary could not continue in this manner. Shortly after taking office, he decided to conquer his disgust and fear (even if he was unwilling to acknowledge the latter) and visit Vaughn at home. He knew that Vaughn spent the entire day buried in documents and books, speaking only if absolutely necessary, and had no friends. He stayed in his office reading until very late at night, so it was after ten when Davey paid him a call at home.

Vaughn's residence was in Shepherd Park on Sixteenth Street NW, in an area in the northernmost part of the city known as the "Gold Coast." It had once been a Jewish neighborhood, and later a home for predominantly black middle-class government and legal professionals. On the side closer to downtown was a large stretch of unrestored apartment buildings, one of the District's neglected corners which, while not as crumbling as Anacostia in the southeast, was an area with a fairly high crime rate and drug trade during the adults' time. Vaughn lived in one of those buildings.

Davey's knock at the door drew a chilly "It's unlocked." He carefully opened the door to reveal a book storeroom. Books were everywhere beneath the light of a dim incandescent lamp, but there were no shelves, or anything else for that matter—not even a desk or chair. Books were stacked in piles, covering the floor. There wasn't even a bed, just a blanket spread over some of the more evenly stacked piles, and there was no space for Davey to find a foothold.

Since he couldn't enter, he just looked at the books from a distance. Apart from the English-language books, he could make out books in French and German, and even a few tattered Latin works. He was standing on a copy of Edward Gibbon's *The History of the Decline and Fall of the Roman Empire;* just ahead was *The Prince,* whose author was obscured by another volume, William Manchester's *The Glory and the Dream.* There was also Jean-Jacques Servan-Schreiber's *Le Défi mondial,* Trevor N. Dupuy's *The Evolution of Weapons and Warfare,* Arthur M. Schlesinger, Jr.,'s *History of U.S. Political Parties,* Immanuel Kant's *A Critique of Pure Reason,* K. Spidchenko's *Economic Geography of the World,* Henry A. Kissinger's *The Necessity for Choice . . .*

Vaughn, who had been sitting on a pile of books, stood up when Davey opened the door and came over, and Davey saw him withdraw a clear object from his left arm, a small syringe. Vaughn stood in front of him holding the syringe in his right hand, and didn't appear to mind that the president had seen him.

"You do drugs?" Davey asked.

Vaughn didn't answer, but just looked at him, and again those incorporeal claws reached out toward him. He was a little scared, and looked around him in the hope that someone else was there, but the building was empty. Once the adults left, there were lots of empty buildings like this one.

"I know you don't like me, but you've got to tolerate me," Vaughn said.

"Tolerate a druggie secretary of state?"

"That's right."

"Why?"

"For America."

Davey was forced to submit under Vaughn's intense, Darth Vader–like stare. He sighed and broke his gaze away from Vaughn's.

"I'm inviting you to dinner."

"At the White House?"

"Yes."

Vaughn nodded, and motioned out the door, and then the two of them went out toward the stairs. As Vaughn was closing the apartment door, Davey took one last look and noticed that in addition to the books and blanket, the room also held an unusually large globe. It stood in one corner, which was why he hadn't seen it at first, and it was taller than Vaughn himself. It was on a stand formed from two intricately carved Greek figures—Athena, the goddess of war and wisdom, and Cassandra, empowered with the gift of prophecy. Together they supported the enormous globe.

★

The president and secretary of state dined in the Red Room, one of the four state reception rooms in the White House, and formerly the drawing room where the First Lady held receptions. The muted light illuminating the garnet-red twill satin fabric edged in gold scroll designs on the walls, the two eighteenth-century candelabras on the mantel, and the French Empire mahogany cabinets gave the room an ancient, mysterious aura.

The two children ate opposite the fireplace at the small round marble table, one of the finest pieces of furniture in the White House collection. It was made of mahogany and other hard woods, and on the inlaid marble surface supported by gilded bronze busts of women sat a bottle of Scotch. Vaughn ate little, but he was a drinker and quickly polished off a number of glasses in succession. Within the space of ten minutes the bottle was practically empty, and Davey had to get two more. Vaughn continued to drink, but the alcohol seemed to have no effect on him.

"Can you tell me about your mom and dad?" Davey ventured.

"I never met them," Vaughn said coldly.

"So . . . where are you from?"

"Hart Island."

They said no more, but ate in silence. Then the implication of what Vaughn had said hit Davey, and he shuddered. Hart Island was a small island outside Manhattan, the site of a baby cemetery where the unwanted children of drug addicts were buried in mass graves.

"Does that mean you're . . ."

"That's right."

"You mean, you were put in a fruit basket and left there?"

"I wasn't big enough for that. I was left in a shoebox. They said that eight were left that day, and I was the only one who survived." Vaughn's voice was as calm as could be.

"Who picked you up?"

"I know him by a dozen names, but none of them are his real one. He trafficked in heroin using a variety of his own unique methods."

"I . . . I imagined you grew up in a library."

"That's true, too, only it was a big library and the pages were made of money and blood."

"Benes!" Davey shouted.

The White House chief of staff, the blond-haired girl with doll-like features, entered the room.

"Turn on some lights."

"But . . . the First Lady used to keep it this dark when receiving guests. For the nobles, she'd have to light candles," she protested.

"I'm the president, not the First Lady, and neither are you. I hate these dim lights!" Davey said angrily.

In a fit of pique Benes turned on all the lights in the room, including the floodlights only used during photographs, and the walls and carpets of the Red Room glared blinding red. Davey felt much better, but he still couldn't bring himself to look at Vaughn. Now all he wanted was for the dinner to be over.

The gilded bronze clock on the mantel, a gift from French president Vincent Auriol in 1952, played a pleasing pastoral melody, informing the two children it was getting late. Vaughn got up and made a farewell, and Davey offered him a ride home, since he didn't want the little freak spending the night.

The presidential Lincoln limousine drove along a quiet avenue. Davey was in the driver's seat; he had stopped the boy who served as driver and Secret Service special agent from coming along with him. He and Vaughn remained silent on the road, but when they reached the Lincoln Memorial, Vaughn gestured and Davey brought the car to a stop. Immediately he regretted doing so: *I'm the president,* he thought. *Why should I follow his signals?* But he had to admit that the boy possessed a power beyond him.

Lincoln's pale seated form loomed indistinctly above them in the night, and the young president looked up at the sculpture's head, wishing that Lincoln could see him, too, but the great man did not move his gaze from the low horizon, where the Washington Monument pierced the night sky in the Reflecting Pool, and beyond it the Capitol at the end of the Mall.

Davey said, not at all naturally, "When he died, Edwin Stanton, the secretary of war, said, 'Now he belongs to the ages.' I believe that when we die, someone will say that about us."

Rather than responding directly, Vaughn said only, "Davey."

"Hmm?" Davey was surprised to hear Vaughn utter his name, since until now he had only called him "Mr. President."

Vaughn smiled, something Davey had never imagined he would do. Then he asked a question that the president was utterly unprepared to answer: "What is America?"

From anyone else, the question would have irritated Davey,

but Vaughn's question set his mind going. Yes, what was America? America was Disneyland, America was supermarkets and McDonald's, America was thousands of flavors of ice cream and a thousand and one hot dogs and hamburgers, cowboy jackets and pistols, moon rockets and spaceships, football and break dancing, the skyscraper jungle of Manhattan and the weird formations in the Texas desert, and presidential candidates debating on TV under the donkey and elephant insignias . . . but ultimately, Davey discovered that the America in his mind was a shattered piece of stained glass, a riot of scattered color, and he stared blankly back at Vaughn.

"And any impressions from your childhood?" Vaughn asked, changing the topic, with a mind that few children could keep up with. "Before the age of four, what was your home like, in your eyes? Was the refrigerator a refrigerator? Was the television a television? The car a car? The lawn a lawn? And the lawn mower—what did it look like?"

Davey's mind spun to catch up, but he still had to respond with a blank, "Do you mean . . ."

"I don't mean anything. Come with me," Vaughn said, and headed toward a side chamber. He could admit that the president had a sharp mind, but that was just by comparison to ordinary people. By his own standard the kid was insufferably dense.

"Why don't you tell me what America is!" called Davey after him.

"America is a giant toy."

Vaughn's voice wasn't loud, but it seemed to produce a larger echo in the hall than Davey's question had, and it stopped the young president in his tracks near the back of Lincoln's statue. It took him a few seconds to recover, and although he didn't entirely get what Vaughn meant, he was a clever child and could sense that it was something profound. He said, "Even now children are treating America like a country. The fact that the country is running as smoothly as it did under the adults is proof of that."

"But that inertia is fading. Children are emerging from the hypnotic spell the adults put them under, and when they look at the world with their own eyes, they'll discover to their delight that it's a toy."

"Then what? They'll play? Play with America?" Davey asked, somewhat surprised at his own question.

"What else can they do?" Vaughn said with a slight shrug.

"How will they play? Football in the streets? All-night gaming sessions?"

They were nearing the memorial's southern chamber. Vaughn shook his head. "Mr. President, you have a lamentable imagination." Then he motioned for Davey to enter.

Davey stepped gingerly past the columns into the darkness. Behind him, Vaughn switched on the lights. Once his eyes adjusted to the brightness, he found to his astonishment that he was in a toy world. He remembered that the south wall of the chamber had been covered in a mural done by Jules Guérin, an allegorical portrayal of Emancipation, paired with a depiction of Unity on the north wall of the opposite chamber, but toys were now piled from floor to ceiling, blocking off the wall entirely. More than he could count—dolls, blocks, cars, balloons, skateboards, and more. It was as if he were at the floor of a colorful valley of toys. Vaughn's voice echoed behind him: "America. This is America. Look around you. Maybe you'll find some inspiration."

Davey scanned the mountain of toys, and suddenly one

object caught his eye. It lay inconspicuous off to one side, half buried in a gaudy pile of dolls, and from a distance looked like nothing more than a black tree branch. He went over and freed it from the dolls, and a grin broke out on his face. It was a light machine gun. Not a toy.

Vaughn explained, "That's an FN Minimi, Belgian made. We call it an M249. It's one of the US Army's standard-issue light machine guns. Small caliber, uses a 5.56-millimeter cartridge, compact and lightweight, but with a decent rate of fire. Up to a thousand rounds per minute."

Davey hefted the black barrel, whose metal physicality somehow felt more appropriate than the flimsy toys surrounding him, in a way he couldn't put into words.

"Like it?" Vaughn asked.

Davey nodded, fondling the smooth cool barrel.

"Then keep it as a memento. A gift from me." Then he turned and headed back to the central chamber.

"Thanks. I've never received a nicer gift," Davey said, cradling the gun and following after him.

"Mr. President, if my gift has inspired you in the way it should, then I am pleased as well," Vaughn said lightly. Just behind him, Davey looked up from the gun at his retreating back. He made no sound as he walked, and passed through the shadows of the hall like a wraith.

"You mean . . . that out of that mountain of toys, I noticed this one first?"

Vaughn nodded. "In that little toy America, you noticed a machine gun before anything else."

Now they were outside, at the top of the steps. A cool breeze brought Davey to his senses, and he realized the implication behind Vaughn's words, and shivered involuntarily.

Vaughn reached over to take the gun from him, and Davey wondered at how it seemed light as a stick in his withered, seemingly weak arms. Vaughn lifted the gun to his eyes and inspected it in the starlight.

"They are the most impressive works of art humanity has ever produced," he said. "Embodiments of the animal's most primitive instincts and desires. Their beauty is irreplaceable. A cold beauty. A sharp beauty. One that grips the soul of every man. They are humanity's everlasting toys."

Vaughn pulled back the bolt with a practiced hand and fired three six-round bursts, shattering the silence in the capital, and the chain of shrill explosions made Davey's skin crawl. Three even tongues of flame issued from the muzzle, the light flickering against the surrounding darkened buildings. Bullets screamed through the night sky as they raced madly over the city, and eighteen casings fell with a pleasing tinkle to the marble steps, the last bars of the whole melody.

"Listen, Mr. President, to the song of the human soul," Vaughn said, his eyes half closed in reverie.

"Wow—" Davey gasped. Then he grabbed the gun from Vaughn's hands and stroked its warm barrel in wonder.

A police car came racing round from behind the memorial and screeched to a halt in front of the steps. Three child police officers got out and shone their flashlights upward to the president and secretary of state. Then they exchanged a few words with each other before getting back in the car and driving off.

Then Davey remembered what Vaughn had said. "But that inspiration is . . . terrifying."

Vaughn said, "History doesn't care whether or not it's terrifying. The fact that it exists is enough. History is for the politician what oil paints are to a painter. There is no good or evil, all that matters is how you control it. There is no bad history, only bad politicians. Now, Mr. President, do you understand your own purpose?"

"Mr. Vaughn, I'm not used to the tone you use, like a teacher addressing a student, but I do appreciate the sense of what you've said. As for a purpose, is it any different from the adults' purpose?"

"Mr. President, I wonder whether or not you understand how the adults made America great."

"They built a fleet of aircraft carriers!"

"No."

"They sent a rocket to the moon!"

"No."

"They built American science, technology, industry, finance . . ."

"Those are important, but they're not it either."

"Then what is it? What makes America great?"

"Mickey Mouse and Donald Duck."

Davey thought in silence.

Vaughn went on, "In self-righteous Europe, in insular Asia, in impoverished Africa, in every corner of the world, in places unreachable by aircraft carriers, Mickey Mouse and Donald Duck can be found."

"You mean American culture permeates the globe?"

Vaughn nodded. "The world of play is dawning. Children of other countries and nationalities will play in different ways. Mr. President, what you need to do is to make the children of the world play according to America's rules!"

Davey took another long moment to think about this, and then he said, "You really have the makings of a teacher."

"These are just the basics, and yet you feel ashamed already. As you should, Mr. President." When he finished speaking, Vaughn walked down the steps without looking back and vanished silently into the night.

Davey spent the night in the Queens' Bedroom, the most comfortable room in the White House, where Queen Elizabeth I, Queens Wilhelmina and Juliana, Winston Churchill, Leonid Brezhnev, and Vyacheslav Molotov stayed during their visits to the United States. Previously he had slept well on the canopy bed formerly belonging to Andrew Jackson, but tonight he lay awake. He got up and paced the room, stopping at times at the window to look out northward at Lafayette Square, stained blue by the Rose Nebula, and then going to the fireplace, above which hung a floral painting and mirror in a gilded frame (a gift from Princess Elizabeth on behalf of her father King George VI in 1951), to stare at his perplexed face.

He sat down in exhaustion in a mahogany chair and began the longest period of contemplation in his life.

Just before daybreak, the young president stood up and went to a corner of the Queens' Bedroom where a large video-game machine had been set up. The device paired oddly with the room's classical décor. He set the machine humming and clanging in an interstellar battle, getting more into it the longer he played, until the sun was high in the sky and his former self-confidence had returned.

The band at the White House banquet played the final notes of "America the Beautiful" and immediately struck up "Hail to the Chief." President Davey went into action and began shaking hands with his young guests.

The first to shake were President Jean Pierre of France and Prime Minister Nelson Green of the UK, the former a ruddy, enthusiastic chubby fellow, and the latter a beanpole. In solemn expressions and formal evening dress with handsome bow ties around high white collars, they looked every inch the gentlemen, as if they had come to show off the traditional style of European adults.

President Davey had reached one end of the table and was ready to make an address. Behind him was the full-length portrait of George Washington, rescued from destruction by Dolly Madison, who took it from its frame before occupying British troops burned the White House in the War of 1812. Now the sight of Davey dressed in a smart tweed suit, with that storied painting as a backdrop, impressed Pierre enough for him to whisper to Green, "My god, look at how handsome he is! In a powdered wig, he'd be Washington. In a beard, Lincoln. In fatigues, Eisenhower. If he was in a wheelchair and a black overcoat, he'd be Roosevelt. He's America, and America is him!"

The prime minister was not impressed with Pierre's superficiality, and replied, without turning his head, "In history, great individuals are ordinary in appearance. Like your Napoleon, a hundred and sixty-five centimeters tall. A short man. They use their internal power to attract people. The pretty ones are mostly just embroidered pillows."

The children expected the president to begin, but he waited, mouth closed, his eyes searching the crowd. Then he turned to the chief of staff and said, "Where's China?"

"We just received a call. They're on their way, and will be

here any minute. Carelessness meant that countries beginning with C got notified late."

"Are you stupid? Don't you know that the Cs include a country with a fifth of the world's population, and two with an area larger than ours?"

Benes protested, "It was a problem with the email system. How is that my fault?"

Davey said, "Without the Chinese children, we can't discuss anything. We'll wait a bit more. Have something to eat and drink, everyone."

But just as the children were surging toward the table, Davey shouted, "Wait!," and, surveying the sumptuous feast, turned to Benes and said, "Did you arrange for this slop?"

Benes opened her eyes wide. "Is something wrong? This is exactly how the adults did it."

Davey said loudly, "How many times have I told you, stop talking about the adults. Don't keep showing off how closely you can follow their stupid rules. This is the children's world. Bring out the ice cream!"

"Ice cream at a state banquet?" Benes stammered, but nevertheless sent someone to fetch it.

"That's not enough!" Davey said upon seeing the place settings of ice cream. "Not those little packages. I want big plates piled high with scoops!"

"How tasteful," Benes muttered. But she carried out his request all the same, and had servers bring in ten trays of ice cream. The trays were so big they needed two kids to carry them, and once all ten were spread out on the banquet table, even at a distance you could feel the chill. Davey picked up a goblet and dipped it into the creamy mountain, and then pried it out by the stem, full of ice cream. Then he held it up and in a few bites swallowed its entire contents, quick enough that the watching children felt their own gag reflex triggered, but Davey smacked his lips in satisfaction, as if he had only taken a sip of coffee.

"So everyone, we're going to have an ice-cream-eating contest. Whoever eats the most, their country is the most interesting. Whoever eats the least, their country is the most boring." Then he scooped up another gobletful of ice cream and took a bite.

Despite the questionable nature of the standard, one by one the heads of state came forward to dip their goblets as Davey had and defend their national reputation. Davey downed ten glasses in succession, and it didn't faze him one bit; to prove their countries weren't boring, the other children took huge bites, as a gaggle of excited reporters snapped photos of the competition. By the end, Davey took top honors with fifteen goblets, while the other leaders turned their stomachs to freezers and more than a few had to race off in search of a White House bathroom.

After the ice cream, they warmed their insides with alcohol, sipping glasses of whiskey or brandy and chatting in small groups. The mix of lively native languages and rigid machine translations into English drew peals of laughter from a few groups. Davey moved among them holding his glass, a large translator hanging around his neck, and at times he interjected his own lengthy opinions. The banquet proceeded in this spirit of pleasant merriment. Servers shuttled back and forth, but no sooner had they put food on the table than it was snatched up. Fortunately the White House had ample supplies. A pile of empty bottles grew next to the piano as the children grew tipsy. Then came something rather unpleasant.

Prime Minister Green and President Pierre, along with the heads of some northern European countries, were engrossed in a discussion of a topic of interest to them when Davey came over holding a large glass of whiskey. Pierre was speaking, with expansive gestures and facial expressions, and Davey tuned his translator to French, and heard the following in his earpiece:

". . . at any rate, as far as I am aware, there is no legitimate claimant to the British throne."

"That's right," Green said, nodding. "It's a worry for us."

"There's absolutely no reason for that! Why not follow France and establish a republic? Yes, the Federated Republic of Great Britain and Northern Ireland. It's entirely justifiable, since the king died on his own, and wasn't sent to the guillotine like ours was."

Green shook his head slowly, and then in the manner of an adult, said, "No, my dear Pierre, that would be unthinkable, both today and in the past. Our feelings about the monarchy are different from yours. It's a spiritual support for the British people."

"You're too conservative. That's the reason why the sun eventually set on the British Empire."

"You're too eager for change. The sun set on France, too, and on Europe. Could Napoleon and Wellington have imagined a world congress like this held not in London, Paris, or Vienna, but in the crude, rude country of cowboys? Forget it, let's not talk history, Pierre," Green said, shaking his head sadly when he saw Davey.

"But reality is just as hard. Where will you find a queen?"

"We're going to elect one."

"What?" Pierre gave an ungraceful yelp, attracting the

attention of more people. Their conversation circle had become the largest at the banquet.

"We're going to get the prettiest, most adorable girl to be queen."

"And her family and lineage?"

"None of that matters. Simply being English qualifies. But the key is that she's got to be the prettiest and most charming."

"That's fascinating."

"You French like revolutions. This might count as one."

"You'll need to find candidates."

Green pulled a sheaf of holograms from a pocket in his evening jacket and passed them to Pierre. Ten candidates for queen. The French president flipped through the holograms, sighing in admiration at each one. Practically every child in the hall gathered round to pass the photos, and they sighed in admiration along with him. The girls in the photos were like ten little suns in their radiant beauty.

"Gentlemen," said the band conductor, "the next song is dedicated to these ten queens."

The band struck up "Für Elise," and in its hands the gentle piano tune remained as touching as ever, even more absorbing than the piano version. Awash in music, the children felt that the world, life, and the future would be as beautiful as those ten suns, and as adorable.

When it finished, Davey asked Green politely, "So what about the queen's husband?"

"Also decided by election. The prettiest and most adorable boy, of course."

"Any candidates?"

"Not yet. There will be once the queen is elected."

"Oh, right. You've got to listen to the queen's opinion," Davey said, nodding in agreement. Then, with that particular brand of American pragmatism, he said, "One more question. How can such a young queen give birth to a prince?"

Green snorted rather than answering, as in contempt for Davey's lack of breeding. Few of the other children present were well-versed in the specifics, so they all just pondered the question and for a while no one spoke. Eventually Pierre broke the silence: "I imagine it's like this. Their marriage is just, well, what's the word, symbolic. They're not going to live together like adults do. They'll have kids after they grow up. Is that it?"

Green nodded, as did Davey, to show he understood. Then Davey cleared his throat, seeming suddenly shy. "Um . . . about the pretty boy."

"What about him?"

Davey tugged at his white gloves and gave a self-conscious shrug. "I mean . . . there's no candidate yet."

"That's right, there isn't."

Davey crooked a finger back toward himself and said, "So how about me. Do I qualify?"

The surrounding crowd tittered, to the annoyance of the president, who barked, "Quiet!," then turned back to Green and waited patiently for his response. Green turned slowly toward the banquet table and picked up an empty glass, and then made a subtle motion for a refill to the server beside him. When his glass was full, he carried it over to Davey and waited until the surface was still. Then he said, "Why not see for yourself?"

The group burst out laughing. The laughter spread until even the servers and army band members were cackling uncontrollably at their president, chief of staff Benes the giddiest of all.

In the center of it all, the president's face contorted. In point of fact, he wouldn't have been found wanting; what disqualified him was his lack of British citizenship. The international mockery annoyed him, of course, but he was most irritated by Green. As he had met with the heads of NATO countries for the past several days, it had been the prime minister who had bothered him the most. No sooner had he arrived in the United States than he began asking for things—steel, oil, and above all, weapons. Three five-billion-dollar Nimitz-class nuclear-powered aircraft carriers and eight two-billion-dollar ballistic nuclear submarines, in one fell swoop, as if angling to re-create the Royal Navy of Admiral Nelson's time.

Even worse, he wanted land. Just the return of a few former colonies in the Pacific and the Middle East at first, but then he rolled out a stinky old seventeenth-century parchment, a map with no lines of latitude or longitude, nothing at all at the north and south poles, and brimming with errors in Africa and the Americas.

Pointing out areas of the map, Green informed Davey of all the places that once were England and remained so (only omitting any mention of North and South America prior to the revolutionary wars). He felt that due to the special relationship Britain had with the US, even if the US was unwilling to aid it in recovering those lands, it should at least permit it to reclaim some of them, since the measly territory it now occupied was tremendously disproportionate to the immense contributions it had made to Western civilization through the ages. The United Kingdom had been a cherished ally of the US in two world wars, and in the second had exhausted its national power to protect the British Isles and prevent the Nazis from crossing the Atlantic, only to suffer such a precipitous decline as a result.

Now the cake needed to be redivided; surely Uncle Sam's children would not be as stingy as their fathers and grandfathers! However, when Davey made the demand that once conditions were ripe, NATO would place a dense installation of medium-range ballistic missiles in Britain to prepare for an advance to the East, he immediately turned as tough as the Iron Lady and declared that his country, and all of western Europe for that matter, would not become a nuclear battlefield. No new missile installations; as a matter of fact, he was going to dismantle some existing ones.

Now on top of that, making jokes at the expense of the president of the United States, in the manner of a fallen aristocrat who can't resist grandstanding like a fool. Davey's anger bubbled over at the thought, and he threw a fist into Green's jaw.

The sudden punch sent the skinny prime minister, smugly holding a wineglass up as a mirror for Davey, tumbling backward over the banquet table. The hall erupted into chaos. Children pressed around Davey shouting angrily, and the prime minister managed, with some help, to get to his feet. Ignoring the caviar and mayonnaise on his clothes, the first thing he did was straighten his tie. He was helped up by the foreign secretary, a brawny boy, who made a dash for Davey but was held back by the prime minister. Even before he stood up, Green's mind had made the transition from overheated to cool, and he understood that now was not the time to lose sight of the bigger picture. Amid the chaos, he was the only one who retained an enviable calm. With aristocratic grace, he extended his right index finger and said to the foreign secretary, in a tone entirely unchanged from usual, "Please draft a diplomatic protest."

Reporters' flashbulbs popped, and the following day, large photos of Green, in evening wear covered in a spectrum of ice cream flavors and raising a genteel finger, ran in every major newspaper, informing all of Europe and the Americas of the prime minister's noble demeanor as a politician. He exploited this stroke of luck to the full, while Davey could only blame drunkenness. Now, facing a crowd of furious young heads of state and sneering reporters, Davey began to defend himself: "What're you calling me? Hegemonic? If America's hegemonic, what about the English? Just wait till you see how hegemonic they can be!"

Green raised a finger to the foreign secretary again. "Please draft another diplomatic protest against this shameless attack on the United Kingdom by the president of the United States of America. This is our statement: We, and our fathers and mothers and grandfathers and grandmothers, are the most courteous people in the world. They have never, and will never, take such uncultured barbaric acts."

"Don't listen to him!" Davey said, waving both hands at the crowd. "I'm telling you, back in the tenth century, England called itself King of the Seas, and they called all the waters they could navigate the British Seas. On these seas, when another country's ship met an English ship, it had to lower its flag in salute, or else the English navy would fire on it. In 1554, Prince Philip of Spain sailed to England to wed Queen Mary, and because the salute was forgotten, he was fired upon several times. In 1570, again because of the naval salute, the English navy almost fired upon the Queen of Spain's ship. Ask him if it's true!"

Davey remained Davey, and his fiery retort rendered Green speechless. He continued, "You want to talk hegemony? That's a word invented by adults. But it's really just a simple thing. A few centuries ago, England had the world's biggest navy, so what they did wasn't hegemonic, it was glorious history. Today, America has the world's biggest navy. We've got Nimitz-class aircraft carriers, nuclear submarines, planes as numerous as mosquitoes and tanks as numerous as ants. But we've never forced anyone to lower their flag to salute US ships! How dare you call us hegemonic? One of these days—"

Before he finished, his jaw was the recipient of a heavy fist, and like Green he went toppling head over heels over the banquet table. He brushed away the arms trying to help him up, but twisted like a fish back to his feet, in the process grabbing a bottle of French champagne as long as his arm and brandishing it in the direction from which the blow had come. But he stopped midswing, and the remaining champagne bubbled out of the bottle and into a foamy pool on the oak floor.

Standing opposite him was Ōnishi Fumio, the prime minister of Japan. The tall, thin Asian boy wore a calm expression, and if you didn't look at his eyes it was hard to believe that he was the one who threw the punch. Davey relaxed his grip and let the empty bottle fall away.

Two days earlier, Davey had seen a report shot by CNN showing the famous statue in Hiroshima of a girl who died as a result of the atomic bomb holding aloft a paper crane. Now there was a mountain of white objects, piled up like snow to half the statue's height. At first glance Davey thought they were the same paper cranes children had always offered at the statue, but when the camera zoomed in for a closer look, he realized what they actually were: paper fighter jets. Groups of children in white hachimakis emblazoned with the sun flag came forward singing "Drawn Sword Corps" and throwing more folded fighter planes toward the statue. Those paper planes spiraled round the girl like white spirits, and piled higher and higher at her feet, bringing her ever closer to burial.

And then the Chinese guests arrived, weary from the journey. Huahua and the ambassador to the US, Du Bin, were accompanied by the American vice president, William Mitchell.

Davey met them at the foot of the stairs and greeted them with an enthusiastic embrace. Then he said to the rest of the children, "Good. Now that children from every country are here, we can begin discussing the important issues of the children's world."

Candytown in America

When the Chinese plane finally reached the end of its arduous journey and arrived in the airspace over New York's JKF Airport, all they could see below them was empty ocean. The tower informed the pilot that the water on the runway was shallow, not even midcalf, so they could safely land using two files of widely spaced black dots as runway markers. Through binoculars they determined that the dots were vehicles parked in the water on the runway. The landing itself produced clouds of spray, and when it dispersed,

Huahua noticed that the airport was under heavy security. Armed soldiers were standing everywhere in the water. When the plane came to a complete stop, it was quickly surrounded by a dozen armored vehicles that had been following it like speedboats through the shallow water. A group of fully armed soldiers in field camouflage jumped out of the vehicles and began running around like weird insects, and they and the vehicles quickly formed a perimeter around the plane. The soldiers, guns in hand, faced away from the plane and looked around warily, as did the machine gunners atop the armored cars.

The hatch opened and several American children hurried up the stair that had been put in place. Most of them were carrying rifles, and one had a large bag. Huahua's two armed guards flanked the aircraft door to prevent them from entering, but Huahua had them make way, since he had seen a Chinese kid at the front of the group, the ambassador Du Bin.

Once the children entered the cabin and had caught their breath, Du Bin introduced a blond-haired boy to Huahua: "This is vice president of the United States William Mitchell, here to welcome you." Huahua took stock of the boy, the large gun he had strapped at his waist that looked extremely out of place next to his tailored suit. Du Bin then introduced another boy, wearing fatigues. "This is Major General Dowell, who's in charge of security for UN attendees."

"This is how we're being welcomed?" Huahua asked Mitchell, which Du Bin translated.

"You can have the red carpet and an honor guard if you'd like. The day before yesterday the president of Finland was given a ceremony on a temporary stage, and had his leg shattered by a bullet," Mitchell said, and Du Bin translated for Huahua.

Huahua said, "We're not here to visit the United States, so we don't need such formalities. But this is a little unusual."

Mitchell sighed and shook his head. "Please forgive our situation. I'll explain in detail on the way."

Then from his bag Dowell pulled out jackets for the Chinese children to wear, bulletproof clothing, he said. Then from another bag he took out a few snub-nosed black pistols and handed them to Huahua and his entourage, saying, "Careful. They're fully loaded."

"Why do we need these?" asked Huahua in surprise.

Mitchell said, "In today's America, if you go out unarmed it's like going out without pants!"

They all deplaned and walked down the stairs, and, closely surrounded by a group of soldiers to shield them from any stray bullets, Mitchell led Huahua and Du Bin to an armored car parked in the water. The others got into separate cars. The cars were dark and cramped and smelled of fuel. The children sat on hard benches fixed to either side, and then the fully armed motorcade sped away.

"The ocean level's rising quickly. Is Shanghai like this?" Mitchell asked Huahua.

"It is. Hongqiao Airport is flooded, but the adults rushed some dikes in place so the water hasn't reached the city yet. It won't last for much longer, though."

"New York is still free of water, but it's not really suited for a UN General Assembly."

The motorcade headed toward the city and eventually reached dry roads. At times, overturned vehicles on the road-side were visible through the armored car's small windows, their sides pockmarked with bullet holes, and some of them on fire. There were also large numbers of armed children, clearly not military, walking along the road in groups, or crossing nervously, clutching guns nearly as big as themselves, their bodies slung with ammo belts. When Huahua's car passed one group, they suddenly threw themselves to the ground as practically simultaneously a rain of bullets from one side impacted on the car's armor shell with a thunderous din.

"None of this looks normal," Huahua said, after a glance out the window.

"It's the times, man. Abnormal is normal," Mitchell countered. "We ought to have received you in bulletproof cars, but yesterday a Lincoln was shot up by special armor-piercing bullets, and the Belgian ambassador was injured. So we're taking these armored vehicles as extra insurance. Tanks would be even better, of course, but the city's elevated roadways won't hold up under their weight."

It was dark when the motorcade reached the city. The buildings of New York's skyline gleamed like a miniature Milky Way. Like every child, Huahua had been full of desire to visit one of the world's biggest cities, and he looked eagerly out the window at the dazzling skyscrapers. But he soon noticed another light flickering in the buildings, the crimson of firelight, and pillars of smoke reaching to the sky. Sometimes a ball of fire rose in the air, and the shadows of the skyscrapers wavered in its magnesium glare. Closer to downtown, he heard the crackle of gunfire, the whine of stray bullets, and the odd explosion.

The motorcade came to a halt, and they received word that the road was barricaded up ahead. Ignoring warnings, Huahua got out to have a look, and saw sandbags piled up into a fortification that cut off the road. Behind the barricade, children were feeding belts into three heavy machine guns. Dowell was negotiating with them.

One of the children behind the sandbags waved a handgun and said, "The game won't be over till midnight. Take a detour!"

Angrily, the major general said, "Don't be cheeky. Do you really want me to call in a squadron of Apaches to take you out?"

Another boy behind the barricade said, "Why can't you be reasonable? We're not playing against you. We arranged it with the Blue Devils this morning. If we don't play, then we're the untrustworthy ones, you see? If you really don't have anyone to play with, then wait back there. We might be done early."

Just then Mitchell walked up behind Dowell, and one of the kids behind the barricade recognized him. "Hey, isn't that the vice president? That might really be a government motorcade."

A kid with a shaved head jumped out from behind the barricade and inspected Mitchell and the others from closer up. Then he waved back at the others. "We shouldn't obstruct official business. Let's let them pass."

The children jumped up and began moving sandbags, but as they were doing so, rapid gunfire sounded from the other end of the street, and then the air around them was filled with the whine of bullets and of armor being struck. Everyone out in the open dove into armored cars or behind sandbags. Du Bin pulled Huahua back into the car, and then they heard a kid behind the barricade shout through a loud-speaker, "Hey, Blue Devil leader! Stop! Stop!"

The gunfire stopped, and from that same direction came a kid's voice over a loudspeaker: "Red Devils, what's the problem? Check your watches. Didn't we decide to start the game at eighteen thirty Eastern time?"

"A government motorcade is passing through. It's a foreign head of state going to the UN General Assembly. Wait for them to leave first."

"Okay. Hurry up, though."

"Then you all send over a few people to help."

"Fine. Here we come. Hold your fire!"

A few children came running from a grassy slope opposite the road. They threw their weapons down into a pile and helped the others move sandbags. Before long an opening was made. When they were done, the Blue Devil children picked up their guns and headed back, but the shaved-head kid called after them, "Don't go yet. Help us rebuild the fortification in a bit. Also, two of us got injured just now."

"So what? We didn't break the rules."

"True. But when the game restarts we won't have even teams. How do we know who wins?"

"That's easy. Mike, you stay on this side. This time you're with the Red Devils. Of course you've got to play for them as hard as you would for the Blue Devils. But you can't tell them our battle plans."

Mike said, "Don't worry. I want it to be interesting, too."

"Great. Red Devils, we're giving you the Blue Devils' best shot. Yesterday on Wall Street he took out three of the Bears. Now that's fair, right?"

Mitchell was about to get back into the car when one of the children called, "Mr. Vice President, we've got something to say to you." Then he was surrounded by a group of children, their faces smeared with black camouflage so that only their teeth and eyes flashed in the firelight. The children began pelting him with questions.

"What the hell are you doing? The adults spent trillions on tons of fun stuff, but kids are only allowed to play with this crap!" said one, smacking the M16 he was holding.

"That's right! Why can't you give us all those aircraft carriers to play on?"

"And fighters and bombers. And cruise missiles. Those would be fun."

"And ICBMs too!"

"Right. Bringing out the big guns would really make it interesting. But all those toys are going unused right now. It's a waste of American wealth. The government should be ashamed!"

"If American kids aren't having fun, you're going to be responsible."

Mitchell spread out his hands. "My apologies to you all. I can't speak for the government here. The president spoke on TV last night about these questions—"

"What're you afraid of? There aren't any reporters here."

"I heard that Congress is going to impeach him. If that happens, that's the end for you Democrats."

"The Republican leader promised on TV last night that if they come to power, they'll let kids play with all of the army, air force, and navy's big boys."

"Ooh. He's awesome. I'm going to vote Republican!"

"I also heard that the army is going to use them for itself."

"That's right. Don't listen to the government. Playing on their own? What's the point of them staging exercises all the time? Bring them out and play for real!"

Dowell barged into the group and found the kid who had said the army would play by itself and seized him by the collar. "You little bastard. If you spread rumors about the US Army again I'll have you arrested!"

The kid struggled to speak. "Then go arrest the commander of the Atlantic Fleet and the chairman of the Joint Chiefs of Staff. They're the ones that said they'll play on their own!"

Another kid pointed in the direction of the ocean, where lights flashed periodically, like a storm on the horizon. "See! The Atlantic Fleet has been firing offshore for the past two days. Who knows, maybe they've already begun to play!"

Mitchell looked around him, and then said in a low voice, "We never said we won't let you play. The president and the government have never said that. But if we play, the whole world has to play. It's suicidal if it's just ourselves, right?"

The other children nodded.

One kid tugged at him and said, "So these leaders are coming to the UN to discuss the games?"

Mitchell nodded. "That's right."

Another kid, holding an antitank rocket launcher, said through smiles, "Awesome! Make it a good talk. You all are responsible for making the world a fun place!"

The motorcade proceeded onward. Huahua asked Mitchell, "If the roads are so dangerous, why not use helicopters?"

Mitchell shook his head. "That would be a simpler solution, of course, but a destroyer in port last week lost ten Stinger missiles, and one of them took down an NYPD helicopter the day before yesterday. The FBI believes the remaining nine are still somewhere nearby, so it's safer if we stay on the ground."

Huahua looked out at the vast ocean, and the colossal illuminated figure rising out of it.

"Is that the Statue of Liberty?" Huahua asked, and when Mitchell nodded, he looked carefully at the symbol of America. But he found something wasn't quite right. "Where's her torch?"

Mitchell said, "Knocked off by some asshole with a recoilless rifle last week. Her left arm had a hole blown in it by a rocket."

Huahua asked, "What are American kids up to?"

Beneath the car's dim red overhead light, Mitchell appeared extremely irked. "What're they up to? I've received dozens of national leaders and that's what you all ask. They're kids. What're they up to? Playing!"

Huahua said, "Our kids don't play like this."

"Even if they wanted to, they don't have the guns."

Du Bin leaned over to whisper in Huahua's ear. "This is Candytown in America. The entire country is playing violent games."

At last the motorcade reached the UN. When Huahua got out of the car to look at the building that at least nominally was the world's office building, he stared in shock. The Secretariat was pitch-black, in stark contrast to the blazing lights in the surrounding buildings; a whole chunk was missing out of the upper left corner of the monument-like building; half of its exterior windows were gone; and there were several other large holes, one still smoking.

As they crossed the glass and cement fragments on their way to the building, a nearby little boy caught Huahua's attention. The kid looked to be only three or four years old, and was holding a gun almost as big as himself. He struggled to hold it level, and aimed it at a compact car a few meters away. The kickback knocked him onto his ass, and he sat there staring straight at the car, but when he realized that nothing had happened, he pulled himself up using the gunstock—his bare bottom, peeking through his open-crotch trousers, had two circular smudges of dirt—and then slammed the muzzle on the ground and loaded another cartridge, and again tried to hold the swaying barrel steady enough to take another shot at the car. Again he fell back to the ground, and again the car made no reaction. The kid stood up again to take another shot. Every time he fired he fell backward, but on the fifth shot there was a boom and the car burst into flames and black smoke. The kid crowed "Woohoo!" and bounded away carrying the huge gun with him.

Will Yagüe, the Argentine boy who was the first secretary general of the UN of the Supernova Era, was waiting for them at the entrance to the building. Half a year earlier, Huahua had watched the televised handover between him and the last secretary general of the Common Era, but the boy in front of him retained nothing of his former dignity. Now he was covered in dust, and he had taken off his tie to stanch the blood on his head. He looked thoroughly beaten down. When Mitchell asked about the situation, he answered irritably, "Another bomb hit the tower just five minutes ago. Look—right there!" He pointed at the smoking crater in the center of the building. "I had just come outside, and a storm of shattered glass rained down. . . . I repeat my demand that you provide adequate protection for the United Nations headquarters!"

Mitchell said, "We've done all we can."

"All you can?" Yagüe snarled, jabbing a finger at the crumbling building. "I asked you long ago to clear out heavy weapons from the vicinity."

Dowell said, "Please let me explain. That one," he pointed at the building's missing corner, "is at least a one-oh-five-millimeter, and has a range of roughly twenty kilometers."

"Then clear out all heavy weapons in a twenty-kilometer radius!"

Mitchell shrugged. "That's not realistic. Carrying out a search and then imposing military controls over such a large area will be tricky. It'll give those Republican bastards an opening. Sir, we're a democratic country."

"A democratic country? I feel like I'm in some twisted pirates' den!"

"Your country isn't much better off, sir. A soccer game has broken out in Buenos Aires with more than a hundred thousand players on a playing field that covers the entire city, with two enormous goals bigger than the Arc de Triomphe set up at either end. A hundred thousand players with a single ball, surging after it wherever it goes. Thousands of people have been trampled to death in the fortnight the supergame has been in progress, and there's no sign of it stopping anytime soon. Your capital has been thrashed to pieces. Play is in children's nature. Sometimes it's even more important than eating or sleeping. You think you can stop them?" Mitchell pointed at the building, "True, this place isn't really suitable for a UN meeting. I also know that the General Assembly building had its roof caved in by a bomb. And that's why we've proposed to hold the session in Washington, D.C."

"Bullshit! This time it's D.C., next time it'll be on an aircraft carrier! This is the United Nations, not the US Congress, and we'll hold it on UN territory."

"But all the heads of state are in Washington already. That's the only place in the country where the games are banned, so it's the only place where security can be guaranteed."

"Bring them back! They have to take that risk, for the good of the children's world!"

"They and their countries won't agree to holding it here. Besides, even if they did return, where are your staff? How many kids are you down to in that building?"

"Those cowards! They've all run off. None of them is worthy of working for the UN."

"Who'd want to stay in this hellhole? We're here for two reasons. First, to give the Chinese children a look, so they can understand why we're not holding the session here. It's their choice whether or not they go to Washington. Second, to invite you to come with us. We've arranged a dedicated workspace for the UN on Capitol Hill, and have outfitted a brand-new team for you—"

"Shut up!" Yagüe shouted. "I've always known you want to replace the UN!" Then, to Huahua, he pointed out places in the distance. "See, those buildings are all untouched. Only the UN has been hit so many times. I wonder who the hell fired all those rockets?"

Mitchell raised a finger and said, "Mr. Yagüe, you are maliciously slandering the United States government. If you did not have diplomatic immunity, we would sue you on the spot."

Yagüe ignored him and tugged at Huahua. "As a permanent member state, you have a responsibility to the UN. Let's stay here together!"

Huahua thought for a moment, and then said, "Mr. Secretary General, the purpose of our visit is to make contact with the other world leaders, to hear their views on the new world and to exchange opinions. If all the heads of state are in Washington, then we have to go there too. We can't do anything by staying here."

Yagüe waved a dismissive hand. "Fine. You all go then. It's clear to me now that the children's era is the most abominable in all of human history!"

Huahua said, "Mr. Secretary General, the world has indeed changed. You can't solve any problems by applying the mentality of the adults' era. We need to adjust to this new world."

Smiling, Mitchell said to him, "You don't appreciate the secretary general's ambition. He once had the notion that the children's world would eliminate all national governments and be unified under the direct leadership of the UN, in which case the secretary general would naturally become the head of Earth—"

"Shut up!" Yagüe said, thrusting a finger at Mitchell. "Wanton slander!" But Huahua recalled that he had indeed voiced such an idea not long after the start of the Supernova Era.

"You go adjust to the new world," Yagüe said. "I'll remain here and see the United Nations through to the end." Then, cradling his head, he turned and walked back into the dark, smoking building.

The motorcade moved on to the outskirts of the city where helicopters were waiting for them, and they took off toward Washington with New York's sea of lights blazing below them in the night.

Huahua asked Du Bin, "Are you aware of our domestic situation?," and seeing Du Bin nod, he asked, "Do you see any similarities between their Candytown period and ours?"

Du Bin shook his head. "I only see how they're different."

"Look down there. New York remains brilliant even through the storm of bullets. Look at the roads, and all those cars and buses driving along like normal."

"True, that's a point of similarity. Even in these conditions, the systems of their society are still functioning normally."

Huahua nodded. "It's a phenomenon unique to the children's world, unimaginable in the adults' time. Back then, if social conditions deteriorated half as much, the country would have collapsed."

"But I wonder how long things will remain normal. The American military apparatus is in a precarious state. American children have in their hands the greatest weapons systems in the world, and it burns them up that they can't play with them. On the other hand, the biggest political transformation in America since the start of the Supernova Era is the ascent of the military to the political stage, and its expanding control over the country. To placate the military, the US government has staged exercise over pointless exercise. But drills will never satisfy the American child."

"The key question now is how are the American children going to play?"

"They probably won't just play among themselves. It's different with light weapons, but when they bring out the big guns there's no way to do it alone. . . . I'm not sure I should go on."

Night now completely covered the North American continent. The only illumination was from the navigation lights on the other aircraft. They seemed to be hanging stationary in the night sky.

"The situation is grim . . ." Huahua murmured, clearly aware of what Du Bin was thinking.

"Exactly. We should prepare for the worst," replied Du Bin in a shaky voice.

World Games

The world leaders continued their meeting in the East Room. The American president started into his opening remarks.

"Boys and girls in charge of the countries of the world, welcome to America!

"First of all, I'd like to express my apologies for having had to receive you in Washington, D.C., I would have preferred to hold this banquet on the top floor of the New World Trade Center in New York. I dislike Washington. This city in no way represents the United States. On a new continent covered in skyscrapers, the city we're in seems like a retreat to medieval Europe. This White House—I mean, it's just a country manor. I wouldn't blame any of you for wondering whether there are stables out back." Laughter from the crowd. "The adults located the beating heart of America here for continuity with the past, not just to L'Enfant's past, but even farther back, for continuity to your homelands," and he gestured to the cluster of European leaders.

"This neatly describes the awkward situation in which we now find ourselves. We're a world of children, but we're still living the lives of adults. Think back to the final days of the Common Era, to our vision of what the coming new world would bring. That vision to an extent mitigated our sorrow at the adults' misfortune, because we were convinced that at the cost of their leaving we had obtained a wonderful new world. But to look at it now, the world remains as dull and boring as ever. Is this the new world we wanted? No, absolutely not! We are seeing disappointment at the new world envelop the globe. This cannot be allowed to continue."

After a round of applause, Davey went on, "We are gathered here today to establish a new order for the children's world. What is the foundation of the new order, you might ask? Not the ideology of the Yalta System, nor the economic development of the post–Cold War period. There can be only one foundation: games! Games are to our era what religion was to the Middle Ages, what exploration was to the Age of Discovery, what ideology was to the Cold War, and economics to the late Common Era. These things served as a basis for existence, a starting point and a destination for the world. Now, in this new world, the dreams of our time ought to become reality!

"Luckily the world's children have more or less realized this and have already begun to play. The purpose of this meeting is to begin games on a global scale, and to turn our entire world into a world of fun!

"Naturally there are an infinite number of possible ways to play, but the games we're going to start here must satisfy two conditions: They must be played between countries, and they must be thrilling. And there's only one kind of game that can satisfy both conditions: a war game!"

Davey held his hands out palms down to calm the applause, and remained in that pose for quite some time, as if the whole world were cheering him on. But in fact there was no applause, just a spell of silence as the world leaders stared blankly at him.

"The war games that American children are playing right now?" asked one kid.

"The very same. But we're going to do it on a national scale to let the whole world play."

"I object!" Huahua shouted, and then leapt up to the dais and said to the children below, "This game is just a disguised world war."

The children flipped their translators to Chinese, and when they finished listening to his words, Russian president Ilyukhin jumped up on the dais and said, "Well said! It'll turn the children's world into hell!"

The other children echoed these sentiments:

"Right. We don't want a world war."

"We're not going to fight! We won't play this game!"

"That's right. Let the American kids play by themselves."

Davey remained composed and smiling, as if he expected this development. Standing between Huahua and Ilyukhin, he clapped his arms good-naturedly about their shoulders, and then leaned toward Huahua and said, "Don't get carried away. It's just a big game. We'll adopt the format of the Olympics. It'll be the first Olympic Games of the Supernova

Era. The war games will be played entirely according to the rules of sports competitions. Every country will compete fairly at a prearranged location, with heats and finals, and gold, silver, and bronze medals. In what way is that a war?" Then he turned to Ilyukhin. "How's a world of fun going to go to hell?"

"A bloodbath Olympics?" Huahua retorted furiously.

"It's just play. Everything has its price; where would the thrill come from otherwise? Besides, countries will participate voluntarily. If you don't want to play, then forget it."

"You're the only country that wants to play," Ilyukhin snorted.

Davey waved a finger back and forth in front of his face. "No, my dear friend, once things have been made clear, I guarantee you that all countries, including yours, will voluntarily take part in these irresistible Olympic Games."

"You've got to be joking."

"We'll just have to wait and see, won't we? . . . Now, let's discuss which country will host the next Olympics. That ought to be a major agenda item for this meeting. If I'm not mistaken, the next city scheduled to host in the adults' era was Manchester."

"Absolutely not!" shouted Green, as if he'd been burned. "Do you really believe England will permit the world's armed forces to enter its territory and turn it into a battlefield?"

Davey smiled faintly at the prime minister. "So is the British Empire simply abandoning the honor it fought so hard to win in the Common Era?" Then he turned to the Turkish president. "How lucky you are. If I recall correctly, Istanbul received the second-highest number of votes after Manchester."

"No. We won't do it!"

Davey looked about him, and then clapped Ilyukhin on the shoulder and pointed down at the prime minister of Canada. "Russia and Canada have the largest uninhabited areas. They're fully capable of holding the Olympics there."

"Shut up!" the Canadian prime minister yelled.

"Since you all proposed the war games, the Olympics really ought to be held in America," Ilyukhin said, to a round of applause.

Davey burst out laughing. "I expected it would come to this. No one wants to hold the greatest Olympics of all time in their own country. But in fact this problem has a simple solution. You're all forgetting that there's a place on Earth that doesn't belong to any country, and is entirely uninhabited. It's as distant and as empty as the moon."

"You mean Antarctica?"

"That's right. And don't forget, it's not too cold anymore."

Huahua said, "That's a gross violation of the Antarctic Treaty!"

Davey smiled and shook his head. "The Antarctic Treaty? That's an adult treaty. It doesn't affect our play. Antarctica was an icebox that would freeze you to death in the Common Era, and that's the condition underlying the treaty. If it had the climate it has now, hah! The continent would have been carved up long ago."

The heads of state were silent, their minds racing as they realized the true nature of the question before them. Antarctica had turned into a habitable new continent since the supernova, and that fact had not escaped the world's attention. For the many countries that had lost sizable portions of land to rising waters, that continent was their last hope.

Davey gazed meaningfully at the young leaders below him. "Once again, I note that participation in the World Games is completely voluntary. Perhaps, as President Ilyukhin said, no one will be willing to attend apart from us. Very well, we'll go. The American children will go to Antarctica. Now let's see which country doesn't want to play!"

No one said anything.

"I told you," Davey said smugly to Ilyukhin. "Everyone wants to play!"

9

The Supernova War

Antarctica

A low rumble came across the sea like spring thunder on the horizon.

"The frequency of the breakaways is increasing," Huahua said, looking in the direction of the sound.

There was another rumble, clearer this time, from a collapse on a mountain of ice close to the shore, and they watched as a chunk of the big silver peak plunged into the ocean, kicking up a high spray. Huge waves quickly reached land and swamped a flock of penguins on the beach; the penguins waddled about in a chaotic scramble once the waves receded.

Lü Gang said, "Last week, Specs and I took the destroyer *Huangshan* around the barrier, and chunks kept falling off all the time. So much crashing. It's like the whole continent is melting!"

"Half the shelf over the Ross Sea has melted. At this rate,

Shanghai and New York will turn into Venice in two months," Huahua said with concern.

Huahua, Specs, and Lü Gang were standing on the Amundsen coast of Antarctica. They had arrived on Earth's southernmost continent a month ago. On that day, after their plane had made its final fuel stop on Tierra del Fuego and crossed the Antarctic coastline for the first time, the pilot had said, "Hey, why does the land look like a panda?" From their high altitude the patchy black-and-white land was vastly different from the expanse of silvery white the children had always pictured in their minds. It was a new face for the continent. A ten-thousand-year-old snowpack was melting, revealing the black stone and dirt of the ground beneath. The patch beside the ocean on which the three children now stood was new ground free from snow. The polar sun hung low on the horizon, casting three long shadows behind them. The wind remained cold, but it had lost its bite, and it carried the damp breath of early spring, a flavor previously unknown here.

"Check this out." Lü Gang bent down and plucked a small plant from the dirt. It was a weird-looking thing, dark green with thick leaves.

Huahua said, "Those things are everywhere. I've heard they're prehistoric vegetation, extinct everywhere else in the world. Their seeds were preserved in the Antarctic soil, and now they've been resurrected after the climate change."

"Antarctica was warm once, long ago. The world keeps on oscillating," Specs said.

The armies of the countries taking part in the World Games were assembling in Antarctica. So far, 102 army divisions, with roughly 1.5 million soldiers, had arrived, including twenty-five divisions from the US, twenty from China, eighteen from Russia, twelve from Japan, eight from Europe, and nineteen from other countries. Even if they managed only a single company, practically all of the countries in the world were participating. Troops were still coming in by sea and air, and many countries were shipping materials and troops through waypoints in Argentina and New Zealand.

Since the majority of armies were using Argentina as a transit base and setting off for Antarctica from ports and airports in the southern part of the country, they made landfall across the Drake Passage on the Antarctic Peninsula. But they eventually realized that the peninsula was too narrow for large-scale war games, and so the gaming region was set in the broader region of Marie Byrd Land. In that vast wilderness, countries were at work building their own land bases; to facilitate bringing in supplies directly from the ocean, the bases were clustered near the shore of the Amundsen Sea, along a long, narrow strip between Thurston Island and Cape Dart, spaced anywhere from fifty to a hundred kilometers apart.

The three children watched the breakaways from the shore for a while, and then reboarded one of the three tracked all-terrain vehicles that were waiting. The small convoy set off to the west, heading to the American base for the first meeting of countries participating in the war games. The original plan had been to go by helicopter, but the three young leaders wanted to see the region up close and in person, so they went overland. Passable roads had not yet been cleared between the different countries' bases, so they had to resort to specialized vehicles originally intended for polar scientific expeditions during the adults' era.

The scenery was monotonous. The left-hand side fluctuated between black exposed ground and white snow cover, and the terrain was predominantly level with low-lying hills. To the right was the Amundsen Sea and its host of icebergs, and a surface littered with chunks of various sizes broken off from the ice shelf. Farther out were the ships of various countries at anchor. The Ross and Amundsen Seas now held more than fifteen thousand ships, forming the largest fleet ever recorded in human history. They included aircraft carriers and supertankers, like ocean-borne iron cities, as well as fishing vessels of just a few hundred tons. It was this gigantic fleet that had delivered more than a million people and an enormous quantity of material to this desolate continent, and had replaced the loneliness of the Southern Ocean with crowded noise, as if an endless chain of cities had sprung out of the water.

After they had driven for over an hour, a spread of field tents and huts appeared alongside the road: the Japanese base. Teams of Japanese children were doing drills on the beach. They sang military songs in unison as they marched exuberantly with uniform steps. But what caught the Chinese children's eye was a huge humpback whale lying on the beach, thick pink slabs of flesh and dark-colored organs visible in its sliced-open belly. A group of Japanese children were clambering over its body like a horde of ants crawling over a fish, hacking away huge chunks of whale meat with power saws, and loading them by crane onto a truck to ship back to camp.

The Chinese children got out of their vehicle and stood quietly off to one side. The whale, it turned out, was still alive, and its mouth twitched and the one cloudy eye that faced upward, big as a truck tire, stared at them lifelessly. A few Japanese kids emerged from the belly of the huge animal drenched in blood, straining under the effort of carrying a huge, dark red organ: whale liver. The crane loaded it onto a truck, where it filled up the entire bed and quivered there, steaming. One kid holding a paratrooper knife climbed aboard and cut a few pieces off the liver and tossed them out to a pack of army dogs beneath the truck. The entire scene, the circle of bloodstained snow, the vivisected whale, the children on top of it slicing pieces of flesh, the blood-smeared crane and trucks, the dogs wrestling for scraps on the bloody snow, and the ocean, stained crimson by two rivers of whale blood, was a surreal picture of horror.

Lü Gang said, "The Japanese fleet has been using depth charges against whales in the Ross and Amundsen Seas, stunning them and then dragging them ashore. One charge can stun a whole pod."

"A century of efforts to protect the whales could be destroyed in a single day," Specs said with a sigh.

A few Japanese children recognized them and jumped off the whale's body and raised their bloodstained gloved hands in a salute. Then they climbed back up and went back to work.

Specs said to Huahua and Lü Gang, "I've got just one question, and I'd like you to answer me truthfully. When you were young, did you ever truly treasure life, in your heart of hearts?"

"No," Huahua said.

"No," Lü Gang said. "When I was at the army with my dad, every day when I got out of class I'd play with the boys from the local villages. We'd shoot birds and catch frogs, and when I saw those little creatures die at my hands, I didn't feel anything in particular. The others were the same."

Specs nodded. "Yeah. It takes a lengthy process of life experience to truly appreciate the value of life. In the mind of a child, life doesn't occupy the same place as in an adult's. What's strange is that adults always associate children with kindness, peace, and other wonderful things."

"What's strange about that?" Huahua said, giving him a look. "In the adults' era, children existed within their restrictions. But more importantly, children had no opportunity to take part as a collective in the cruel struggle for survival, so of course their true nature wouldn't be exposed. Oh, for the past couple of days I've been reading the copy of *Lord of the Flies* you gave me."

"It's a good book. Golding was one of the few adults who really got children. It's a shame that the others mostly judged the hearts of children using the measure of great men,* rather than recognizing our basic nature. This was their last and greatest mistake. And that mistake has introduced too many variables into the progress of history in the Supernova Era," Specs said somberly.

The three children watched in silence for a while longer before returning to the car and setting off again.

*

* An inversion of an aphorism from the *Zuo Zhuan*, which warns against ascribing mean motives to virtuous people.

If any adult had survived the supernova, they would have thought they were in a nightmare. When all the world's nuclear weapons winked out in space in the final days of the Common Era, the coming children's world was, in the adult imagination, a paradise of global harmony, a world brimming with childlike innocence and friendship, in which the children would join hands kindergarten-style and, out of their innate purity and goodness, build a wonderful new Earth. There were even suggestions that all human historical records be obliterated: "Our final hope is that children retain a decent image of us in their hearts. Should those gentle children look back on our history from their wonderful new world of peace and see all the war, power, and plunder, they will realize what sort of unreasonable, deviant creatures we are."

But what the adults could never imagine was that less than a year into the Supernova Era, the children's world would erupt into a world war. So grim were its rules of competition, so bloody and barbaric its methods, that they were unprecedented not only in the Common Era but throughout the entirety of human history. The Common Era had no cause to worry about its own image in the hearts of children, since what made them unreasonable in children's eyes was their restraint and moderation, and their patently ridiculous misgivings and moral codes. International law and behavioral norms were cast aside overnight as everything was flung out into the open, and no one felt the need to hide anymore.

China's high command was initially of divided opinion about sending troops to Antarctica to take part in the war games. The importance of the Antarctic Games was undeniable, but

Xiaomeng brought up a pragmatic question: "Our own neighborhood isn't very stable. India, for example, is only sending one division, and will retain a million-strong army inside the country. Who knows what they're planning to do? If we want to fully participate, we'll need to deploy a sizable proportion of army forces, plus at least two-thirds of the navy. Having two of our three fleets far from home will create a local defense vacuum. Add to that the current domestic situation, and the rising ocean levels and widespread flooding along the coast, and other potential large-scale natural disasters that need major support from the military."

Huahua said, "Both issues are resolvable. First, India is contained by Pakistan, which will also leave a major force at home. We can launch a diplomatic offensive so that under pressure from other major powers, India will be forced to deploy forces to the games in equivalent measure to us. As for natural disasters, the absence of the military is of course detrimental, but it's not something we can't handle."

Lü Gang brought up another, more unsettling question. "Our armed forces are intrinsically a force for territorial defense. They are untested and incapable of waging a long-distance, intercontinental war. Our navy, for example, is based on ideas derived from land-war theories. It's only an offshore defensive force, not a deepwater fighting force. The majority of the ships in the fleet can go no farther than James Shoal, which for a modern navy hardly even counts as leaving the backyard. Now we've got to voyage to Antarctica. Before they left, the adults told us time and again not to engage in wars across continents or oceans. You're all aware of that."

"But the world is very different from what the adults imagined. We can't be inflexible," Huahua said.

Specs then laid out his own viewpoint. "If the climate continues to follow the same pattern, half of our country will be drowned or rendered uninhabitably hot. Our future is linked to Antarctica, and so a global contest for the south pole is unavoidable. When the country first contemplated embarking on Antarctic expeditions, one national leader said, 'In the midst of pressing concerns, taking an idle move like this shows vision.'* But for us, sending the army to Antarctica is not an idle move. It is a matter of urgency, and a mistake may cost us the game."

Huahua added, "Set aside Antarctica's strategic significance for the time being and consider the war games on their own. The outcome may determine seating order in the children's world."

They all agreed that Huahua's point could have profound implications for the future, and so the question of taking part in the Antarctic Games was settled.

News of the games spread round the country, and it brought the Candytown period to a swift end. The country awoke with a start from its two-month slumber, "as if a tray of ice cubes had been dumped under the covers," in the words of a later historian. But careful consideration reveals that this was nothing unusual. Nothing is a more powerful stimulant to society than war.

Apart from excitement and tension, the new direction that

* Wu Heng (1914–1999), a geologist who chaired the National Antarctic Research Committee (later the Chinese Arctic and Antarctic Administration) in the early eighties ahead of China's first expedition, attributed this remark to Marshal Chen Yi (1901–1972).

Antarctica gave the children was a major factor in waking them out of the Candytown period. In the children's minds, the far-off south pole, a wonderfully mysterious place, became their only hope for shaking off the boredom of life. They had faith that their army would be able to win for the Chinese children an expanse of land on the continent, where the children who settled there could start new lives. In the televised broadcast of the order mobilizing troops to Antarctica, Huahua had this to say:

"Our territory is a paper covered with the adults' drawings. Antarctica is an empty page where we can sketch whatever we desire, and build the paradise of our dreams!"

His statement led to a serious misunderstanding. A rumor began circulating saying that the country would simultaneously execute two five-year plans, the boring one drafted by the adults for domestic use, and the glorious one the children had depicted in the virtual country for Antarctica. There they would build their parks. The idea whipped up all of the country's children into a frenzy. For a time, the "Antarctic Park" was the hottest topic online and in the media, and the entire country focused its attention on the far-off war games. After the mobilization order was issued, the tidiness of the Inertia period returned. Children returned to their jobs and resumed work, and soon the country was humming again.

The Supernova War was the first children's war in human history, and from the start it demonstrated their society's idiosyncrasies. The adults of the Common Era had no capacity to imagine a war that took the form of a game and proceeded according to the rules of a sports tournament.

Despite the deployment by all the countries of over a million troops, and the bases lined up at fifty-kilometer intervals, peace and calm reigned. There was even communication and interchange among the bases. Were it the adults' era, war would already have broken out. For example, sea transport lines between the countries and their Antarctic bases were fragile and it was impossible to obtain supplies locally from the untilled land, which meant that a strike severing those supply lines would cause a disastrous collapse of an enemy's land base. The children did the opposite: the fleets of major powers assisted weaker countries in transporting personnel and material to take part in the games.

Why this occurred is one of the strangest aspects of the children's war: None of the countries had yet learned who their opponents would be. They were all just athletes at the Olympics, and only when the order of play was set would they know who they would be fighting. And they would be pitted against different opponents in each competition. Although diplomacy was constantly being conducted both openly and in secret, no alliances were formed, and all countries maintained complete nonalignment as they waited on the Antarctic playground for the start of the war games.

After they left the Japanese base, it was another two-hour drive before the Chinese children reached the American base. It was their first visit, and the scale of the place amazed them. It stretched out along the coastline for twenty-odd kilometers, dense clusters of tents and temporary buildings as far as the eye could see. Some of the buildings were quite tall, and sprouted forests of antennas from the rooftops. Radar antennas were distributed in large quantities throughout the base, half of them in white radomes that looked as if some gigantic bird had laid a clutch of eggs at random.

Surrounding the base was a web of rough roads on which all manner of military vehicles were passing by, kicking up clouds of dust alien to Antarctica and befouling every last stitch of snow along the way. Nearer to the impromptu harbor along the coast, mountains of goods of all kinds were piled up near the water. A row of large landing craft had just arrived and opened their black maws toward the shore to disgorge tanks and armored vehicles. The giant iron beasts crossed the shallows to dry land, and the ground shook as they rumbled on both sides of the Chinese children's snow track. An unending line of transport planes flew low overhead, their enormous shadows flitting across land and sea in the direction of the airstrips, which had been set up in a hurry out of specialized perforated steel plates.

The summit of participating countries was held in an expansive hall constructed out of inflated building material. It was brightly lit and heated to springtime, and the ceiling was filled with balloons in all colors. A military band was playing a cheerful tune, as if this were a holiday celebration. When the Chinese children entered, most of the other leaders were already there. President Davey came over to greet them, and then led them to a long table in the center of the structure where other leaders were munching heartily. Over a hundred metal helmets were laid out on the table, each of them brimming with some sort of shiny substance.

"Try it. Krill from the Ross Sea."

Huahua picked up one of the translucent krill, and then peeled and ate it. "Raw?"

Davey nodded. "Don't worry. Everything is clean in Antarctica." He handed Specs a glass of beer, and then took a few chunks of ice out of a tray on the table and dropped them in the glass, where they hissed and fizzed. "Natural Antarctic ice. It's got high gas content. The finest restaurants in Europe used to source it specially. It's quite expensive."

"It's all going to disappear pretty soon, judging from the oil slick along the shoreline," Specs said.

"I'd like to discuss a topic not on the agenda of the meeting," Huahua said, finding Ōnishi Fumio on the opposite side of the table and pointing a finger at him. "You need to stop the Japanese children from overfishing whales. If this goes on, whales will be wiped out in Antarctica in short order."

Ōnishi set down his krill and answered with a sneer, "Focus on the games. Otherwise you'll be wiped out."

"That's right, focus on the games," Davey called out eagerly. "That's the goal of this meeting. It's been four months since the last one in D.C., and now that every country has brought a decent amount of naval and land forces to Antarctica, the games can begin. The thing is, no one knows how to play! That is the focus of this discussion. First off—"

"Mr. President, I should be chairing this meeting!" Yagüe said from one end of the table, banging on it with an empty helmet.

"Oh, fine. Mr. IOC President, if you please," Davey said with a slight nod.

Throughout the first, and final, UN session of the Supernova Era, Yagüe in his capacity of secretary general had tried to restore the doomed international organization, but eventually even he came to the realization that his efforts were pointless, and he ended up sitting all by himself in the ruins of the UN Secretariat with nothing to do. The tower was dark and rumored to be haunted. It was said that when the light of the Rose Nebula shone through the collapsed roof of the General Assembly building, Roosevelt seated in his wheelchair would appear on the half-ruined rostrum, with the UN secretaries general taking turns pushing him. If it was moonlight that shone in through the roof, the hall would echo with the sound of slapping, as if Khrushchev's ghost were rapping his delegate desk, not with a shoe, but with Kennedy's skull. . . . These rumors gave Yagüe the creeps, bad enough that he had to resort to liquid courage at night. Just as he reached his breaking point, he received an invitation from the newly re-formed International Olympic Committee, tasked with organizing the war games, and gladly accepted this new position.

Yagüe waved to either side. "Stop eating, everyone, and sit down. Act like you're in a meeting."

The leaders took their seats along the table and put on their translation earpieces, although some of them still snitched a krill or two from the helmets in front of them.

"I told you to stop eating! Mr. President, please have someone take all that away!" Yagüe said.

Davey looked sidelong at him. "Mr. Chairman, you need to understand your position here. You're just the moderator of the games. You have no power to give orders."

Yagüe stared at him for a few seconds, and then spat to one side. "Fine. Then let's begin. I'm sure you all know the national leaders present, so there's no need for introductions. However, also present today are each country's top military commanders. Shall we have them introduce themselves?"

The young generals took turns. In their tailored officers'

uniforms with gleaming golden stars on their epaulets and colorful ribbons and medals on their lapels, they cut far more impressive figures than the adult generals had and added considerable luster to the venue.

The last to make an introduction was the chairman of the Joint Chiefs of Staff of the United States, General Scott. When he first took office, he had waffled over modeling himself after Eisenhower or Bradley or Patton or MacArthur, and had changed styles daily, to the bafflement of his young staffers. Today he had chosen MacArthur. He had ordered a staffer to prepare him a corncob pipe, but such a thing couldn't be found in Antarctica. The staffer brought him a big, shiny black briar, sending the general into a rage. Now he didn't salute as the other generals had done, but waved the pipe at everyone and said, "You twerps, just you wait! I'm gonna beat you so hard you'll piss your pants."

His words elicited laughter. "General Scott, we're intrigued by your pips," said the chief of general staff of the Russian Armed Forces, Marshal Zavyalova, her tone sarcastic. Scott had seven stars on his shoulder.

"You have reservations about the number of stars? True, the highest rank ever created by the US Army was a six-star general, and that was a posthumous, ceremonial promotion. But I want seven stars on my shoulder. Patton himself could covet decorations, so why can't I wear one more star? The president hasn't criticized me, so what are you going to do?"

"I'm just wondering why you're not wearing eight stars. That would be more symmetrical."

"No, the layout would be too rigid. I'd prefer nine!"

Lü Gang put in, "Just slap on an American flag, why don't you?"

Furiously, Scott said, "You're mocking me, General Lü. I can't permit this! I won't!"

"Can you go a single day without getting into a fight?" Davey said.

"He's mocking me!" Scott said, pointing at Lü Gang.

Davey grabbed the pipe out of Scott's hand and threw it onto the table. "From now on, no messing around with that wacky crap. Also, take three of the stars off that idiotic shoulder mark. Don't give the media anything to gossip about."

Scott's face reddened as he realized that the day's choice of style had been a mistake. MacArthur was inappropriate for the president's presence.

Yagüe rapped the table again with the helmet serving as a gavel. "Okay now, let's continue. There are two items on the agenda for today's meeting. First, to set out general principles for the war games, and second, to determine the events. We'll proceed to the first agenda item. Our proposal for general principles are as follows: To make the games thrilling and fun, the six major military powers taking part, namely the United States, Russia, the European Union (counting as a single country during the war games), China, Japan, and India, as permanent members of the World Games, must abide by the package principle; that is, they must take part in all events. Other countries may selectively participate in the events as they so choose."

The general principles gained unanimous approval from all countries, and Davey said with delight, "Excellent. A commendable beginning."

Yagüe rapped the helmet again. "Next we'll move to the second item, determining the events."

"I'll propose one first," Davey called out. "Carrier battle groups!"

The other children were shocked into silence for a moment, and then Yagüe asked tentatively, "Isn't that a little too . . . big? A carrier group? With all the aircraft on the carrier, and the escort of cruisers and destroyers and submarines? It's too big."

Davey said, "That's the point! Don't kids want to bring out the big guns?"

Huahua stood up. "American kids, maybe. We can't play that game, though. China doesn't have an aircraft carrier."

"Japan doesn't, either," said Ōnishi.

Prime Minister Jairu of India said, "We've got one, but an old model with traditional propulsion. And we can't put together a battle group."

"What you mean is that it'll be the EU, Russia, and us, and you all watch from the sidelines?" Davey asked.

Yagüe nodded, and added, "That's not in line with the package principle."

Huahua shrugged. "That can't be helped. We can't fabricate an aircraft carrier."

"And you all won't let us make one," Ōnishi said, and snorted.

Scott pointed at the two of them and said, "The games have only just begun and already you've spoiled them!"

Standing up, Lü Gang suggested, "How about this. We use our cruisers and submarines against your carrier groups?"

"No way!" Davey shouted.

"He's a smart kid," Lü Gang whispered into Huahua's ear after sitting down, and Huahua smiled slightly and nodded.

Davey was actually well aware that the adults' aircraft

carriers were an entirely different beast in children's hands. Child naval aviators had only just learned to fly solo, and their strike rate against ship and ground targets was very low. At the same time, carrier group combat was a highly sophisticated technical process that children could not master in such a short time, so in an actual battle, ships launched from the carrier might be unable to locate their targets. More dismaying to the US Navy was carrier security. Carriers had few defensive capabilities of their own, but relied on the escort in the carrier group for protection. The hardware and software of the Aegis-based carrier defensive system that consolidated the various weapons systems of cruisers, destroyers, and submarines was so complicated it made even the adults' eyes blur, and there was no way that children could operate it normally. Although the carrier had as usual sailed out surrounded by attending ships, it was actually quite poorly defended, and its ponderous bulk made it an excellent target on the open sea. Lots of weapons were scary to the American children; the Chinese Navy's C-802 antiship missile (the "Chinese Exocet"), for instance, presented a huge combat threat. It only took a single missile breaking through the Aegis perimeter and striking the carrier to sink it. As the commander of the Pacific Fleet said, "Right now our aircraft carrier is as fragile as an egg float-ing on the ocean." A tyrant of the waves in former days, now the best it could do was serve as a transport craft for fighter jets. But it could not be permitted to sink. It was a spiritual support for the American children, a symbol of American power, and so during this event, America's carriers were off cruising the Pacific, far from shore. Davey had only been bluffing.

"Very well," Davey said with a sigh. "Let's make it a destroyer game."

The permanent members approved unanimously, and Yagüe wrote the event down in a notebook. Then he looked up and said, "Continue suggesting—"

"Submarines!" shouted Prime Minister Green.

"That won't be any fun, a bunch of kids playing cat and mouse in the dark," said Marshal Zavyalova, but Yagüe wrote it down anyway.

"Don't stick to the ocean. How about a land game?" Huahua asked.

"Fine. A tank game!" Russian president Ilyukhin said.

"That's a major category, so we should be more detailed," General Scott said. "I have a suggestion: head-on combat. Tank formations start from a distance and advance toward each other simultaneously, and commence firing."

"That's well-suited to the flat geography here. To make it more fun, restrict it to the tank's gun. Don't use guided missiles," said Marshal Zavyalova. No one objected.

"Then there ought to be threshold distance. The two sides can only start firing when they're within that distance," Lü Gang said, seizing on the key issue. The Abrams, T-90, and Leclerc had far more advanced fire-control systems than the Chinese children's Type 99.

"Thirty-five hundred meters," Scott said.

"No, a thousand meters," Lü Gang said.

The children began arguing, but Yagüe interrupted, "Fine, fine. The technical details can be sorted out by each event's task force. We're only deciding on the events in general."

"This is critical. We need to decide it now," Huahua said, refusing to give an inch. But they were outnumbered and ultimately a distance of three thousand meters, highly unfavorable to the Chinese children, was decided upon.

"We propose another tank event," Huahua called out, raising a hand. "Ultra-close wall smashing!"

"What's that?" The other children were mystified.

"The rules are that opposing tanks each start out behind two parallel brick walls, and when the start command is given, they topple the wall and attack each other. The walls erected on-site are only separated by ten to twenty meters."

"Hah! Now that's a thrilling game!" Davey said, laughing. Scott whispered to him that since the Bradley weighed fifty-seven tons, heavier than both the Chinese Type 99 and Russian T-90, and could go from 0 to 30 kph in just seven seconds, it wouldn't be outclassed in wall tumbling, so he didn't object to the event.

"There's an even more thrilling tank game. Foot soldiers versus tanks!" Marshal Zavyalova said.

"Awesome!" Lü Gang exclaimed, and everyone else agreed.

"There's bound to be lots more fun tank games, but let's set out these for the time being. We can add new ones as we please," Yagüe said, writing down the events.

"Jet fighters!" Scott shouted.

No one objected, but someone asked whether the event would be divided into two parts—air-to-air missiles, and guns.

Marshal Zavyalova shook her head. "I don't see the point. Kids aren't proficient at flying yet, and it's tough enough to manage dogfights. Add in extra restrictions, and I'm afraid it won't be any fun." And so the event was decided upon.

"Infantry with light weapons," called out Huahua.

"Hmm. That's a basic event. But it needs to be subdivided. First, define light weapons," Marshal Zavyalova said.

"Anything under twenty millimeters."

"Then maybe we should first divide into two games, fortified positions and charges. In the first, the two sides shoot at each other from within their fortifications. The second is like the tank-charge game, where the two sides advance toward each other and open fire when they reach a certain distance. That distance . . . doesn't need to be set right now."

"It's like a Russian-style pistol duel," someone murmured.

"Armored helicopter duels!" Davey shouted.

China and India opposed that game, and Japan remained neutral, but with the US, Russia, and the EU in support, the event was approved.

"Grenades!" Huahua shouted. "Oh, right. That should be a subdivision of the infantry and light weapons."

"Why are you only pitching that backward stuff?" Davey asked the Chinese children.

"Why are you only pitching the advanced stuff?" Huahua asked back.

Again, it was Yagüe who smoothed things over. "It's all good. Everyone has the same goal, to play fun games. You've got to be understanding. If everyone only picks their strong events and rejects their weaker ones, how are we going to have games to play?"

"Grenades are a basic weapon. Why can't they be included?" Lü Gang asked.

"Fine. Put them in, then. Don't imagine we'll be push-overs, though," Davey said caustically.

"We should also subdivide grenades into fortifications

and charges," Marshal Zavyalova said. "And with basic weaponry in mind, have you considered artillery?"

As they realized the potential, the children shouted out different artillery games.

"Five-kilometer artillery fights!"

"Ten-kilometer large-caliber!"

"Thirty-kilometer rockets!"

"Self-propelled rockets against a moving target! Heh, on the Antarctic plain that'll be like a sea battle."

"Mortars! Who can forget mortars?"

"That's right. Mortars at close range. And they can be mobile, too. That'll be tons of fun."

Scott cut them all off, saying, "Let me make a suggestion. Contests at ranges beyond five kilometers can take advantage of aerial reconnaissance and fire correction."

"Opposed! That makes the game too complicated, and increases the chance of fouls," Lü Gang said.

"In favor! It makes the game more interesting," Prime Minister Green said.

"Stop!" Yagüe rapped the helmet loudly. "I said before, technical details are up to the task force to decide."

When Yagüe finished recording the artillery games, Davey jumped to his feet. "You're all interested in quite a lot of events. I'll suggest another one. Bombers and ground-based air defense!"

Yagüe raised an eyebrow, considering the question. "The game would be like tanks versus infantry. The two sides would be unbalanced, so you'd need to swap roles, which increases the number of heats, and complicates administration and judging. We ought to minimize this sort of game."

Huahua chuckled, and shot Davey a grin. "I'd wager that

President Davey didn't consider the role-swapping issue. He probably only imagined that the US would do the bombing, and someone else would do the defense. Is that right?"

Davey slapped his head. "Uh, yeah, I overlooked that part."

"Cognitive inertia. So how about it, do American kids want our H-20 and the Russians' Tu-22M to bomb their defenses?"

"Uh . . . since the chairman just mentioned the administration and judging difficulties, we can just take a pass on this event."

Scott interjected, "We can add a ship-to-shore game, like landing versus land defense."

"That's also incredibly hard to organize and administer. And it'll take an awfully long time. And it might not be any fun. I say forget it," Marshal Zavyalova said. Yagüe and the other children followed with similar sentiments, and the game did not pass.

"This one ought to work: Missile versus missile!" Davey suggested, undaunted.

Ilyukhin nodded approvingly. "Great. An excellent game. You can subdivide it into close and midrange guided missiles, and ICBMs."

"Ooh, ICBMs!" exclaimed Davey, waving his hands wildly. "This is the best game so far!"

"But no using TMD or NMD," Ilyukhin said coolly.

"What? Of course we need to use NMD and TMD!" Scott shouted.

"But most of the permanent member countries don't have them, so it doesn't fit the package principle."

"Who cares! We're going to use them. We support this a

hundred and twenty percent! Otherwise, we're pulling out of the games," Davey shouted while his arms flailed about uncontrollably.

"Fine. Use them if you want," Lü Gang said with a dismissive wave.

"NMD? They can't even get Aegis going." Zavyalova punctuated her criticism with a snort of contempt.

Davey let out a long breath. "Good. Now let's move on." Then he sat down and looked smugly at the other children.

Huahua raised a hand. "Land mines!"

"Interesting. How do you play?" asked the children.

"Opposing teams set up two minefields over an area to be determined by the task force. In the center of each field is the team flag. The first to clear a path to the opposing team's flag is the winner."

Davey curled his lips and said sarcastically, "Fine, give the kindergartners something to play. Write it down, Mr. Chairman."

Now a head of state from an island in the Pacific stood up. "Some of the smaller countries want me to say a few words for them. You've got to give us at least a few chances to play."

"Can't you play with the rest of us in those traditional events, the ones the Chinese kids proposed?" Davey asked.

"You're not getting it, Mr. President. Take my country, for example. Right now we have just one company on Antarctica, fewer than two hundred troops, and even in the simplest infantry game, I estimate we'll lose combat effectiveness after just one round."

"You all can propose other games."

"I've got one," said Lê Sâm Lâm, the prime minister of Vietnam. "Guerrilla war!"

"Wicked! How do you play?"

"The two opposing teams attack each other's base using a small guerrilla force. The specific rules are as follows—"

"Shut up!" Davey shouted, leaping up and banging the table. "You ought to be ashamed of yourselves for proposing such a vile idea!"

"That's right. You should be ashamed!" Green joined in.

"It's . . . it's going to be a little disruptive," Yagüe said to Lê Sâm Lâm. "Back at the meeting in Washington, we reached a consensus that country's bases are sacrosanct. Your proposal disturbs the very foundation of the games."

The event was vetoed.

"Antarctica has turned into a private club for major powers. What's the point of us even being here?" Lê Sâm Lâm grumbled.

Yagüe ignored him and said to everyone else, "Our meeting has already achieved some stunning results. Do any other countries have suggestions for new games?" His gaze halted on Ōnishi, far off at the other end of the table, and he called over to him, "Prime Minister Ōnishi, you've been silent throughout the proceedings. I recall that at the first UN session, you conveyed Japan's intense desire to gain the right to speak at the UN, but now that Japan is a permanent member state of the World Games, you've gone silent."

Ōnishi made a slight bow, and then said slowly, "I'll propose a game none of you have thought of yet."

"Let's hear it," Davey said, and everyone looked expectantly at the Japanese prime minister.

"Cold weapons."

The children all looked at each other. Someone asked, "Cold weapons? What are those?"

"Swords." He said nothing beyond that terse reply, but sat there motionless as a statue.

"Swords? None of us have any," Scott said, somewhat confused.

"I do," the Japanese kid said, and then from beneath the table took out a long military sword and eased it out of its scabbard. The children gasped at its icy glint. The sword was so thin that its cutting edge seemed almost threadlike. Ōnishi stroked the surface gently with a finger. "It's crafted from the finest carbon alloy, and is sharper than anything." Then he blew across the blade, and the children heard a sustained buzz from the sword. "This is a two-layered blade; when one edge gets dull, the other is exposed, so it remains sharp forever without honing." He placed the sword gently onto the table, where it dazzled the children with its cool light and sent chill wind down their spines. "We can provide ten thousand of these for the games."

"That's a little too . . . barbaric," said Davey timidly, and the other children nodded along.

Ōnishi didn't bat an eyelid. "Mr. President, and the rest of you, you all should be ashamed of your weak nerves," he said, brandishing the weapon. "It's the foundation of all of the games you all have already suggested, the soul of war. Humanity's very first toy."

"Very well. Include a cold-weapons event," Ilyukhin said.

"Except this kind of military sword . . . isn't really necessary, is it?" Davey asked, averting his gaze from the sword on the table, as if the glare hurt his eyes.

"Then rifle bayonets," Marshal Zavyalova said.

The children's enthusiasm had vanished. They all stared at the sword in silence, as if they had just awakened from sleepwalking and were trying to figure out what they were in the process of doing.

"Anyone else have a suggestion?" Yagüe asked.

No one answered. There was no sound in the hall, as if the sword had taken away their very souls.

"Okay then. We should get ready to start the games."

One week later, the opening ceremony of the first Olympic Games of the Supernova Era was held on the broad plain of Marie Byrd Land.

More than three hundred thousand children took part in the opening ceremony, standing in a huge dense crowd. In the distance, the low-hanging sun of this half of the year was mostly below the horizon now, with only a tiny arc shedding a ruddy glow across the mottled monochrome landscape, glinting off the packed mass of helmets. In the dark blue of the sky a few silver stars had begun to twinkle.

The ceremony itself was simple. First there was a flag-raising, in which all of the participating countries dispatched representative soldiers to carry the five-ring Olympic flag around the venue, and then that symbol of peace was run up a tall flagpole over the Supernova Era battlefield. Child soldiers fired into the air in a salute that rippled across the crowd, gunfire trailing off in one area only to be picked up in another, like the rise and fall of ocean waves. On a platform beneath the flagpole, IOC president Yagüe stood waving for what seemed like ages until the shots finally quieted down and he could make his speech. As he opened up his notes, a kid next to him passed him a helmet. He did not immediately understand why, and shoved it aside in annoyance without noticing that the world leaders and other besuited VIPs on the platform were wearing helmets. He pressed on with his speech.

"Children of the new world, welcome to the first Olympic Games of the Supernova Era—"

Just then he heard a burst of rat-a-tat noises, like a shower of hailstones, and after a moment of confusion, he realized it was the sound of bullets hitting helmets and the ground, celebratory gunfire returning to earth. Now he grasped the helmet's purpose, but before he had sense enough to reach for it, he received a sharp crack on the noggin. A bullet in free fall raised a welt on a scar from a previous head injury, one due to falling glass at the UN Secretariat a few months before. It probably was only a 5.56×45 mm NATO round, since if it had been a 7.62×39 mm round from one of the Chinese or Russian children's older AK-47s, it might have knocked him out. Amid laughter, he put on his helmet, fighting back the pain, and reached a hand inside to massage his head. As bullets rained down, he said in a loud voice:

"Children of the new world, welcome to the first Olympic Games of the Supernova Era. This is a war games Olympics, a fun Olympics, a thrilling Olympics, and a real Olympics! Children, the boredom of the Common Era has come to a close, and human civilization has returned to its childhood, to a happy, uncivilized age. We have left the dreary ground and returned to the freedom of the trees, we have shrugged off the clothes of hypocrisy and grown luxurious downy coats. Children, the new motto of the Olympic Games is: 'Take part! Sharper, Fiercer, Deadlier.' Let the world go crazy, children! Next, I'll describe the events."

Yagüe unfolded that creased piece of notepaper and began reading: "After negotiations by all member states, the events of the first Olympic Games of the Supernova Era have been decided upon, and fall into three categories: land, sea, and air events.

"In the land-events category: Tank battles, tank versus infantry (heavy weapons), tank versus infantry (without heavy weapons), artillery battles (five-kilometer large-caliber guns, fifteen-kilometer rockets, self-propelled mobile rockets, and one-kilometer mortars), infantry battles (machine guns), infantry battles (grenades), infantry battles (cold weapons), guided-missile battles (short-range, midrange, cruise missile, ICBM), land mines.

"In the sea-events category: destroyer battles, submarine battles.

"In the air-events category: fighter-jet battles, attack-helicopter battles.

"Gold, silver, and bronze medals will be awarded in all events.

"Mixed categories, such as air versus land, or sea versus air, were discussed, but due to the complexity of organization and judging, they were not formally included.

"Now, will the representatives of the world's children taking part in the games take the oath."

The representatives, a lieutenant colonel in the US Air Force, a lieutenant in the Russian Navy, and a lieutenant in the Chinese Army, took the oath as follows:

"I swear first to abide by the rules that govern the games, and to accept all penalties if I break them; and second, to do my best to keep the games thrilling and fun, and to show my opponents no shred of mercy."

Cheers and gunfire rang out on the plain.

"All armed forces to the battlefield!"

For more than two hours, infantry and armored divisions from every country swarmed past the flagpole, and at the tail end, tanks, armored vehicles, and mobile rocket launchers mixed with crowds of people into a chaotic flood of iron whose dust clouds blotted out the sky. On the sea in the distance, the countries' ships fired en masse, their guns flashing brilliant white in the blue-black twilight, shaking the ground with their noise and light.

When calm was restored but before the dust had settled, Yagüe called for the last item on the program: "Light the torch!"

The whine of engines filled the air, and the children all looked up to see a fighter jet coming in from the east. In the near-dark sky it was visible only as a silhouette, and seemed cut out of cardboard. As it drew near, they could make out the ugly shape of an A-10 Warthog, its two large engines looking like aftermarket attachments to the tail section. As it passed over a large clearing in the crowd, it dropped a napalm bomb that exploded with a deep rumble, sending flames and black smoke leaping skyward. The crowd on the plain was lit up with orange firelight, and the children ringing the clearing could feel the waves of heat.

The sun was entirely below the horizon now as the Antarctic continent began its long nighttime. But it wasn't a dark night; lit by aurora australis, greatly intensified by the radiation from the supernova, every inch of the sky was filled with dancing bands of color, while on the vast land below, the Supernova Era's nightmarish history continued its march forward.

Games of Blood and Iron

The thirty-five tanks in Lieutenant Wang Ran's battalion advanced at full speed in an attack formation, but in front of them was only an open plain dotted with patches of unmelted snow. They had covered a considerable distance without seeing the enemy. This was the head-on tank vs. tank game. Their starting point was a low-lying depression, an excellent cover position for an armored division, and difficult to locate in this section of the plain.

Under the norms of regular combat, they could enter under cover of night with a considerable gap between vehicles and carefully camouflage themselves once everyone was in place, and then the following day wait until the enemy drew near to attack. But such an approach was impossible now, because the enemy knew their position, and they knew their enemy's, and each side was fully aware of the other's strength. The intelligence was 100 percent accurate; they had informed each other directly. They even knew the type and amount of ammunition carried by each of the thirty-five Abrams tanks they were about to fight, and were completely conversant with the defects in tracks and fire-control systems owing to a memo received the previous day from the US Army commander. Everything proceeded as clearly and openly as the unobstructed plain under the southern lights.

The only things they could exploit were their attack-formation design and their shooting skills. Wang Ran had been a driver, but his tank had been destroyed in the games two days ago, and he had barely escaped with his life. The gunner in his current tank had been killed in that game, and he had been put into the position as an emergency replacement. Although he was not at all sure of himself, he was still looking forward to it, since being a gunner was a totally different feeling. He sat up in a much higher seat listening to the roar of the engine and enjoying the feeling of speed. The most satisfying part was when the tank crested a medium-size rise in the ground, since in that instant the tracks left the ground and the Type 99 was entirely airborne, and when it descended again Wang Ran had a delightful sense of weightlessness. For a brief moment the fifty-ton iron beast was as agile as a glider, but in the next instant it landed heavily on the ground, which shifted beneath the impact of its tracks as if it were soft mud. He sunk down with it, like a weighty mountain settling in place. Throughout the whole jump his every cell screamed with excitement, like in a cavalry charge.

"First of all we simplified tank combat into two opposing tanks traveling toward each other across a two-dimensional flat plane. Such conditions don't actually exist, just like the points and lines of geometry don't really exist in the real world, but this allows you a clear view of the essential elements of tank combat. In this age, the key to victory is to fire first, and to hit with the first round. The two have a multiplicative relationship, not an additive one; if either is zero, the outcome is a zero. The interesting thing is that they are in opposition: the earlier the fire, the farther from the target, and the lower the first-round hit rate; and vice versa . . ."

This was a lesson given by an adult officer to the young armored forces a year ago, and his words echoed in Wang Ran's brain, even though he now felt it was all bullshit. Now, Wang Ran could be that colonel's instructor, since the colonel had never been in actual tank combat; otherwise he'd have taught Wang Ran and the others some more useful information. Sure, the colonel had mentioned that the modified Abrams fire-control system gave it a first-round hit rate of 78 percent outside of one mile, but he didn't comprehend the actual implications of that figure. Wang Ran understood. The goal he and his young brothers-in-arms had had upon joining the armored division, to be a hero with dozens of tank kills, was the biggest joke in the world. Their only goal now was to hit one enemy tank before they were destroyed themselves, to not lose on the exchange. It was by no means an easy goal; if every Chinese tank were able to achieve it, the Chinese kids wouldn't lose the game.

Both sides fired flares, and their surroundings lit up in green light. Wang Ran looked through his scope at the yellowish haze ahead of them, the dust cloud kicked up by tank #105 to their forward left. All of a sudden the yellow dust in his field of vision turned red with flickering firelight. The scene cleared up and he saw #108 slow down, trailing smoke and fire, and then it was far behind them. Ahead to the right another tank was on fire, and was also left behind. At no time did he hear the two tanks get hit. Suddenly a column of dust was kicked up straight ahead of them, and they ran directly into it, stones and shell fragments clattering on the tank's outer armor. The shot, a high-speed fin-stabilized armor-piercing round, had fallen short of the target. Now his tank was at the head of their formation, and Wang Ran heard in his earpiece the voice of the lieutenant colonel in command of their battalion, from her command vehicle: "Targets sighted directly ahead! Fire at will!"

More bullshit. Just like in the previous engagements, in

the crucial moment they never provide you with the information you want. They're just a distraction. Now the tank slowed down, evidently so he could fire. Wang Ran looked ahead through his viewfinder, and in the light of the flares he saw first the dust clouds blocking out the sky over the horizon, and then, at the base of the cloud, he saw the black dots. He adjusted the focus until the Abrams tanks resolved, and his first impression was that they were nothing like what he had seen in photographs, where they looked as powerfully sturdy as two square iron ingots bolted together. Here, trailing long dust clouds behind them, they looked smaller.

He caught one in the crosshairs, and then pressed the button to lock it, turning the M1A2 into a magnet to attract the 120 mm smoothbore cannon, so that no matter how the tank pitched or rocked, the barrel would remain stubbornly trained onto its target like a compass needle. He pressed the fire button and saw the spurt of fire from the barrel and the dust kicked up ahead of them by the vented air. Then off in the distance the shell exploded in fire and smoke. It was a clean explosion, no dirt, and Wang Ran knew it was a hit. The tank continued to advance, trailing smoke, but he knew that it wouldn't make it very far before it stopped.

He moved the crosshairs to capture another target, but then from outside the tank came a deafening noise. His helmet and earphones had excellent noise-shielding, but he knew it was a loud noise because it rocked his entire body numb. The viewfinder went dark, and his legs suddenly felt burning hot, like the time when he was young and his father carried him into a hot tub. But the heat turned scorching, and he looked down at the inferno he was now standing in: flames were everywhere in the lower part of the cabin.

The extinguishers went on automatically, filling the cabin with fog and suppressing the fire. Then he realized that a black, branch-like object beneath his feet was twitching. A fire-scorched arm. He grabbed the arm, not knowing whether it belonged to the driver or the loader, but neither would have been so lightweight. He quickly learned the reason: he had pulled up just the upper half of a body, blackened all over, the lower part of the chest still in flames. His hand shook, and the half torso slipped down again. He still couldn't make out who it was, or why the hand was still moving. He opened the hatch and climbed out as fast as he could. The tank was still moving forward, and he rolled off the back and crashed heavily to the ground, surrounded by clouds of smoke from the tank he had just exited.

After a breeze cleared the smoke, Wang Ran saw his tank at a standstill ahead of him. The smoke had ebbed, but flames were spurting from the interior. It had been hit by a shaped charge, he now knew, one designed to cut through armor by concentrating explosive energy into a high-temperature jet, turning the tank into a furnace. He moved backward, passing a number of other burning tanks, and his burned trousers dropped in shreds from his legs. He turned around at the sound of a dull thud behind him; his tank had exploded and was now a ball of thick flame and smoke. Now he felt an intense pain in his legs and sat right down on the ground, surrounded by explosions and fires, beneath flickering southern lights dulled by the thick smoke in the night sky. He felt the chill wind, and then the colonel instructor's words echoed in his mind once again:

". . . group engagements are more complicated. Now, our tank group and the enemy's can be thought of in mathematical terms as two matrices, and the entire course of battle as the multiplication of these matrices . . ."

Bullshit. Complete bullshit. Even now Wang Ran had no idea how matrices were multiplied. Surveying the battlefield, he carefully counted the number of destroyed tanks on each side. The relative damage rate needed to be calculated.

Three days later, and still dragging his injured leg, Wang Ran got into a third tank, this time as driver. They reached the match location before it was light. More than a hundred tanks were parked along a long brick wall for the wall-smashing game, waiting for the start command. When the command came, they and their opponents, parked behind a parallel wall ten meters beyond theirs, would push the walls over and attack each other. The event required fast reflexes, and the key to victory lay in the attack formation, not shooting skills since there was basically no need to even aim when it came time to shoot. Their instructors back in the Common Era would never have imagined that their students would be firing upon enemy tanks at a distance of just a few meters, much less that the command to shoot would be issued by a Swiss judge, surveying the battle from a helicopter far overhead.

For the next several hours, that wall was all of the outside world Wang Ran could see through the tank's forward window. It flickered between indistinct and crystal clear as southern lights danced overhead. He inspected it in minute detail, down to the last fracture of every brick and the shape of every segment of still-wet cement, enjoying the interplay of light and shadow on the wall from the aurora australis that he couldn't see. He discovered for the first time that the world had so many things to enjoy, and he made a decision: If he made it out of this game alive, he would enjoy every inch of the world around him as if it were a painting.

His earpiece broke its five-hour silence with the command to attack. The voice came so suddenly, right in the middle of his careful study of the pattern of cracks in the thirteenth brick in the fourth row up, that he froze for a second. But just one second, and then he slammed the accelerator and sent the giant steel beast leaping forward to smack down the wall alongside the other tanks. As bricks scattered and dirt flew, he realized he was already in the enemy's armored formation. In the brief, chaotic battle that followed, the constant noise of smoothbore cannon fire and exploding shells, blinding flashes outside, the turret above him spinning rapidly, and the ammo loader grinding away as the smell of propellant filled the cabin, he knew that the gunner had only to fire as quickly as possible in all directions with no need to even aim. The firing frenzy lasted less than ten seconds, until there was a thunderous noise and the world exploded before his eyes.

When Wang Ran regained consciousness he was lying in the battlefield first-aid station. Standing next to him was a reporter for the army newspaper.

"How many tanks do we have left in the battalion?" he asked weakly.

"Not a one," the reporter said. He should have known. The tanks were close enough to set a world record for armored-vehicle combat. The reporter added, "But I should congratulate you: One to one-point-two! We turned around the relative damage rate for the first time! Your tank destroyed two of theirs, one Leclerc and one Challenger."

"Zhang Qiang's amazing," Wang Ran said, nodding, despite his splitting headache, in recognition of his tank's gunner.

"So are you. Only one was due to shooting. You flipped the other on impact!"

Wang Ran felt drowsy again owing to lack of blood, and he dropped off with the sounds of frenzied shooting echoing in his ears like a rainstorm beating down endlessly on a metal roof. But all his eyes saw were those abstract patterns on the brick wall.

The commander of Wang Ran's armored division stood on a low hill watching the last of her battalions roll out. When the steel skirmish line reached the enemy's position and the tanks switched on their smoke generators, all she could see was a band of white smoke. A rapid series of explosions followed, and although from this vantage point she couldn't see the enemy's tanks, she could see the explosions of the shells they fired at hers, lighting up the band of smoke with dazzling balls of light. At times a silhouette would momentarily be visible amid the fog and explosions. The thirteen-year-old commander had the sudden sense of familiar recognition: back on the morning of the first Spring Festival she set off firecrackers, she had been so frightened after lighting them she had thrown the entire long strand on the ground, where it cracked and thundered, sending hundreds of tiny flashes into the drifting smoke. . . .

But the battle didn't even last as long as the firecrackers had, and in fact to the commander it seemed even longer than it actually was. Afterward she learned that the shooting had only lasted for twelve seconds. In twelve short seconds, enough to take six breaths, the commander's one remaining division was annihilated. The Type 99s sat in flames before her; under the thinning smoke it was almost as if they were torches obscured beneath a gauze curtain.

"What's the damage rate?" the commander asked a staff officer beside her, unable to keep the tremor out of her voice. She stood on the crossroads between heaven and hell, a ghost asking God which road to take. The staffer took off his wireless earpiece and uttered the fiery, icy figure they had obtained at the price of a hundred-odd children's lives.

"One-point-three to one, sir."

"Tolerable. Not over the limit," the commander said, and let out a long breath. She knew that in the invisible distance, enemy tanks equivalent to ten-thirteenths the number of her own were also aflame. The game was still in progress, but she had completed her mission, and kept their relative damage rate below the limit.

Second Lieutenant Wei Ming, one of Huahua's classmates, took part in the heavy-weapons subcategory of the tank vs. infantry games with his armored platoon. Unlike the light-arms subcategory, which restricted soldiers to antitank grenades, soldiers in this game were able to use antitank guns and guided missiles against their opponents. By no means did this given them an easier time of it, because while the other game pitted a platoon against a single tank, they were facing three main battle tanks or five light tanks simultaneously.

Today was a group match, and Wei Ming and his young comrades had spent the night poring over the battle plans. The previous day they had watched their company's Second

Platoon use the country's most advanced antitank missile, the HJ-12, which their adult instructors had raved over, in particular the three types of guidance it utilized, including its cutting-edge visual pattern matching. In the game itself, all three of the missiles Second Platoon had fired were jammed and went wide of their targets, and only five soldiers survived. The rest were taken down by the guns and cannons of three Leclercs. The M1A2 tanks that Wei Ming's platoon now faced had an even more powerful jamming system, so they had decided to use the more outdated, wire-guided HJ-73 missiles. They had less range, but were resistant to jamming, and the warheads had been improved to increase the armor-penetration capability from 300 mm to 800 mm.

Now their preparations were complete. Three antitank missiles were set up in a line in their small base, no grander-looking than three white-painted wooden pegs. The Indian judge at their side motioned to indicate that the game had begun, and then scurried off to hide behind a line of sand-bags and train her binoculars on them. The tank vs. infantry game was not easy on judges; it had already killed two and wounded five.

Wei Ming was operating one of the three missiles. During training in the adults' time, he had posted the highest total performance in this discipline, owing to his love of playing with a video camera back home. Missile operation consisted of keeping the target captured in the crosshairs from start to finish to guide the missile in its flight.

Dust appeared on the horizon, and through binoculars Wei Ming saw a large group of tanks. With an entire infantry regiment taking part in today's game, all but three of the M1A2s were attacking other targets. Wei Ming quickly picked out the three that were on their preset path, tiny shapes that didn't seem at all ferocious from far away.

Letting go of the binoculars, he dropped down to the missile to track one of the tanks in the viewfinder, keeping the crosshairs steady on the black spot that showed indistinctly through the dust. When he was certain it was within his three-thousand-meter firing range, he pressed the button to fire, and the missile next to him took off with a whoosh, trailing the wire behind it. He heard two more whooshes as the other two missiles took off. Now fire flashed from the front of the three M1A2s, like they were opening their eyes, and two or three seconds later the shells landed to the right and back of them, and then a few earsplitting explosions and a storm of dirt and stones rained down on them. More shells followed, and Wei Ming involuntarily shielded his head with his arms amid the explosions. He recovered quickly, but when he turned to the viewfinder all he could see was the horizon, rocking unsteadily. By the time he found the target again and locked it in the crosshairs, he saw a column of dust rising up to the tank's right side, and he knew that his missile had gone wide. Looking up from the eyepiece, he saw two other dust columns behind the tanks. All three missiles had missed. The tanks charged toward them, clearly recognizing that without any missiles the base was no longer a threat. It had become a light-weapons game, but the platoon was facing not one but three tanks.

"Ready antitank grenades!" Wei Ming shouted, taking out one of his own and crouching in the shell scrape as the tanks grew ever closer. With magnetic material in its head, the grenade was heavy in his hand.

"Sir . . . how does it work? I never learned!" a kid next to him said anxiously. Indeed they had never learned how; the adults who had trained them had never imagined their charges would be going up against the world's most ferocious main battle tanks armed only with hand grenades.

As the three iron beasts closed in, Wei Ming could feel their vibrations in the ground beneath his feet. He ducked as machine-gun rounds zipped overhead, and had to estimate the tanks' distance. When he sensed they were charging into the base, he stood up and hurled his grenade at the middle tank, and at the same moment saw a flash from the muzzle of the turret machine gun pointed straight at him, and a bullet whisked just past his ear. The grenade traced an arc through the air and stuck to the side of the M1A2's sloped turret a little to the front of the smokescreen outlet, scaring the American kid manning the gun back inside.

Other kids in the platoon came up and hurled their grenades, some of which stuck to tanks, others landing on the ground. The kid next to Wei Ming collapsed to the ground outside the trench with a gaping bullet wound to the back, dropping a grenade that tumbled to a spot two or three meters away. It lay there unexploded; perhaps the kid had forgotten to pull the firing pin. The other grenades exploded, but the three tanks charged onward through the flames and smoke over the trenches, completely unscathed. Wei Ming leapt backward out of his trench and tumbled out of the path of the oncoming tank treads, but many of the other kids were crushed. Then, with a tremendous crash, one tank tipped over into a trench and came to a stop, after hitting and dragging under its tracks a kid right in the middle of throwing a grenade, which exploded, severing the track and dislodging a wheel into the air.

The far-off judge put up a green signal, declaring the game finished. The turret of the crippled Abrams opened with a clang and a helmeted American kid emerged, but at the sight of Wei Ming's machine gun trained on him, he ducked mostly back inside, leaving just half a head poking out as he called through his translation unit, "Follow the rules, Chinese kids! Keep to the rules! The game is over. Stop fighting!" Once Wei Ming lowered his weapon, he came out, with three other kids on his heels, and climbed off the tank, hands on the guns at their waists as they looked warily around at the surviving Chinese kids on the ground. Then they headed off toward the US base. The last kid, who had a huge translation unit strung round her neck, stopped, turned back toward Wei Ming, saluted, and said what her translator then translated as, "I'm Lieutenant Morgan. You all played well, Lieutenant."

Wei Ming returned a salute but said nothing. All of a sudden he noticed movement at Morgan's chest, and a cat poked its head out of the kid's armored division jacket and meowed. Morgan took the cat out of her jacket and showed it to Wei Ming. "This is Watermelon, our crew mascot." To Wei Ming, the cat's ringed markings did make it resemble a watermelon. With another salute, Lieutenant Morgan turned and walked off.

Wei Ming stood still for a while watching the Antarctic horizon shimmer under the spectrum of the southern lights. It was a long time before he walked slowly over to the edge of the trench and his two crushed comrades, and then sat on the soggy ground and burst into tears.

★

The fighting taking place on the Antarctic continent was an unprecedented form of battle, and one unlikely to be repeated: a game war. In this war, enemies fought using the format of an athletic competition. High command on both sides set the time and location of the battle, determined the strength of each side, and chose or drafted rules of battle that they all would abide by. Then they fought according to the arrangements, while an impartial jury observed the fighting and decided the ultimate victor. All participating countries had equal status, there were no alliances, and they took turns fighting. Below is a transcript of a conversation between two countries' high command arranging a competition:

COUNTRY A: Hey, B.

COUNTRY B: Hello.

COUNTRY A: Let's set out the next tank game. How are we going to play tomorrow?

COUNTRY B: How about another head-on charge?

COUNTRY A: Good. How many are you mobilizing?

COUNTRY B: Oh, 150.

COUNTRY A: That's too many. Some of our tanks are in a tank vs. infantry game tomorrow. Let's say 120.

COUNTRY B: Fine. How does Arena 4 sound?

COUNTRY A: Arena 4? Not the greatest. It's hosted five head-on charges and three ultra-close wall-toppling games, so there are wrecked tanks all over the place.

COUNTRY B: Wrecks can act as cover for both sides. It'll add variables to the game and make it more fun to play.

COUNTRY A: That's true. Arena 4 it is. But the rules need to change a bit.

COUNTRY B: The jury can handle that. Set the time?

COUNTRY A: Let's start at 10 A.M. tomorrow. That way we'll both have enough time to assemble.

COUNTRY B: Great. See you tomorrow.

COUNTRY A: See you tomorrow!

Careful thought reveals that this form of warfare is not entirely inexplicable. Rules and agreements suggest the establishment of a system, and a system gains inertia once established; a violation by one side implies the system's collapse, with unforeseeable consequences. The key point is that this warfare system could only have been established in a children's world where game thinking was determinative, and could never be reproduced in an adult world.

If anyone from the Common Era had witnessed the game war, what they would have found most surprising would not have been the sports-like form, since such wars could be found, if not quite so glaringly, back in the old days of cold-weapons warfare; no, they would doubtlessly have been shocked, mystified even, by the nature of the roles played by the participating countries. Enemies were established according to the order of play. People later referred to the "athlete role" of the belligerents who competed in battles set up in a manner never before seen in human history.

One other key characteristic of the game war was the specialization of the fighting. Every battle was a single contest of weapons. Integration of forces and cooperative operations were basically nonexistent.

Not long after the Olympics started, the land-based Supernova War transformed into a huge tank battle. Tanks were the children's favorite weapons; nothing better embodied their fantasies about fighting. During the adults' era, a remote-controlled tank was guaranteed to be a welcome gift. Once war broke out, their fascination transferred to real tanks and they sent them out onto the battlefield with abandon. All together, the countries brought nearly ten thousand tanks to Antarctica to engage in unbridled tank combat on an immense scale, with hundreds to upward of a thousand tanks pitted against each other in each fight.

On the open plain of Antarctica, these groups of iron monsters raced, fired, and burned. Everywhere you looked were fragments of destroyed tanks, some of them on fire for two or three days and, when the wind let up, releasing long, thin columns of weird black smoke from clusters of wrecks all over the plain. From a distance the land looked like it had a wild head of hair.

Compared with the grandeur and brutality of the tank battles, air combat was a much chillier pursuit. Dogfights ought to have been the most competitive fights of all, but the child pilots had trained for less than a year and had put in less than a hundred hours in high-speed fighters, meaning they had mastered only normal takeoff, landing, and level flight, at best.

The superior skill set and physical fitness required for air combat was simply unattainable for the vast majority of them. Hence, combat between opposing fighter formations could barely even get started; far more planes were lost owing to accidents than were shot down by the enemy. During dogfights, most of a pilot's concentration was devoted to not crashing, with little energy left for attacking. Moreover, the acceleration produced by a modern fighter in air combat could be over six gees, to as much as nine when evading a radar lock or a tracking missile, more than the children's fragile cerebral blood vessels could take. There were, of course, a few prodigies, like the American flying ace Carlos (the F-15 pilot who twice evaded missile tracking), but they were in the minority, and avoidable if not provoked.

It was even chillier on the water. Due to the Antarctic's particular geographic location, ocean supply lines were the lifeline for the armies of every country. A cut supply line was the worst of all possible disasters, and would be like abandoning the children on another Earth.

So as to guarantee transport, no country dared to risk any of its sea power, and hence during naval battles, the opposing sides' ships stayed far away from each other, usually beyond the line of sight. Attacks at that distance required technical sophistication, but giant missile attack systems had a very low hit rate in the children's hands. Few strikes actually hit the target, and only a few transport ships were sunk during the games.

It was the same below the surface. Piloting structurally complicated submarines through the inky depths, relying only on sonar in a cat-and-mouse game with the enemy, was a game that required rich experience and top skills the children could not possibly have attained in such a short time.

As in air combat, submarine battles didn't work. Not a single torpedo struck its target during the whole games. Moreover, since Antarctica had no submarine base, and constructing one was far more complicated than setting up a bare-bones port for surface ships, all countries were forced to use logistics bases in Argentina or Oceania. Conventional subs were ill-equipped for lengthy activities in the Southern Ocean, and few countries had nuclear attack subs. In the course of the underwater games, just one conventional sub was sunk, and that owed to its own malfunction.

During the Olympic Games period of the Supernova War, most of the fighting was concentrated on land, which saw quite a number of peculiar forms of combat brand new to the history of warfare.

Most terrifying of all were the infantry games. Although all games of this type used light weapons, they saw casualties in far greater numbers.

The biggest infantry games were firearm duels, and were played in the fortifications and assault categories.

Fortification infantry games involved opposing sides firing at each other from fortifications across a separation, and they could last as long as several days. But as the children discovered, firing from fortified positions meant there was very little exposure, which minimized the lethality of ordinary firearms. They would rain bullets at each other in volleys so dense they would collide in midair, and the spent casings piled up to calf height in the firing positions, but in the final analysis, apart from chipping away the outside layer of the enemy's fortifications, they achieved very little.

And so they switched to scope-equipped precision sniper rifles, which cut ammo expenditure to a thousandth of what it was and boosted combat successes by a factor of ten. Now the game saw the young gunners spending most of their time lying low observing the opposite position, scanning inch by inch for the slightest discrepancy in the stones and patches of snow, and sending over a bullet at any potential firing gaps.

Ahead of the line was empty ground, with no creature

stirring across the broad plain as the children hid in their bunkers. The characteristic snap of a sniper rifle and then the zip of a bullet through the air, *pop—zip pop—zip,* only intensified the chilly quiet of the battlefield, as if somewhere out under the southern lights a lonely ghost were randomly plucking a zither. The children chose a striking name for this game: "Rifle Fishing."

The most thrilling and savage of the infantry games were the grenade events, which were also subdivided into fortifications and assault categories. In the former, fortifications were constructed before the game began, with the two sides separated by just twenty meters, the distance a child could throw a grenade. Once the game started, the children popped up from their defense works, made their throws, and then ducked back down again to avoid the incoming ones.

Wooden stick grenades were used most often, since they were relatively powerful and could be thrown relatively far; egg-shaped grenades were far less common. The game required high levels of strength and courage, and a particularly strong nerve.

After the start command, grenades flew like hailstones, and even within the fortifications the rapid pace of the violent explosions could spook your soul out of your body, to say nothing of keeping you from jumping up to counterattack. The integrity of the fortification was the decisive factor. If an enemy grenade managed to pierce or tear away part of the roof, then it was all over. The game had one of the highest casualty rates, and the kids dubbed it "Grenade Volleyball."

The assault subcategory of grenade games had no fortified positions. Opposing sides faced each other across open ground, when they closed to within throwing distance, commenced throwing. Then they threw themselves to the ground or beat a retreat out of the fragmentation area to protect themselves. This game mostly used egg-shaped grenades, since it was easier to carry more of them. Attacking and evading, the two sides invariably intermingled, and everyone then just chucked their grenades at crowded areas. It was nothing short of a nightmarish scene of madness: dense smoke and fire of explosions on the open ground, crowds of kids running and diving and occasionally pulling a grenade from a bag and tossing it up, smoking grenades tumbling about on the ground. . . . The children called this game "Grenade Football."

Artillery games acquired fanciful nicknames as well. The five-kilometer howitzer subcategory, in which parties towed their units into position and finished aiming before receiving the start command, whereupon they commenced firing immediately, was known as "Cannon Boxing." Artillery games with self-propelled mobile batteries had far more variables and were known as "Cannon Basketball." Mortars, in which opposing sides were only separated by one or two thousand meters, within line of sight, was a thrilling, physically demanding game the children dubbed "Mortar Soccer."

Contrary to their enticing names, the games saw some of the most brutal forms of combat in history. During the battles, weapons exchanged fire more directly than they ever had before, and the casualties they caused topped the ranks of their particular category of combat. For example, in the tank battles, even the winning side saw at least half its tanks destroyed. Blood flowed in rivers by the end of every game in the War Olympics. As for the little soldiers, they prepared for eternity with every sortie.

This led to the later identification of the fundamental misperception the people of the Common Era had where children were concerned. The Supernova War taught people that children placed less value on life than adults, and thus had a much stronger tolerance for death. If necessary, they could be meaner, colder, and crueler than adults. Later historians and psychologists agreed that were this cruel, crazy form of war set in the Common Era, the unimaginable psychological pressures produced would have pushed all participants into a collective mental breakdown.

True, no small number of children fled on the brink of battle, but mental breakdowns were rare. Later generations were in awe of the grit they displayed on the battlefield, particularly in the baffling heroics of heroes who emerged during battle. During the grenade games, for example, there were children known as "pitchbacks," who never used their own grenades but picked up the ones thrown by the enemy and tossed them back. Although few managed to survive the games, it still was an honor to be a pitchback. They were described in a popular fighting song:

Oh what a joy to be a pitchback, one as great as me!
I've got a craze for hand grenades, and I pick up all
    I see.
As quick as a lick I snatch them up when they're
    smoking in the muck,
Like Ali Baba in the treasure cave,
But I'm . . . not . . . gonna . . . get . . . stuck!

Out of all the games of the War Olympics, cold-weapons events had to be counted among the most barbaric and terrifying. In these games, the opposing sides battled each other with bayonets and other bladed weapons, returning warfare to its most primitive form. Below is an account of one young soldier who took part in an event:

I found a nearby rock and honed my rifle's bayonet one last time. The squad leader saw me sharpening it yesterday and I got an earful. He said bayonets were not to be sharpened, since it would damage their rustproofing. I didn't care, and kept on grinding. This rifle never seems to have a sharp enough bayonet. And I wasn't expecting to survive the game anyway, so why the hell did I need rustproofing?

The kids on the jury inspected our guns one by one to make sure they weren't loaded. And they took away the bolt, and they body-searched me for pistols or other hot weapons. All five hundred Chinese kids were searched, but the judges didn't find anything, since each of us had buried a grenade in the snow at our feet before they came to inspect. Once they left, we dug them up and tucked them into our clothing. We weren't trying to break the rules; it's just that the previous night a Japanese captain came to us in secret and told us that he belonged to an antiwar group, and that the Japanese kids were planning to use a scary weapon in the cold-weapons games. We asked him what it was, but he wouldn't say. He only said it was a weapon that we'd never guess. An extremely terrifying one. He told us to be on guard.

When the game began, infantry formations on both

sides started advancing toward each other. A thousand bayonets glinted like ice under the shifting southern lights, and I can clearly remember the howl of the wind that drove over the unmelted snow, like it was singing some desolate war song.

I was in the back of our formation, but since I was at the edge I had a pretty good view of up front, and I saw the Japanese kids gradually getting closer. They weren't wearing steel helmets, but had tied on white cloth head-bands, and they sang as they walked. I saw the bayonet-fixed rifles in their hands, but didn't see the fearsome weapon the Japanese captain had mentioned the previous night. Suddenly, the enemy formation changed shape, thinning out into columns spaced around two paces apart, creating parallel passageways through their formation. Then I saw clouds of snow and dust rising behind them, and coming through the clouds a horde of black objects surging through the formation like a flood. I heard deep whines, and when I got a better look, my blood curdled.

It was a huge pack of army dogs.

The dogs charged past the enemy formation and in the blink of an eye had reached our own. Up ahead the front half of our formation was in disarray, and I heard pitiful screams. I couldn't tell the dogs' breed, but they were huge, standing a head taller than me, and mean as hell. The tussle between kids and dogs up front stained the ground with fresh blood. I saw one dog leap up with a torn-off arm in its jaws. . . . The Japanese kids were closing in and fell out of formation and swarmed toward us, bayonets leveled, joining the dogs in their attack on the Chinese kids. Most of my comrades up front were already beaten to a pulp by the teeth and blades.

"Grenades away!" the regiment commander shouted, and without a second thought we pulled the pin and slung the grenades into the mess of people and dogs, and rapid explosions sent blood and flesh flying.

Those of us remaining charged across the blast zone, trampling on the corpses of our comrades, the enemy, and the dogs to reach the Japanese army, and then turned ourselves into killing machines fighting with bayonets, rifle butts, and teeth. I fought a Japanese second lieutenant first, and he came screaming at me with his bayonet aimed for my heart, but I parried with my gun and it got me in the left shoulder. I was shaking with the pain of it and I dropped my rifle on the ground. Instinctively I grabbed his rifle with both hands right at the bayonet socket. I could feel my own hot blood trickling down the barrel. He gave the gun a few yanks back and forth, and somehow the bayonet detached. With my right hand, which could still move, I yanked the bayonet out of my left shoulder, and then held it shakily and moved toward him. The little punk stared at me, and then ran off carrying his bayonet-less rifle. I didn't have any energy for a chase, so I looked around and saw a Japanese kid holding one of my comrades on the ground, strangling her with both hands. So I crossed the few steps toward them and stabbed the bayonet into the guy's back. I didn't even have the strength to pull it out. My vision went dark as I saw the ground coming to meet me, brown and muddy, and I fell smack into it, getting a faceful of that mix of our blood and the enemy's and the Antarctic snow and earth.

I woke up in the first-aid station three days later and learned that we had lost the game. In the jury's reasoning, even though both sides had broken the rules, our violation was more serious, since the grenades we had used were most definitely hot weapons. The dogs used by the Japanese kids were warm weapons at best.

From Zheng Jianbing, *Blood Mud:*
The Chinese Army in the Supernova
War. Kunlun Publishing House, SE 8.

As the Olympics progressed, the outcome that gradually took shape was well afield of anything the advocates of this form of warfare had anticipated.

From a purely military perspective, the game war was nothing like traditional warfare. The more or less fixed position and arrangements predetermined by the two sides meant their forces' geographic positions were for the first time relatively unimportant. The aim of the battle was not to occupy a city or a strategically important position, but purely to exhaust the enemy's strength on the battlefield. Ever since the start of the games, the children's attention had focused on one key point, and now, from high command all the way down to the front-line trenches, the one thing in everyone's mind and on everyone's lips was relative damage rate.

In the adults' era, the relative damage rate for particular weapons received some attention as a factor in war policy, but it rarely was the most important factor. High command could still elect to achieve a particular strategic or tactical objective no matter the cost. But in the children's war, the relative damage rate took on an entirely different significance, primarily because in their world, heavy weapons were a nonrenewable resource; there was no way for them to manufacture such complicated war machines in such a short time.

When a tank was destroyed, they had one fewer tank; a plane shot down, one fewer plane. Even comparatively simple weapons like howitzers couldn't be resupplied. Relative damage rates, then, became almost the sole determiner of victory.

On a technological level, the Supernova War was akin to the First World War, in which the land armies' regular forces played a decisive role. In contrast to high-tech weapon disparities, there was not as great a disparity in the game war in relative damage rates between the parties' conventional weapons.

Tanks were this war's most important weapons. NATO's land-war theory held that armored ground forces were inseparable from low-altitude assault power; without fire cover and aerial reconnaissance provided by armored helicopters, tank groups were sitting ducks on the battlefield. As one American armored commander of the Common Era put it, "An Abrams without an Apache has its pants down."

The children's training had been so brief that low-altitude helicopter strikes had as little impact on the Supernova War as the high-altitude air power of fighters and bombers, and helicopters crashed or were shot down in even greater numbers than other aircraft. An Apache piloted by two inexperienced, overwhelmed children flying back and forth over the battlefield proved an excellent target for shoulder-fired missiles. So on the Antarctic battleground, the attack helicopters most desired by army aviation pilots weren't the

American Apaches but the coaxial-rotor-equipped Russian Kamov Ka-50s, whose distinguishing feature was the first-ever helicopter ejection seat.

Surviving an ejection through a helicopter's rotors would be especially difficult, so the Ka-50's solution was to blow off the rotors before ejecting, giving the pilot a high chance of surviving a direct hit. In an Apache, on the other hand, if the young pilots were hit while in flight, they simply had to wait it out until the end. Absent low-altitude support and cover, the tank games did not display much of a disparity in relative damage rates.

Time flew by, and before they knew it six months had passed. In that time, ocean levels worldwide continued to rise, swamping the coasts and turning Shanghai, New York, and Tokyo into water cities. Most children in these areas moved farther inland, and the remainder adapted themselves to the liquid life, rafting between skyscrapers and preserving some semblance of life in these formerly bustling metropolises. In Antarctica, meanwhile, the climate continued to warm up, even during the long night, bringing mild, early-winter weather and average temperatures above −10°C. The continent's temperate weather only served to further underscore its crucial nature.

Negotiations for dividing up Antarctica were set to begin, and the key bargaining chip for every country was its performance in the war games, a fact that motivated all children to redouble their efforts. Fresh troops were constantly arriving in Antarctica, swelling the scale of the games, and the fires of war continued their march across the continent.

The United States, on the other hand, was mired in disappointment and dejection, despite being the instigator of the games. Because high-tech weapons were no threat in the hands of children, the country had not dominated the games in the way its children had hoped, and the multipolar shape of the games worried them ahead of the upcoming Antarctica Talks.

One last event, the ICBM fight, was about to begin, and it was on this that the American children were pinning their final hopes.

"Are you kidding? It's really heading our way?" Marshal Zavyalova asked the advisor.

"That's what the radar warning center says. I doubt they're mistaken."

"Maybe it'll change trajectory?" President Ilyukhin ventured.

"Not a chance. The warhead's in the terminal guidance phase, in an unpowered free fall. It's coming in like a stone."

In the command center, everyone in Russian High Command was concentrating on the first ICBM fight with the US. The American children had fired an ICBM from their own territory, ten thousand kilometers away, directly at the Russian command center, a serious violation of the game's rules. Both sides had set their target areas in advance, and Russia had provided a target zone more than a hundred kilometers distant. There shouldn't have been any mistake.

"What are you afraid of? At least it's not a nuclear warhead," Ilyukhin said.

"A conventional warhead is frightening enough. It's a

Minuteman III. Those were deployed in the 1980s, I think. They can carry three tons of conventional high-explosive warheads. If it lands within two hundred meters we'll be destroyed!" Zavyalova said.

"And what if it lands right on our heads? We'd be dead even if it wasn't carrying anything!" a colonel advisor said.

Zavyalova said, "It's not out of the question. The Minuteman is one of the most accurate ICBMs there are. Hundred-meter precision."

They heard a low wailing in the air, as if a keen blade were rending the sky in two. "It's coming!" someone shouted, and everyone held their breath, skin crawling, waiting for the coming impact.

There was a dull thud outside and a gentle tremor in the ground. They poured outside and saw a shower of dirt falling back to the ground about half a kilometer away. Ilyukhin, Zavyalova, and the others jumped into vehicles and hurried over to it. A crowd of soldiers were digging into a crater with shovels, hoes, and a backhoe.

"The warhead apparently released a small drag chute at around ten thousand meters, so it didn't burrow too deep," an air force colonel said.

Half an hour later, the bottom part of the buried ICBM's warhead was exposed, a metal sphere 2.3 meters in diameter with three scorches on the perimeter from blasting bolts. The children inserted a drill rod into a gap they found, and were able to pry apart the metal shell. In wonder they stared at the cornucopia of boxes, all shapes and sizes, lying in a dampening cushion. Then, very carefully, they opened one. Inside were small foil-wrapped objects containing lumps of a brown substance.

"Explosives!" warned one kid.

Zavyalova picked up one of the "explosives" and looked it over. She gave it a sniff, then bit a piece. "Chocolate," she said.

They opened other boxes, which held not just chocolate but cigars as well. As the other kids were divvying up the chocolate, Ilyukhin took out a fat cigar and lit it, but he'd only taken a few puffs before it blew up in a ball of streamers, and the kids burst out laughing at him standing there stunned with a cigar butt hanging from his lips.

He spat out the cigar butt, and said, "Three days from now, it'll be our turn to fire on the American kids' command center."

"I've got a bad premonition," Specs said during a meeting in the Chinese command center.

"Agreed. We ought to move our command center immediately," Lü Gang said.

"Is that really necessary?" Huahua asked.

"The American kids attacked the Russian command center in the ICBM game, violating the principle that bases were untouchable. Our base might be hit as a target, and that warhead might contain more than just chocolate and cigars."

Specs said, "My premonition goes deeper than that. I've got a feeling there's going to be a sudden change in the situation."

Out the window of the command center, the first white of dawn had appeared on the horizon. The long Antarctic night was coming to an end.

★

From the desolate plains of northwestern Russia close to the Arctic Circle, a range-extended SS-25 Sickle whooshed into the air from a multifunction missile launcher and crossed the globe in the space of forty minutes. When it reached the sky over Antarctica, the warhead came down in a smooth parabola and hit a patch of snow inside the American base, just 280 meters from the command center. After the launch, American NMD and TMD fired six antiballistic missiles to intercept. The children watched on their screens in breathless anticipation as two glowing dots smacked almost exactly into each other. But each was a letdown, since the intercepting missiles' suborbital trajectories through the atmosphere passed by each other separated by dozens of meters.

After a moment of shock, the American children went about digging out the warhead, and discovered that what the Russian children had rocketed to them from twenty thousand kilometers away was a copious amount of vodka in shock-resistant bottles, and a pretty box with a note saying it was a gift for Davey. Inside was a Russian doll, and inside that one another one, ten in all, each of them with an uncannily accurate representation of Davey's face. The outermost was laughing, but farther in the expressions grew less happy and more worried, until the last thumb-sized one had Davey mouth open, bawling.

Enraged, Davey threw the dolls into the snow and seized General Scott with one hand and General Harvey, who was in charge of strategic missile defense, with the other. "You are both relieved of duty! You idiots. You guaranteed that NMD and TMD would work. You—" He broke off and turned to Scott. "Didn't you say they put us into a strongbox? And you—" He turned to Harvey and shouted, "Where the hell were your prizewinning prodigies? Are they any better than a pack of online hackers?"

"Uh . . . all six tries only missed by a smidgen," Scott said, red-faced.

Harvey, who hadn't slept in three days, pushed Davey aside without regard for presidential dignity and shouted, "You're the idiot! You think those two systems are there to play around with? The TMD software alone runs to nearly two hundred million lines of code!"

An advisor came over and handed Davey a printout. "This is from Mr. Yagüe. It's the latest agenda for the Antarctic Talks."

The children from US High Command stood silently at the edge of the giant crater with a warhead from the other side of the world down at the bottom. Davey was quiet for a moment, and then said, "We have to seize the absolute advantage in the games before negotiations begin."

Vaughn said, "That's impossible. The games are practically finished."

"You know it's possible. You're just unwilling to take up that line of thought," Davey said, jerking around to fix a stare on the secretary of state.

"Surely you don't mean the new game?"

"That's right. The new game. That's exactly it. We should have started earlier!" Scott answered for Davey.

"There's no way of knowing where it'll take the Antarctic Games," Vaughn said. He looked off in the distance, and the depths of his eyes reflected the white light of dawn on the horizon.

"You love to complicate the simplest things in order to show off your knowledge. Even an idiot can see that the new game will give us an absolute advantage throughout the continent, in one stroke. It'll totally clear up the direction of the games." Davey took the printout the advisor had just delivered and waved it in Vaughn's face. "As clear-cut as this memo. There's nothing that's unknown about it!"

Vaughn reached out and took the paper from Davey's hands. "You think this paper is cut-and-dry?"

Davey gave him a puzzled stare, and then looked at the paper. "Of course."

With his withered hands, Vaughn folded the paper in half, and said, "That's once." Then he folded it again. "That's twice." Again. "Three times. . . . Now, Mr. President, do you find this clear-cut? Something easy and predictable?"

"Of course."

"Well then, I dare you to fold it thirty-five times." Vaughn held up the thrice-folded printout.

"I don't get it."

"Answer me. Do you dare?"

"Why wouldn't I?" Davey went to take the paper from him, but Vaughn caught his hand. At the cold, clammy touch, he felt like a snake was crawling across his back.

"Mr. President, you're speaking as the supreme decision maker, and every one of your decisions will make history. Think it over again. Do you really dare?"

Davey stared at him in utter confusion.

"You have one last chance. Before you make your decision, wouldn't you like to predict the outcome, just like you've predicted the outcome of the new game?"

"The outcome? The outcome of folding a piece of paper in half thirty-five times? Don't make me laugh," Scott said derisively.

"For example, how thick will that folded paper get?"

"Around as thick as a Bible, I'd guess," Davey said.

Vaughn shook his head.

"Around knee-high," Harvey said.

Again, Vaughn shook his head.

"As high as the command center?"

Vaughn shook his head.

"You don't mean it'd be as high as the Pentagon?" Scott said mockingly.

"This sheet of paper is around zero point one millimeters thick. Calculating with that value, after thirty-five folds, it would be 6,871,950 meters thick, or around 6,872 kilometers. That's roughly the radius of the Earth."

"What? For just thirty-five times? You've got to be joking!" Scott said loudly.

"He's right," Davey said. He was no dummy, and had quickly made the connection to the Indian legend of the king and the chessboard.

Vaughn tucked the folded paper into Davey's shirt pocket. Looking around at the dumbstruck young commanders, he said slowly, "Never be too optimistic about your own judgment, particularly when it comes to the course of history."

Davey bowed his head and dejectedly accepted his loss. Then he said, "I admit that our minds are simpler than yours. If everyone had a mind like yours, the world would be a really scary place. Still, we can't be certain of success, nor can we be certain of failure. Why not give it a try? We want to! There's no way we can be stopped!"

"Mr. President," Vaughn said coldly. "That is your right. I've said all I need to."

In the first rays of dawn over the Antarctic wilderness, the Supernova Era advanced into the most dangerous place in its young history.

A Thousand Suns

Before the start of their ICBM match with the American children, the Chinese children secretly moved their command center. They loaded all personnel and communications equipment into fourteen helicopters and flew forty-odd kilometers inland. Here the geography was somewhat different from the coast, and featured conical hills where the snow hadn't entirely melted. The command center was set up in tents backed up against one hill, fronting on a broad plain in the direction of the base.

"Second Artillery Corps Command called to ask what we should load into the warhead," Lü Gang said to Huahua.

"Hmmm . . . how about tanghulu?"

Then the children scanned the sky near the coast through binoculars, and a young advisor wearing an earpiece provided them with a general direction, using data transmitted to him by the distant radar warning center about the approaching American ICBM.

"Heads up. They say it's getting close. Heading 135, inclination 42. Just over there. You should be able to see it now!"

The early-morning Antarctic sky was a deep, dark blue, and scattered stars were still visible, but it seemed blacker than it had during the long night owing to the greatly diminished southern lights. A point of light stood out against the dark blue, moving rapidly but slower than a shooting star. It had a short fiery tail visible through binoculars, caused by air friction during reentry. Then the light disappeared, and nothing was visible in the blue heavens, whether by naked eye or through binoculars, as if it had melted into the infinite darkness. But the children knew that the missile's warhead had entered the atmosphere and was following a precise, gravity-guided trajectory toward its target.

"Good. It's target is the base. Or more precisely, the command center!" called the advisor with the earpiece.

"What'll be in the warhead this time?"

"Maybe Barbie dolls."

The Antarctic dawn was suddenly bright as midday.

"A supernova!" exclaimed one child in fear.

This was a familiar sight to the children, one they knew in their bones. Indeed, it closely resembled a supernova blast, and the blinding light threw the land and hillside into sudden, sharp clarity. But this time, rather than turning blue, the sky turned deep purple. The light came from the direction of the ocean, and when the children looked toward it, they saw the new sun hanging over the horizon. Unlike the supernova, this sun was a ball larger than the actual sun and so fierce they could feel its heat on their faces.

Realizing what had happened, Lü Gang shouted, "Don't look at it. It'll hurt your eyes!"

They all shut their eyes, but the intensifying glare penetrated their eyelids and remained painfully bright, making them feel like they had fallen into an ocean of radiance. They clapped their hands to their eyes, but the light pierced the gaps between their fingers. They stayed in that position until the world darkened again, and then carefully removed their hands. It took their burnt-out eyes some time to readjust.

Lü Gang asked them, "How long do you think that sun lasted just now?"

They thought back on it, and said it seemed like at least ten seconds.

He nodded. "I think so too. Judging from the duration of the fireball, it might have been in the megaton class."

Now that their vision had returned, the children looked out toward where the sun had appeared and vanished. Something white was rapidly expanding on the horizon.

"Cover your ears!" Lü Gang shouted. "Quickly! Cover your ears!"

They covered their ears and waited, but no explosion came. The mushroom cloud on the horizon, silvery white in the morning light, now touched the sky. The contrast it posed with the land and sky was frankly surreal, as if a gargantuan fantastic image had been superimposed upon a realistic painting. The children stared in silence, and some of them subconsciously lowered their hands from their ears.

Lü Gang shouted again, "Cover your ears! Sound takes two seconds to reach us."

They covered their ears tightly, and then the ground began to rumble beneath their feet like the surface of a charged drum, throwing dirt and snow knee-high in the air, and sending the snow cover down the hill as if it had melted. The noise penetrated their flesh and bones, bored into their skulls, and they felt as if their bodies were being broken apart and scattered to the four winds, leaving their terrified souls to quiver on the ground.

Lü Gang shouted, "Get behind the hill for cover. The shock wave will be here any moment!"

"A shock wave?" Huahua cocked an eye at him.

"That's right. It might die down into a stiff wind by the time it reaches us."

As the children retreated to the back of the hill, a sudden squall picked up around them, ripping the tents from their stakes and sending the equipment inside flying. Half the helicopters on the hillside were knocked over before flying snow whited out the entire scene, but they heard the sound of flying stones pelting airframes. The gale lasted for about a minute before rapidly slackening and finally dying away altogether, letting the snow and dust return gently to the ground. As the curtain fell, it revealed a hazy firelight on the horizon. The mushroom cloud was less distinct now but far larger, and now took up half the sky. The wind had blown its top portion to one side, giving it the look of a gigantic monster with a wild head of hair.

"The base is destroyed," Lü Gang said soberly.

All communications from the base had been severed, and when they looked toward it through the dust that had yet to settle, all they could see was the dim fire on the horizon.

An advisor came over to tell Huahua that the American president was calling him. Huahua asked, "Will replying give away our position?"

"No. The transmitter is in a different location."

Davey's voice came through the wireless receiver. "Hey, Huahua, looks like that atom bomb didn't have your name on it. You really are clever fellows to think of moving your command center. I'm glad you're still alive. I'd like to let you all know that we're starting the new game! Nuclear bombs!" He laughed. "It's the greatest! Wasn't that new sun pretty?"

Huahua said angrily, "You shameless pack of pissants. You've trampled over every rule of the games! You've wrecked their very foundation!"

Davey laughed. "What rules? Fun is the only rule!"

"Your adults were a bunch of scoundrels to leave you with strategic nuclear weapons."

"Hey now, they only left a few behind carelessly. Our stockpiles were huge. You eat a big piece of bread and you're bound to drop some crumbs. Besides, don't you wonder if there might be any crumbs remaining from the Russians' big hunk of bread?"

"That's the crucial thing," Lü Gang whispered into Huahua's ear. "They won't dare try a nuclear strike against Russia since they're afraid of retaliation. With us, they don't have that worry."

"Don't sweat the small stuff if you don't have to," Davey said over the radio.

"We're not sweating it," Specs said coldly. "In this insane world, there's no point to getting mad on moral grounds. It's too tiring."

"Right, right. Listen to him, Huahua. He has the right attitude. That's how to keep it fun." Then Davey cut off the connection.

The Chinese children immediately contacted other Antarctic Games participants to set up an alliance to punish the American children for breaking the rules, but the outcome was a disappointment.

Huahua and Specs called Russia first. Ilyukhin said perfunctorily, "We have learned of what has befallen your country and express our deepest sympathies."

Huahua said, "This abominable violation deserves to be punished. If this vile precedent is allowed to stand, they will move on to drop atom bombs on other countries' bases, or even on land outside of Antarctica! Your country ought to stage a nuclear counterattack on the violator's base. You may be the only one left with that capability."

"Of course such conduct deserves punishment," Ilyukhin replied. "I expect that all countries are hoping you will stage a nuclear counterattack to preserve the integrity of the rules. My country also desires to punish the wrongdoer, but Russia has no nuclear weapons. Our venerable fathers and mothers fired all the nuclear bombs into the sun."

The talk with the EU was even more depressing. The incumbent rotating president, Prime Minister Green of Britain, asked innocently, "Why would your country believe that we have retained nuclear weapons? This is shameless libel of a united Europe. Inform us of your current position and we will deliver a memo of protest."

Huahua set down the phone. "Those little punks just want to play it safe on the mountaintop and watch the tigers fight it out."

"Very wise," Specs said, nodding.

Communications were provisionally restored between the command center and the Chinese base, and an unbroken stream of frightening news began coming over the radio. G Group Army, stationed at the base, suffered a devastating blow; total casualties were still unknown, but it had likely lost all combat effectiveness. The majority of base installations had been destroyed. Fortunately, as the geographic scale of the games had grown, the other two group armies formerly stationed on base had moved over a hundred kilometers away, preserving two-thirds of the Chinese children's Antarctic forces. However, the port they had spent two months building had been seriously damaged in the nuclear strike, posing a major supply problem for these forces.

An emergency meeting of high command convened in a hastily raised tent at the foot of the hill. Just before it began, Huahua said he had to step out for a moment.

"This is urgent!" Lü Gang reminded him.

"I'll only be five minutes," Huahua said. Then he went outside.

About half a minute later, Specs left the tent, too, and seeing Huahua lying motionless on a patch of snow staring straight up at the heavens, he went over and sat down beside him. The dust had settled and a warm, gentle breeze blew through the air, bringing with it the moisture of melting snow and the scent of damp earth. In the sky over the ocean, the expanding mushroom cloud had lost its shape, but had grown even larger, and it was hard to tell where it ended and the clouds began. The other half of the sky was painted by the rays of dawn over the opposite horizon.

"I really can't keep it up anymore," Huahua said.

"No one's doing any better," Specs said lightly.

"It's not the same. This is impossible!"

"Think of yourself as a computer. You're just cold hardware, and reality is just data. Accept your input and perform your calculations. That's how you keep it up."

"Is that the strategy you've used since the supernova?"

"I did that before the supernova. It's not a strategy. It's my nature."

"But I don't have that nature."

"Getting out is easy. Just run out in any direction without taking anything with you. Keep going and you'll get lost pretty quick, and before long you'll freeze or starve to death in the Antarctic wilderness."

"Not a bad idea. I just don't want to be a deserter, is all."

"Then be a computer."

Huahua propped himself up and looked at Specs. "Do you really think that everything can be accomplished purely through cold deduction and calculation?"

"Yes. Hiding behind what you imagine to be intuition is actually a complicated set of calculations and deductions. So complicated as to be imperceptible. We need only two things right now: calm, and more calm."

Huahua got up and patted the snow off his back. "Let's go back."

Specs caught him. "Think carefully about what you're going to say."

Huahua gave Specs a thin smile under the morning light. "I've thought about it. For a computer, our current situation is really nothing more than a simple arithmetic problem."

The children were silent for a long time at the start of the meeting, still dazed by the nosedive their already grim situation had taken.

The commander of D Group Army broke the silence by pounding on the table and shouting, "Were our adults really that honest? Why didn't they leave us any?"

The other children echoed similar sentiments:

"That's right. Why not even a few?"

"They left us empty-handed!"

"If we had just one, the situation would be completely different!"

"Right! Even one would be good."

"That's enough," Lü Gang said. "Stop it with the useless talk." Then he turned to Huahua. "What are we going to do?"

Huahua stood up and said, "The two group armies in the interior need to evacuate immediately to save their strength in the event of a further nuclear strike by the enemy."

Lü Gang stood up and began to pace briskly. "You ought to know what that means. If all of our assembled and combat-ready land forces stand down and evacuate, it will take a long time to reassemble them. We'll lose all combat capacity on Antarctica!"

Specs said, "It's like reformatting our hard drive."

Lü Gang nodded. "That's exactly what it is."

"But I agree with Huahua. Evacuate immediately," Specs said firmly.

Bowing his head, Huahua said, "There's no other way. If the group armies remain in a dense, combat-ready form, the enemy's next large-scale nuclear strike could wipe out the entire army."

Lü Gang said, "But if they divide up into a large number of small forces distributed across a wide area, it will be hard to guarantee supplies. They may not survive very long."

B Group Army commander said, "We'll take things as

they come. Now is not the time for overthinking. The danger grows with every second we stay here. Give the order!"

D Group Army commander said, "Over our heads a sword is dangling by a thin strand of hair. It could drop at any moment."

Most of the children supported a swift evacuation.

Huahua looked at Specs and Lü Gang, who both nodded. Then he crossed to the front of the conference table and stood there. "Good. Give the evacuation order to the two group armies. There's no time to plan out the details, so let the forces disperse themselves into battalions. Speed is paramount. Also please be crystal clear about the consequences of this decision, and prepare yourself mentally. The Antarctic mission is going to be very difficult for us from now on."

The children stood up. An advisor read over the draft of the order, but no one proposed any changes. All they wanted was speed, as much as possible. The advisor took the order to the radio, but all of a sudden a solemn voice broke in, "One moment, please."

The children turned to look at the speaker, Senior Colonel Hu Bing, the liaison officer for the five special observers. Saluting Huahua, Specs, and Lü Gang, she said, "Sirs, the Special Observer Team will now carry out its final duty!"

The mysterious body organized by the adults before they left consisted of five senior colonels, three from the army and two from the air force. In the event of war, they had the authority to know all confidential information and to listen in on all of the high command's deliberations. However, the adults had guaranteed that the team would never interfere. That was how it had been throughout the games, where during every military meeting of the high command, those five children had sat silently to one side, listening. They didn't even take any notes. They just listened. They never spoke, and even after the meetings adjourned they had little interaction with anyone. Gradually the other children in the high command forgot they were there.

Once, when Huahua asked them who was team leader, Hu Bing had answered, "Sir, the five of us have equal power. There is no team leader, but when it is necessary I will serve as liaison."

That only deepened the mystery of their mission.

Now the five officers gathered in an odd formation, an inward-facing circle, and stood solemnly at attention, as if a flag were being raised in the center. Hu Bing said, "We have a Situation A. Vote."

Each of the five raised a hand.

Hu Bing turned toward the ammo boxes serving as a conference table and pulled a white envelope from her uniform. Holding it in both hands, she lowered it decorously to the center of the table, and said, "This letter was sent from the last president of our country in the Common Era and is addressed to the country's current leadership."

Huahua picked up the envelope and opened it. Inside was a single sheet of paper with a letter handwritten in fountain pen. He read it aloud:

Children,

When you read this letter, our worst fears have come to pass.

In the last days of the Common Era, we can only make predictions about the future according to our own way of thinking, and on the basis of these predictions, do the work we are able to as well as possible.

But still those fears kept pricking at our hearts. The minds and actions of children are entirely different from adults. The world of children might follow an entirely different track from our predictions. That world might be one unimaginable to us, and we're powerless to do much for you.

We can only leave you with one thing.

It is the last thing we wanted to leave behind for our children. When we left it, it felt like taking the safety off of a handgun and placing it on the pillow next to a sleeping infant.

We have been as careful as possible, and have appointed a Special Observer Team made up of five of the most dispassionate children, who will vote, based on the situational danger level, whether or not to hand over this legacy to you. If, after ten years, it has not been handed over, it will self-destruct.

We had hoped they would never need to carry out this vote, but now you have opened the envelope.

We write this letter at the final assembly point. We have reached the end of our lives, but our minds are still clear. A child keeping watch at the assembly point delivered this letter to the SOT. We had thought that we had said all we needed to, but in the course of writing this letter, so many things come to mind.

But now you have opened it.

Opening the letter means that your world is entirely beyond our imagining. Everything we want to say no longer has any meaning, apart from one thing:

Take care, children.
On the last day of the Common Era,
at the Final Assembly Point #1, China

The letter closed with the former president's signature.

The child leaders focused their attention on Hu Bing, who gave a formal salute, and said, "The SOT will now conduct the handover. One Dongfeng 101 ICBM, with a maximum range of twenty-five thousand kilometers, carrying one thermonuclear warhead with a yield of four megatons."

Lü Gang stared at them. "Where is it?" he asked.

"We don't know. And we don't need to," she said. Then another senior colonel on the SOT set a laptop on the table and opened it. It was already running, and the screen displayed a world map. "Any location on this map can be enlarged for more detail, to a maximum 1:100,000 scale. Double-click on the strike target and the wireless modem will transmit a signal through via a satellite link to the destination, and the missile will fire automatically."

The children crowded round to stroke the computer, many of them with tears in their eyes, as if they were touching the adults' warm hands reaching out to them from the beyond.

The CE Mine

The supernova did not bring massive changes to every part of the world. In a small village in the mountains of southwestern China, for example, life hardly changed at all. Sure, the adults were gone, but there weren't all that many in the Common Era anyway, since they were all working far from home. The farm work the children did now wasn't all that much heavier than what they were used to. Their day-to-day lives were the same as before, going to work at sunrise and resting at sunset, although they were even more unaware about the outside world now than they had been in the adults' time.

But for a period before the adults died, it seemed as if great changes were coming to their lives. A highway was put in past the village into the mountains leading to a valley sealed behind barbed wire. Every day, large trucks in great numbers would go in fully loaded and return empty. Their contents were covered in green canvas tarps, or packed into big boxes, containing who knows what, and if all of it was piled together it would probably have been as high as the hill behind the village.

Day and night the unbroken stream of trucks traveled the highway, going in full and coming back empty. There was also the occasional plane with blades like electric fans that flew into the valley dangling objects beneath it that weren't there when it flew out again. This went on for about half a year before things went quiet again. Bulldozers tore up the highway, and the village children and the critically ill adults had to wonder: Why didn't they just leave the highway alone rather than expending so much effort to destroy it? It wasn't long before the grass grew over the plowed-under right-of-way and it was more or less reabsorbed by the surrounding hillsides. The barbed wire around the valley was torn down, too, and the children were once again able to hunt and cut firewood. When they reached the valley they found that nothing had changed. The forest was the same old forest, and the grass was the same old grass. They had no idea why a thousand outsiders, in military uniforms and plain clothes, had spent the last half year messing around here, much less where all the cargo on the endless river of vehicles had gone. It all seemed like a dream now, and gradually it was forgotten.

They had no way of knowing that beneath the mountain valley was buried a sleeping sun.

Historians called it the Common Era Mine. The ICBM was referred to in this way for two reasons. First, because it occupied the world's deepest missile silo. The 150-meter shaft was covered over by a further twenty meters of earth, making it undiscoverable even during substantial excavations in the mountain valley. Before launch, directional blasting would blow apart the earthen cover and expose the shaft's mouth. Second, because it waited unattended for the trigger signal, like a mega-landmine buried inside the country awaiting its target's approach. The CE Mine stood ninety meters tall, and if set outside would have risen like a metallic spire. Now it was in a deep sleep in the silo, with just a clock and a receiving unit operating. Listening silently on its locked-in frequency, the unit no doubt received all kinds of noise from the outside world, but it was waiting for a long string of digits, a prime so large that it would take the fastest computer in the world until the end of time to match it by brute force. And there was only one other copy of this number in existence, saved on the five observers' laptop computer. When the timer ticked up to 315,360,000 seconds, that is, ten years after it was started, the CE Mine would wake up to the end of its life, switch on its systems, and fly out of the silo through the atmosphere to an orbit five thousand kilometers above the Earth, where it would self-destruct, leaving a gleaming star visible even in daylight for ten seconds or more.

But when the counter had reached just 23,500,817 seconds, the unit received that huge prime, and after it two other numbers precise to the third decimal place. A simple program in the receiver checked the two numbers; if the first was outside the 0–180 range, or the second outside 0–80, nothing would happen, and the unit would continue listening. But this time, the two numbers, while close to the boundary, were still within their respective ranges, which was enough; the program required nothing further. As dawn approached, the mountains of the southwest still slumbered and the valley was cloaked in a light mist, but the CE Mine awakened its sleeping power.

The warmth of electric current coursed through its enormous body. The first thing it did upon waking was extract the two coordinate values from the receiver and put them into the target database, which immediately added a point to the 1:100,000 scale map of the Earth. In a flash the central computer generated flight path parameters, and, learning from the target database that the target was located on a level plain, set the warhead for airburst at an elevation of two thousand meters. Were it conscious, it would have noticed something strange, since in the countless simulated launches run after its installation to test the reliability of the system, the continent in which this target area was located was the only one it had never tested. But this didn't matter. Everything proceeded according to the program. In its electronic mind, the world was exceedingly simple; all that mattered was the target far off on the Antarctic continent. The rest of the world was just coordinates describing the target point, a point flashing on the very top of the Earth's transparent spherical coordinate system, luring it to the completion of its exceedingly simple mission.

The CE Mine switched on the fuel tank heating system.

Like most ICBMs, it was propelled by liquid fuel, but for the purposes of long-term storage, the propellant was a solid-liquid conversion fuel ordinarily found in a gel-like state and needed to be melted before firing.

The layer of earth atop the silo was blasted away, exposing the CE Mine to the gaze of the dawn sky.

The deep boom of the explosion was heard by a few of the lighter sleepers in the village, who could tell it came from the direction of the valley, but they thought it was only distant thunder and ignored it.

The next sound that came to the village was enough to keep them from going back to sleep, and it startled even more children awake. This time it was a low rumble, as if some gigantic beast was rousing itself deep within the earth, or a faraway flood was surging in their direction, threatening to swallow up the whole world. The paper of their lattice windows trembled. The sound increased in volume and shifted from a deep rumble to a high-pitched roar that shook the tile-roof houses.

The children all ran outside in time to see a gigantic fire dragon climb slowly skyward out of the valley. The fire was too intense to look at directly, and it spread an orange aura over the surrounding hills. The children watched it ascend and increase in speed, going higher and higher and turning into a point of light as its sound grew more muffled. Eventually the light flew due south and soon dissolved into the dawn sky.

Counterattack

The Antarctic morning turned overcast followed by heavy snow, but Davey's mood remained bright. The cocktail party held at the base the previous night to celebrate victory in the games had lasted late into the night, but he had slept very well. Fully refreshed, he was breakfasting with the generals and senior officials who had come to Antarctica. He valued this breakfast opportunity, since children tended to be in a good mood in the morning, rather than irritated and annoyed from the frustrations and work of the day. Many things could be talked through at breakfast.

The army band played pleasant music in the pressurized hall for the children to listen to as they ate, and everyone was in a good mood.

At the table, Davey said, "I predict that the Chinese children will announce their withdrawal from the games today."

Seven-star general Scott, who was cutting a piece of steak, grinned. "Nothing special about that. After yesterday's strike, do they have any other choice?"

Davey raised a glass in his direction. "Getting them off of Antarctica is a whole lot easier now."

Scott said, "And then knocking out the Russian kids and driving them off. And then Japan and the EU—"

"We've got to be a little careful about the Russians. Who knows whether or not they've got any bread crumbs in their bag?"

Everyone nodded, understanding the implication of those bread crumbs.

"Can we be truly certain that the Chinese kids don't have any bread crumbs?" Vaughn asked, spearing a live krill with his fork.

Davey shook a fist at him. "They don't have any! I told you they wouldn't. Their bread was too small to leave behind any crumbs! Our gamble succeeded, I'm telling you!"

"When are you going to get more optimistic?" Scott said with a sidelong glance at Vaughn. "You bring a blanket of gloom and depression wherever you go."

"On my deathbed, I'll be more optimistic than any of you," Vaughn said coldly, and swallowed the krill whole.

Then a colonel came in carrying a portable phone, and bent down to whisper something into Davey's ear before passing the phone to him.

Laughing as he took the phone, Davey said gleefully, "It's the Chinese kids. I told you, they're definitely going to drop out of the games!" Then he spoke into the handset: "Is this Huahua? How're you doing?"

All of a sudden he froze, and his expression turned unnatural, his characteristic sweet smile freezing in place for a few seconds before vanishing entirely. He set down the phone and looked around for Vaughn, just as he did in every moment of crisis. When he found him, he said, "They've informed us that they're still in the game, and have just launched a nuclear missile at our base carrying a four-megaton warhead that will strike its target in twenty-five minutes."

Vaughn asked, "Did he say anything else?"

"No. He hung up right after that."

All eyes focused on Vaughn. He gently set down his knife and fork, and said calmly, "It's real."

Just then another officer came running in and nervously reported that the warning center had detected an unidentified projectile heading in their direction. The warning system had first detected the object when it took off from southwestern China, but by the time the warning had navigated the multiple layers of confirmation, the object had already passed the equator.

All of the young generals and officials stood up at once, eyes wide and faces white, as if a gang of armed assassins had burst into their plush restaurant.

"What do we do?" Davey asked in bewilderment. "Can we hide out in the new underground hangar we just dug?"

The seven-star general shouted, "The underground hangar? Bullshit. One blast from a four-megaton nuclear bomb will turn the whole area into a crater a hundred meters deep. And we're smack in the center of it!" He grabbed Davey and threw his typical insults back in his face. "You moronic asshole! You're the one who's stuck us here. You're gonna make us die here!"

"The helicopters," Vaughn said. His simple statement pulled everyone to their senses and they surged toward the exits. "Wait," he added, and they stopped as if nailed to the ground. "Immediately notify all the planes to take off at once, and to take as much equipment and personnel as possible. But don't explain why. We must remain calm."

"And the other branches? Order a total evacuation of the base!" Davey said.

Vaughn shook his head gently. "There's no point. In the little time we have, no vehicle will be able to escape the blast radius. It would only cause chaos, and in the end no one would escape."

The children scrambled for the exits. All but Vaughn, who remained behind, sitting at the table and wiping his fingers on a dinner napkin. Then he slowly got up and made his way outside, waving to the band as he passed to signal that it was nothing important.

Out on the tarmac the children fought to board the three Blackhawk helicopters. Scott managed to scramble into the cabin of one, and when the rotors started up, he looked at his watch and said through tears, "Only eighteen minutes left. We're not going to make it!" Then he turned to Davey. "You're the fool who got us stuck here. You're not gonna get away, not even in death!"

"Keep your composure," Vaughn, the last to climb aboard, said coldly to Scott.

"We're not going to make it!" Scott choked out through tears.

"What's so scary about dying?" A rare smile came to Vaughn's face. "If you're willing, General, you've got another seventeen minutes to become a true philosopher." Then he turned to another officer next to Scott. "Tell the pilot not to climb, since the bomb will probably detonate at around two thousand meters. Fly with the wind, at top speed. If we can make it thirty kilometers or so, we should be outside the blast radius."

Three helicopters inclined their rotors and accelerated inland. As Davey looked out through the porthole at the Antarctic base spread out below them, it seemed to gradually transform into an intricate sand-table model, and he shut his eyes tight against the pain.

The sky was foggy, and now that nothing was visible below them, it was almost as if the three helicopters were holding stationary. But Davey knew that they might already have flown beyond the base. He checked his watch. Twelve minutes had passed since they had received the warning.

"Maybe the Chinese kids are just trying to scare us?" he said to Vaughn, who was sitting next to him.

Vaughn shook his head. "No, it's for real."

Davey pressed against the porthole and looked outside again, but there was nothing but fog.

"The World Games are over, Davey," Vaughn said. Then he closed his eyes, leaned back against the cabin wall, and said nothing more.

They found out later that the three helicopters had flown for roughly ten minutes prior to the nuclear explosion, putting them around forty-five kilometers away, outside the blast radius.

The first thing they saw was the outside world drowned in light. In the words of one young pilot, who had not been informed of the situation, "It was like flying through a neon light tube." The glare lasted for around fifteen seconds and was accompanied by a giant roar, as if the planet below them was exploding. All at once they saw blue sky, a circular region centered on the blast that expanded rapidly outward. It was the nuclear shock wave dispersing the cloud layer out to a radius of one hundred kilometers from the hypocenter, they later learned.

Smack in the center of the blue towered a mushroom cloud. It started off in two parts, one huge ball of white smoke and fire that took shape at two thousand meters after the initial fireball cooled, and a second on the ground where the shock wave kicked up dirt into a low pyramid whose apex extended upward into a thin spire that joined up with the huge smoke ball. The white ball instantly darkened in color as it absorbed the dust sent up by the pyramid, and flames flickered intermittently throughout the surface. Now the fog beneath the helicopter had been banished like the clouds, giving them a clear view of the land. The pilot later recalled, "The ground got fuzzy all of a sudden, like it had turned to liquid, as if an endless expanse of floodwater was surging toward us, and all of those little hills were islands and reefs. I saw cars on temporary roads flip over one after another like matchboxes. . . ."

The three helicopters were battered about like leaves in a storm. A number of times they dropped perilously close to the ground and were pelted by flying stones and sand; then they were flung high into the air. But they didn't crash. When they finally landed safely on snowy ground, the children jumped out of the cabin and looked back seaward at the tall mushroom cloud, even darker now. The morning sun, still below the Antarctic horizon, was high enough to just light up the top of the cloud, painting its rippling outline in gold against that slowly expanding dark blue circle of sky.

Blizzard

"Now this is Antarctica!" Huahua said, standing in the driving snow and bone-chilling wind. Visibility was poor through the endless whiteness of earth and sky, and even though they were on the coast, there was no distinguishing land from water. The young leaders of all the countries in Antarctica were closely gathered together as the blizzard swirled around them.

"That's not really accurate," Specs said. He had to shout to make himself heard over the howling wind. "It rarely snowed in Antarctica before the supernova. It's actually one of the driest places on Earth."

"That's right," Vaughn said. He was still only lightly dressed, and stood at ease in the cold wind, which had the children burrowing into their coats and shivering anyway. It was like the cold didn't affect him at all. "Higher temperatures filled the air in Antarctica with moisture, and now the dramatic drop in temperature is turning that moisture to snow. It might be the biggest snowfall on the continent for the next hundred thousand years."

"Let's go back. We'll be frozen stiff if we stay here," Davey said through chattering teeth, as he stomped his feet.

And so the heads of state returned to the pressurized hall, identical to the one on the US base that had been vaporized by the atomic fireball of the CE Mine. They had gathered here with the intent of holding talks about Antarctic territory, but the long-anticipated conference was entirely meaningless now.

The CE Mine had ended the Antarctic war games. The children of every country had finally agreed to meet at the negotiating table to discuss the question of Antarctic territory. Each country had paid a heavy price during the war games, but now that the contest had unexpectedly returned to its starting point with no major power commanding a decisive advantage, negotiations seemed impossible for the foreseeable future. The children had no clear idea of whether war would break out again on the continent, or if events would follow another path. In the end, however, all of their problems were solved by a sudden change in climate.

Signs had actually started appearing more than a month ago when autumn made its return to the northern hemisphere after a two-year absence, first with a hint of a chill, and then rains, cold weather, and fallen leaves piling up on the ground. After analyzing worldwide climate data, various countries' meteorological agencies concluded that the impact of the supernova on global climate was only temporary, and it now was returning to a pre-supernova state.

The ocean may have stopped rising, but it fell far more slowly than it had risen, leading many young scientists to predict that it might never return to its previous level. Still, the worldwide flood was over.

In Antarctica, temperatures hadn't changed as much, and the small drop was taken by most children to be a function of the long night. They expected the rising sun to dispel the cold and for Antarctica to welcome its first spring. Little did they know that the white figure of Death loomed near on the vast continent.

In what later proved to be a wise decision, countries began withdrawing personnel from Antarctica once they reached the conclusion that the climate would recover. The war games had claimed the lives of five hundred thousand children, half in conventional games and half to nuclear explosions, but the death toll would have been four to five times worse if they had not effected an immediate withdrawal as the climate began to return to normal.

Their bases were largely built to withstand winter temperatures no colder than around −10°C, and were incapable of sustaining the bitter −30°C temperatures that were to come. In the first month, the temperature changed only gradually, allowing the withdrawal of 2.7 million children at a speed that would have astonished the adults. However, equipment still needed to be evacuated, and countries also desired to maintain a certain presence, so nearly three hundred thousand children remained behind as the climate changed. The temperature plummeted nearly 20°C in a single week, and blizzards swept the continent, turning it into a white hellscape.

An emergency evacuation of the remaining children left more than two hundred thousand on the shore, since the worsening weather had grounded virtually all aircraft, and the ports had all iced over in the space of a week, preventing ships from entering. Because most young heads of state were still gathered on the continent for the territorial negotiations, they naturally assumed the role of evacuation command. Leaders wanted to assemble their own country's children, but the crowds on the shore were a mixture of all countries, leaving them at a loss as to how to proceed.

In the pressurized hall, Davey said, "Now that you've seen how things are out there, we have to come up with a solution, and quickly. Otherwise more than two hundred thousand people will freeze to death on the seashore."

"In a pinch, we could retreat to the inland bases," Green said.

"No," Specs said, "most base facilities were dismantled earlier in the withdrawal. And with minimal fuel remaining, all these people wouldn't survive very long. Going back and forth would waste tons of time and miss any chance to evacuate."

"We can't go back," someone added. "Even if the bases

were in perfect order, in this kind of weather we'd still freeze to death in those buildings."

Huahua said, "All our hopes are on the ocean now. Time is too tight to transport so many people by air even if the routes were passable. The critical question is how to deal with the frozen harbors."

Davey asked Ilyukhin, "When can your icebreakers get here?"

"They're in the middle of the Atlantic. It'll be ten days at the earliest before they make it here. Don't count on them."

"How about blasting a channel through the ice with heavy bombers?" Ōnishi suggested.

Davey and Ilyukhin shook their heads, and Scott said, "Bombers can't even get off the ground in this weather."

Lü Gang asked, "Aren't the B-2 and Tu-22 all-weather bombers?"

"Pilots aren't all-weather."

Marshal Zavyalova nodded. "The adults didn't actually think that all-weather meant wretched stuff like this. Besides, even if they did take off, visibility is so poor that it would be impossible to blast a precise channel. They'd just punch a few holes in the ice, and ships still couldn't get in."

"What about large-caliber naval guns? Or mines?" Pierre ventured.

The generals shook their heads. "Same problem with visibility. Even if they could make a navigable channel, there's not enough time."

"Besides," Huahua said, "it'll damage the ice surface and render the one viable solution impossible."

"What solution?"

"Walking across the ice."

★

The several kilometers of snow-blown coastline was densely dotted with abandoned cars and hastily erected tents, all covered in a thick layer of snow that made it a piece with the snowy plain behind and the frozen ocean on either side. When the children saw the group of young leaders walking toward them along the coast, they came out of tents and cars and ran over, surrounding them with a huge crowd of people. The children were shouting something, but their words were carried away by the wind. A few Chinese children were close to Huahua and Specs, and called to them, "Class Monitor, Studies Rep, what are we going to do?"

Huahua didn't reply immediately, but climbed on top of a tank buried in the snow next to them and shouted down to the crowd below, "Children, walk across the ice. Walk to the edge of the ice shelf, where lots of ships are waiting for us!" He realized his voice wasn't carrying very far in the gale, and crouched down to say to the nearest kid, "Pass that on back!"

His words spread through the crowd, passing to other nationalities through translation units, or through gestures that made his meaning clear enough to keep it from getting distorted.

"Have you gone crazy, CM? The wind is so stiff out on the ocean and the ice is so slippery, we'll be blown away like sawdust!" yelled one of the children.

Specs said, "If everyone holds hands, we won't blow away. Pass that back."

And so, lines of children soon appeared out on the ice,

almost a hundred in each, all holding hands and walking through the blizzard. As they crept away from the shoreline they looked like stubborn wriggling bugs. The line of national leaders advanced onto the ice first. Huahua had Davey to his left and Specs to his right, followed by Ilyukhin. Dense, windblown snow tumbled over their feet, making the children feel as if they were walking through the white deluge of surging rapids.

"So that's how this period of history ends," Davey said to Huahua through his translation unit, with the volume turned to maximum.

Huahua replied, "That's right. Our adults had an old saying, 'This too shall pass.' No matter how hard things might get, time always just keeps going forward."

"Makes sense. But things are going to be even harder. The passion that Antarctica sparked in children's hearts has turned to disappointment, and American society may lapse back into violent games."

"Chinese children might return to their indifferent stupor, and the interrupted Candytown might return." He sighed. "It's gonna be tough."

"But I might not be involved in any of that."

"Is Congress really going to impeach you?"

"Those sons of bitches!"

"But you might end up luckier than me. A head of state isn't a job for anyone."

"Yeah. Who would have thought that a thin page of history could fold up to be so thick?"

Huahua didn't quite get Davey's last reference, and he didn't bother to explain. The bitter cold and strong ocean wind prevented them from speaking, and it was all they could do to keep moving forward, or occasionally help up companions who slipped on the ice.

A little more than one hundred meters away from Huahua, Second Lieutenant Wei Ming was also trudging arduously through the blizzard. During a sudden lull in the wind, he heard the call of a cat. At first he thought it was just a figment of his imagination, but when he looked around he noticed a stretcher he had just passed on the ice. It was buried in the snow and he had mistaken it for a snowdrift. The meowing was coming from underneath. He left his column and slipped and slid over to the stretcher, where the cat had jumped down and was shivering in the snow. He picked it up, and then recognized it: Watermelon.

Pulling the army blanket off the stretcher, he saw Morgan lying there, clearly seriously wounded. Her face wore a white beard of frost, and her eyes glittered with fever. She didn't appear to recognize Wei Ming, and when she spoke a few words, her voice was as weak as a thread in the driving wind. Without a translation unit, Wei Ming couldn't understand her anyway. He tucked the cat back under the blanket, pulled it over Morgan, and then went around to the front of the stretcher and started pulling. He made slow progress; when the next column of children caught up to him, a few members broke away and came over to help him carry the stretcher forward.

For ages, swirling snow was all the children could see in the expanse of white around them, and although they strove to move forward, they felt as if they were frozen in place on the ice. But just as they were too numb to move, hazy black silhouettes of ships appeared ahead of them, and they were informed via radio not to proceed any farther. They had reached the edge of the ice shelf, where the ice was not frozen solid, and they could fall through at any time. The ships would dispatch landing craft and hovercraft to fetch them. By the time they received the message, over a thousand children had already fallen through crevasses into the icy sea, but the vast majority of them managed to reach the edge of the ice.

Smaller black shadows, separate from the distant fleet, gradually took shape through the snow, dozens of landing craft pushing through the floating ice. When they reached the solid ice, they opened their rectangular maws to let the children swarm aboard.

Wei Ming and the other children carried the stretcher onto one of the landing craft. It was a vessel especially for the wounded, so his companions left at once and he never knew what countries they were from. Under the cabin's dim yellow light, Wei Ming saw Morgan staring blankly at him from the stretcher. She clearly hadn't recognized him yet, so Wei Ming picked up Watermelon and said, "You can't take care of him anymore. Why don't I take him with me to China?" He set the cat down and let it lick its master's face. "Don't worry, Lieutenant. We went through so many devilish games and made it out alive, and life will go on. We've survived the impossible, so blessings must be in store. Goodbye." Then he put Watermelon into his backpack and left the boat.

★

Huahua and a few generals from other countries were coordinating the boarding, and preventing the children who were temporarily unable to board from crowding too far forward and collapsing the ice shelf with their numbers. Farther back on the ice, children from different countries clustered together into large masses to shelter from the cold as they waited. All of a sudden Huahua heard someone call his name, and he turned around to see Wei Ming. The two former classmates embraced.

"You came to Antarctica too?" Huahua asked incredulously.

"I came a year ago with B Group Army's advance team. I've actually seen you and Specs quite a few times from far off, but it didn't feel right to disturb you."

"Out of our class, I think Wang Ran and Jin Yunhui also joined the army."

"Correct. They came to Antarctica too," Wei Ming said, his expression faltering.

"Where are they now?"

"Wang Ran was evacuated last month with the first batch of wounded, but I don't know if he made it back home. He was seriously injured in the tank games. He managed to stay alive, but his spine was severed, and he'll probably never walk again."

"Oh . . . and Jin Yunhui? I recall he was a fighter pilot?"

"Correct. A J-10 in the First Airborne Division. His fate was much happier. He crashed into a Su-30 during a fighter game, and both planes were blown to bits. He was posthumously awarded a Nebula medal, but everyone knows he only hit the enemy plane by accident."

To cover up his own sadness, Huahua asked another question: "Any other kids from our class?"

"We kept in touch the first few months, but by the start of Candytown, most of them, like all the other kids, left their assigned jobs. I don't know where they ended up."

"Didn't Ms. Zheng leave a kid behind?"

"Correct. At first, Feng Jing and Yao Pingping were looking after him. Xiaomeng sent someone to look for the kid, but Ms. Zheng's final instructions were 'You may not use your connections to give him any special treatment,' and so they didn't let anyone find him. At the start of Candytown, the kid's nursery was hit by an epidemic, and he ran a high fever. He survived, but the fever took away his hearing. The nursery was disbanded near the end of Candytown, and the last time I saw Feng Jing, she said he had been transferred to another one. No one knows where he is now."

Huahua was too choked up to speak. A deep sadness came over him, and the numbness he had begun to acquire at the harsh pinnacle of power instantly melted away.

"Huahua," Wei Ming said, "do you still remember our graduation party?"

Huahua nodded. "How could I forget?"

"Specs talked about how the future can't be predicted. Anything could happen. He proved it using chaos theory."

"That's right. He also mentioned the uncertainty principle . . ."

"Who would have thought back then that we'd run across each other in a place like this?"

Huahua could no longer hold back his tears. The wind

blew them cold on his face almost immediately, and then they froze. He looked up at his classmate. Wei Ming's eyebrows were white with ice, and the skin on his face was dark and rough and patchy with scars and frostbite and the visible and invisible nicks and scratches left by life and war. His child's face was already weathered by time.

"We've grown up, Wei Ming," Huahua said.

"Correct. But you've got to grow up faster than us."

"It's hard for me. And for Specs and Xiaomeng, too."

"Don't let anyone know. You can't let the country's children know that."

"And I can't talk to you about it?"

"I can't help you, Huahua. Give my regards to Specs and Xiaomeng. You're the glory of our class. The absolute glory."

"Take care of yourself, Wei Ming," Huahua said with feeling as he shook his classmate's hand.

"You too." Wei Ming gripped his hand for a moment, and then turned and disappeared into the snow.

Davey boarded the aircraft carrier USS *John C. Stennis*. Anchored close to shore, this supercarrier launched in the 1990s was a black iron island in the blizzard. Across the runway on the snow-covered flight deck, Davey heard the sound of shots from the gun platform, and asked the captain who had greeted him what was going on.

"Lots of kids from other countries want to board. Marines are preventing them."

"You dumbass!" Davey roared. "Let every kid aboard who can, no matter where they come from!"

"But . . . Mr. President, that's impossible!"

365

"That's an order! Tell those marines to get the hell away!"

"Mr. President, I have to be responsible for the safety of *John C. Stennis*."

Davey smacked the captain across the head, knocking off his hat. "And you're not responsible for the lives of the kids on the ice? You're a criminal!"

"I'm sorry, Mr. President. As captain I cannot execute your order."

"I am the commander in chief of the United States of America, for the time being at least. If I so desired, I could have you thrown into the sea this instant, just like your hat. Dare me to try?"

The captain hesitated, and then said to a marine captain, "Tell your people to withdraw. Let anyone who wants to come aboard."

An unending stream of children from different countries surged up the gangway and onto the deck. The wind was fiercer here, and the leeward side of fighter jets was the only respite from it. Lots of children had fallen into the ocean while boarding the landing craft, and their soaked clothing had now frozen into sparkling coats of ice.

"Let them into the cabins. These kids won't last long out here before they freeze to death," Davey said to the captain.

"Can't do that, Mr. President. The cabins are full to bursting with the American kids who came aboard first."

"And the hangars? There's tons of space in there, enough for a few thousand people. Are those full too?"

"They're full up with planes!"

"Then bring the planes up onto the flight deck."

"Impossible. The flight deck already has too many other fighters that the horrible weather forced to make an emergency landing here. See, the elevator to the hangars is completely blocked!"

"Then push them into the sea!"

And so, one after another, the ten-million-dollar fighter planes were pushed over the side of *John C. Stennis* and into the ocean, and the broad flight deck quickly filled with more planes brought up from the hangars on the enormous elevator. The international group of children left the deck for the warm refuge of the cavernous hangars, which soon held thousands of occupants. Once the children had warmed up a bit, they gasped in wonder at the sheer size of the carrier. But on the flight deck out in the snowstorm, over a hundred drenched children had frozen to death.

The final evacuation took three days, and then the huge fleet of more than fifteen hundred ships carrying the last three hundred thousand children off of the continent split into two groups bound for Argentina and New Zealand. More than thirty thousand children succumbed to the cold during the evacuation, the last group of casualties in the Supernova War to die in Antarctica.

The Amundsen Sea returned to its empty state free of its covering of ships. The snow had stopped, but the wind was as fierce as ever, scouring the cold air over the water. As the sky cleared up and a crack appeared in the clouds over the horizon, the newly risen sun shed golden light over Antarctica, onto the deep blanket of snow that now covered the once-exposed rocks and dirt. Perhaps, in some distant future, crowds of people would again set foot on this frigid land in search of the snow-covered bodies of five hundred thousand children, the wreckage of countless tanks, and the two ten-kilometer craters the nuclear blasts left behind. During the continent's brief springtime, three million children from all over the world had fought each other amid flames and explosions, unleashing their lust for life. But now the epic tragedy of the Supernova War seemed little more than a bad dream in the long night, a mirage beneath the brilliant southern lights. In daylight, the land was a lonely expanse of white. It was as if nothing had ever happened.

10

Genesis

A New President

Davey burst into the Oval Office in a panic, and then let out a long sigh. He picked at the frostbite patches on his face, the mark carried by most children who returned from Antarctica. The girl Benes was sitting in the high-backed presidential chair leisurely clipping her nails. When she saw Davey enter, she rolled her eyes and said, "Mr. Herman Davey, you've been impeached and have no authority to return to this office. And in fact, you don't have any authority to be in the White House at all."

Davey rubbed his temples and said, "I want to leave, but that pack of thugs out there want to kill me!"

"You deserve it. You screwed everything up. You've done a worse job than any president in US history."

"You . . . you have no right to say that to me! Why are you sitting in the presidential chair? You think you can just ignore etiquette when I'm away?"

Benes looked up at the ceiling. "You're the one who needs to pay attention to etiquette."

Davey was about to explode when Vaughn came in and said, "What you probably don't know is that Frances Benes was elected the second president of the United States of the Supernova Era."

"What?" Davey exclaimed, staring at the blond-haired girl clipping her nails in that hallowed seat. He looked back at Vaughn, and then burst out laughing. "Don't joke around. That idiot doesn't even know how to count!" He chuckled.

Benes furiously smacked the table, but then held her hand to her mouth to soothe the pain. Then she pointed a finger at Davey and said sharply, "Shut your mouth or you'll be charged with defaming the president!"

"You've got to be responsible to the republic!" Davey said, pointing at Vaughn.

"She's the choice of all American children. The new president was selected in a fair election."

Davey spat in Benes's direction. "When we were off facing death in Antarctica, you were back here flirting with the media!"

"Slandering the president!" Benes shouted at Davey, opening her eyes wide, but then her face dissolved into a pleased smile. "Do you know why they voted for me? I look like Shirley Temple. That's where I've got you beat. You may be handsome, but you don't look like any movie star."

"If those old black-and-white movies hadn't been playing on TV all day, who would even remember Shirley Temple?"

"That was our campaign strategy!" Benes said with another sweet smile.

"The Democrats are blind."

Vaughn said, "It's actually fairly easy to understand. After the war games, the people needed someone more moderate to represent their will."

Davey frowned in distaste. "And this Barbie doll can represent the will of America? Right now the whole country is consumed by the Antarctic failure. The country is going to slide back into violent games. The crisis facing the republic right now is far more frightening than the Antarctic war, since we could collapse at any moment. At this critical juncture, to put the American children in the hands of this—"

"Mr. Vaughn will find a solution for us," Benes said with a nod in his direction.

Davey was stunned for a moment, but then nodded thoughtfully. "I get it. Mr. Vaughn is using us as tools to realize his ideas. The country and the world are his stage, and any individual is a puppet whose strings he can pull at will. Yes, that's what he thinks. . . ." Then he jumped to his feet in exasperation and pulled an object from his pocket: a full-lug snub-nosed revolver, which he leveled at Vaughn. He said, "You're far too sinister and frightening. I should blast your brains open. I've been fed up with that head of yours for a long time."

Benes yelped and reached for the alarm, but Vaughn stopped her with a gentle wave. "You're not going to pull the trigger. If you do, you're not walking out of this old house alive. You're an exemplary American. In whatever you do, you act according to one iron law: Outputs always need to exceed inputs. That's your fundamental weakness!"

Davey put away the gun. "Of course outputs should exceed inputs!"

"But that's not the way to make history."

"I'm not making history anymore. I'm tired of it!" Davey said, and bounded to the door, where he took one last look around the Oval Office, where so many of his dreams remained. Then he ran out alone.

Carrying a motorcycle helmet, Davey exited the White House by the back door. He found the Lincoln Town Car he had parked there and got inside. He put on the helmet, and then found a pair of sunglasses in the car and put those on. Then he started the engine and headed off. Just outside the White House a hundred children were gathered, looking to settle their score with him, but his car didn't attract their attention and they let him pass.

He glanced out at the crowd as he did so and saw they had hung a banner:

HERMAN HERMAN GO AWAY, FRANCES
HAS NEW GAMES TO PLAY!

Davey drove aimlessly around the capital. Very little of D.C.'s population was left, since the majority of children had moved in search of work to larger cities with denser concentrations of industry, so apart from the government it was practically a ghost town. It was past nine in the morning, but the city showed no signs of waking up. His surroundings were as silent as the dead of night, which only heightened the impression he had of the city: It was a tomb. He thought fondly of bustling New York. That's where he came from, and that's where he'd return.

The Lincoln was too flashy, he thought, and such a high-end thing no longer suited him. He parked it in a secluded spot by the Potomac River and from the trunk retrieved the FN Minimi light machine gun that Vaughn had given him. He checked the translucent plastic magazine; it was almost half full. He hefted the gun level and aimed it at the Lincoln a few meters away, and then *ratatatat* let fly a burst. The muzzle spurted flame three times, and the recoil dropped him back on his ass. He sat there staring at the car for a moment, and when nothing else happened, pulled himself up by the barrel, adjusted the gas valve to the fastest rate of fire, and again leveled the swaying gun. Again he fired at the car, the rapid reports echoing across the river, and again he fell back onto the ground. There was no reaction from the car. He stood up again, two round dirt stains on the butt of his jeans, and sprayed the car again, emptying the magazine. With a boom the Lincoln burst into flames and started smoking, and Davey crowed "Woohoo!" and bounded away, carrying the gun with him.

Benes finished clipping her nails and turned to plucking her eyebrows, using tweezers and a small mirror. Vaughn pointed to two buttons on the presidential desk, and said, "Lots of people are very curious about those buttons. The media has even speculated that they are tied to the fate of the nation, and if the president presses one, it will immediately contact all NATO countries. Press the other, and a nationwide war alert is issued, scrambling bombers and dispatching nuclear bombs from their silos . . . things like that."

But in fact, one button called for coffee, and the other alerted housekeeping to clean the room. During the time she had spent with Vaughn, Benes had discovered that he was sometimes quite eager to talk to her. He proved a good conversationalist, although he held forth only on insignificant and nonessential topics, and deflected serious matters with practiced evasion.

She said to him, "I know my own strengths, and I don't share the outside world's misapprehensions about those two buttons. I'm not too clever, I know that, but I'm better than Davey's reverse cleverness, at least."

Vaughn nodded. "You're certainly clever about that."

"I'm riding on this horse of history but I'm not holding the reins. It can trot wherever it pleases. Not like Davey, clutching the reins and forcing it to the edge of a precipice."

Vaughn nodded again. "That's very wise."

Benes set down her mirror and looked at Vaughn for a moment. "You're clever. You can create history. But you need to give me most of the credit."

"Not a problem," Vaughn said. "I don't have any interest in having my name in the history books."

Benes gave him a playful smile. "I've noticed that. Otherwise you'd have been president already. But you still ought to say something to me when you want to make history, so I'm able to speak to Congress and the press."

"That's what I'm going to tell you now."

"I'm listening," Benes said with another smile, setting down her tweezers and mirror and commencing to paint her nails.

"The world will enter a period of brutal struggle for control. A redivision of land and resources. There's no returning to the adults' model of the world. The children's world will operate on an entirely new concept, a new model that no one can foresee. But one thing is certain: If America wants to command the same position it did in the Common Era, or even if it wishes to survive at all, it must awaken its slumbering might!"

"That's right. Strength is ours!" Benes said, shaking a fist.

"So, Madam President, do you know the source of America's strength?"

"You mean it's not aircraft carriers and spaceships?"

"No—" Here Vaughn shook his head meaningfully. "Those things are extraneous. Our strength took shape earlier, during the opening up of the West."

"Oh, yeah! Those cowboys were so handsome!"

"They lived lives far less romantic than in the movies. In the Wild West they faced a constant threat of hunger and disease, and their lives were always in danger from attacking wildfires, wolf packs, and Native Americans. With just a horse and a revolver, they rode off smiling into a cruel world to forge the American miracle, pen the American epic, their strength drawn from a desire for hegemony over the new world.

"Those knights of the West were the true Americans; theirs was the true American spirit. That is where our strength derives. But where are those riders now? Before the supernova, our fathers and mothers hid themselves inside the hard shells of skyscrapers, under the impression that they had the world in their pocket. Ever since the purchase of Alaska and Hawaii, they no longer expanded into new territory, no longer dreamed of new conquests, but turned slow and lazy, and the fat on their bellies and necks grew thick. They turned numb, became fragile and sentimental, trembled uncontrollably at the slightest casualty in war, and wailed and agitated disgracefully outside the White House. Later, when a new generation saw the world as nothing more than a scrap of toilet paper, hippies and punks became the new symbols of America. Now in the new era, children have lost their way and anesthetize themselves through violent games in the streets."

Benes asked soberly, "But how can America's strength be awakened?"

"We need a new game."

"What kind of game?"

Vaughn then uttered a sentence Benes had never heard him say before: "I don't know."

"No!" the girl president exclaimed. "You do know. You know everything! You've got to tell me!"

"I'll think of it, but I need time. Right now I'm only certain of one thing: The new game will be, and can only be, the most imaginative and dangerous game in history, so I hope that you won't be overly surprised when you hear what it is."

"I won't. Come on, think up something soon!"

"Leave me alone here for a while, and don't let anyone come in. Including you," Vaughn said, and waved her away.

The president made a silent exit. She headed straight for the basement, to the White House security control center crammed with monitors of all sizes, one of which had a direct view of the Oval Office. No president liked being under surveillance, so the system was only operable in special circumstances with the president's express permission. The old equipment hadn't been used in years, and it took the young special agents on duty in the basement quite a while to bring an image up on the screen. Vaughn was standing motionless in front of the huge world map in the office, lost in thought. In the cramped basement room, under the curious gaze of the other children, President Benes stared unblinking at the screen, like a child waiting long into the night on Christmas Eve for Santa to arrive with a sack of toys. One hour passed, then another ... all through the afternoon, Vaughn stood there like a statue. Finally losing her patience, Benes turned to the kids on duty and ordered them to notify her immediately if Vaughn made any movements.

"Is he dangerous?" asked an agent with a big-bore revolver at his backside.

"Not to America."

She had spent the previous day busy with various presidential duties and had not slept a wink the previous night. Now an acute drowsiness hit her, and without knowing it she slept the entire afternoon, waking up only after it was dark. She snatched up the phone and inquired about Vaughn's status, but the kids on duty in the basement informed her that he had spent the entire day motionless in front of the map; during the entire time he had only murmured one thing to himself: "God, would that I had Wegener's inspiration!"

Benes hurriedly called in a few advisors to study that statement. One advisor told her that Wegener was a geologist from the Common Era, a German. On one occasion, on his sickbed, bored out of his mind and staring at a map of the world, he suddenly realized that several continental borders matched, giving him an idea: Long ago the surface of the Earth might have had just one continent. It had subsequently been broken up by some unknown force, and the various pieces of the crust had drifted apart, forming the world of the present day. This was the beginning of Wegener's epochal continental drift theory. There was, Benes realized, no mystery to Vaughn's words; he was only aching to come up with a continental drift theory of international politics. And so she sent the advisors away and went back to sleep on the sofa.

When she next awoke it was after 1:00 A.M. She grabbed the phone and called the basement, and learned that the weird kid in the Oval Office was still standing motionless. "We wonder if maybe he died on his feet," one of the special agents said. Benes had them transfer the feed to her room. A shaft of light from the Rose Nebula fell through the window and directly onto Vaughn, who appeared wraithlike with the indistinct map beyond him. She sighed, switched off the monitor, and went back to sleep.

She slept till it was light and she was awakened by the ringing of her phone.

"Madam President, the guy in the office wants to see you."

Benes flew out the door, still in her pajamas, and raced to the door of the Oval Office, where Vaughn's ghastly gaze was waiting for her.

"We have a new game, Madam President," Vaughn said gravely.

"We do? Tell me!"

Vaughn held out his hands, each of which held an oddly shaped piece of paper. She snatched them eagerly to take a look, and then raised her head in confusion. They were two fragments that Vaughn had cut out of a world map: one was America, the other was China.

A Visit

In a small motorcade heading toward Capital Airport, Huahua sat in the lead vehicle with a bespectacled interpreter next to him. The minister of foreign affairs was in the car behind them, and the third held the US ambassador, an eleven-year-old boy named George Friedman who was the son of a former military attaché. A truck at the rear of the motorcade held an army band, and several of the band members were practicing on their instruments, squawking audibly even at this distance.

Two nights before, the Chinese children in the NIT had received an email from the US president. Its contents were simple:

> I really, really want to visit your country. I would like to go immediately. May I?
>
> Best Regards,
> Frances Benes
> President of the United States of America

When the motorcade reached the airport, a flashing silvery-white dot was already circling overhead. The children in the control tower signaled permission to land, and the dot rapidly increased in size. Ten minutes later, Air Force One touched down. Due to the young pilot's limited technical abilities, the big metal object bounced back up again a few times before landing for good, and then traced a dangerous S curve right up to the end of the runway, where it finally stopped.

The hatch opened. A few small heads poked out and watched anxiously as the airstair was brought in from a few hundred meters away. Once it was in place, the first to exit was a pretty blond-haired girl whom Huahua recognized from TV news as the new president. Right behind her were a few senior officials he didn't know. They crowded into each other, jostling into Benes so that she nearly tripped. She righted herself and turned back to them to shake a fist and shout a few words of warning, and they slowed down.

The president continued a graceful descent, keeping a clear picture in mind of the history she was making. At the two-thirds point, a gaggle of reporters with cameras strapped round their necks pushed their way out of the hatch and down the stairs, overtaking the officials. The fastest made it to the ground a step ahead of Benes and turned around to train his lens on her. She erupted into fury, bounded down the rest of the stairs to grab the photographer by the collar, and started shouting angrily at him.

The interpreter told Huahua, "The president says that she was supposed to descend first, so that she would be the first American to set foot in China in the Supernova Era. But the reporter stole it from her. The reporter is arguing that he only came down first so he could get a photo of her, but the president is calling him a jackass, and says that she made it very clear aboard the plane that no one was to go in front of her. They were already being privileged; when Nixon came to China he went down by himself, and when he was shaking hands with Zhou Enlai everyone else was still stuck on board. That reporter is the AP's old pro in the White House and he's furious. He's saying, 'Who the hell are you? You'll be gone in four years, but we'll still be in the White House!' Now the president is saying, 'Go to hell. I'll still be there in four years. I'll be there in eight. I'll be there forever!'"

Now all the children had come down the stairs, and the argument had turned physical. The president extracted herself from the scrum and strode over to greet the Chinese children.

"I am overjoyed to meet you on the cusp of the rebirth of human history. Wow, your face is covered in frostbite scars. They're medals of valor! Do you know that in America there are lots of special beauty salons now that give kids frostbite scars using dry ice? They do good business!" Benes said to Huahua through the translator.

"I wish I didn't have these medals," Huahua said. "They itch like crazy, and I think they'll be that way every winter. I really don't want to have to relive that time in Antarctica over and over. Our two countries suffered such immense trouble and loss due to the World Games."

"That's why we're here. We have a new game!" Benes said with a smile and a bow. Then she looked into the distance. "Where's the Great Wall?" And around her. "And the pandas?" Clearly she imagined that she would see the Great Wall as soon as she set foot in Chinese territory, and that pandas would be as common as dogs are in the US.

Then a thought struck her. Glancing about again, she asked, "Where's Vaughn?"

It took a few kids shouting back at the plane for a while before Chester Vaughn emerged. He came down slowly, his arms cradling a thick book. "He's always reading," she said to Huahua. "He didn't even realize we'd landed."

Shaking his hand, Huahua glanced at the book. It was a volume of Mao Zedong's commentary on the *Twenty-Four Histories,* a thread-bound Chinese edition.

Vaughn's eyes were half closed, as if he were in a trance,

and he took a deep breath. "It's the air I've dreamed about," he said.

"What?" Benes asked in wonder.

"The air of antiquity," he said, practically inaudible to anyone but himself. Then he stood silently in place, detached, taking everything in.

New World Games

Warily, the children entered the solemn, mysterious hall. Deep red carpets, snow-white armchairs arranged into a large semicircle, and behind them elegant embroidered silk screens and a magnificent cloisonné vase the size of a person . . . all of it was spotless, and they passed through air so still it felt like swimming through the phantoms of history.

"Wow. This is China's White House?" Benes asked softly. Behind her, two other American kids were carrying a roll of paper, a full two meters long, and they set it gingerly on the carpet as the Chinese children looked on curiously.

"That's right," Xiaomeng said. "The adults used to receive foreign heads of state here. You know, this is our first time in here, too."

"Your first time? Why didn't you come before? You're the supreme leaders of the country, so surely it ought to be your workplace."

"We work in the NIT. I was kind of scared to come here, since it seemed like as soon as I came in I'd have all those pairs of adult eyes watching us from some place, like they were saying, 'Children, you're being stupid!'"

"I felt the same way my first time in the White House, but I got over it eventually. I don't like adults watching us. Still, I'm really grateful that you've brought us here, because a historic meeting should be held in an exceptional setting so that we won't feel embarrassed when it is written into the history books."

The children sat down in the armchairs.

"Now we'll explain the new world games," Benes said.

Huahua shook his head. "You can't simply place world games however you please. We've done them once with your idea, so now it's time to listen to someone else's."

"Naturally we won't force anyone to play our game. You can come up with your own rules, and we'll use whichever is more fun. Do you have anything new?"

Xiaomeng shook her head. "We've got too many other things to do right now. The end of the Antarctic Games obliterated the children's dream for a new world on that continent, and now a dark mood of loss and disappointment has descended upon all of society. There are signs of a reemergence of Candytown."

Benes nodded. "It's the same in the US. The streets are ringing with gunfire again, since violent games are the only way for kids to find thrills. Or any meaning in life at all. We really need a new game to give them some kind of spiritual support, so they can escape the current danger."

"Very well," Huahua said. "Then let's discuss your new game."

When Xiaomeng and Specs nodded their agreement, Benes's excitement bubbled over. "Thank you! Thank you! Now, before we get to the idea of the game, I'd first advise you to mentally prepare yourselves for the shock of the unimaginable. We may have a far better tolerance for that than the adults, and our tolerance has only been strengthened by the supernova, but the shock we're preparing will still be a challenge for our Chinese friends."

"You're bluffing," Huahua said dismissively.

"You'll find that out soon enough."

"Then out with it."

Now the young president grew nervous. She quickly crossed herself, and with her eyes half closed, she said, "God bless America," in a voice audible only to herself. Then she leapt up from the chair and began to pace energetically, before stopping short and clasping her hands to her chest. She said, "First I'd like to make a request. Would our Chinese friends share with us your impressions of our country?"

The Chinese children's remarks came out in a jumble:

"America is skyscrapers covered in mirror glass glittering in the sun."

"In America, a river of cars flows morning till night, unceasingly."

"America has Disneyland and lots of other fun places."

"Americans love football."

"American farms use huge machines, so one family can till a huge area!"

"In American factories, it's all robots and assembly lines, and a whole car can be assembled in a matter of seconds!"

"Americans have been to the moon, and they want to go to Mars. They fire tons of rockets off every year."

"America has lots and lots of nuclear weapons, and huge aircraft carriers. No one messes with them."

The impressions shared by the Chinese children sketched a rough outline of America that happened to match exactly with what Benes had been hoping for. All was going according to plan, so she determinedly took the next step.

"I have long been aware that China is a great and mysterious country, but as a newly arrived guest, I know far less about your country than you do of mine. So let me ask you: Does your country have anything that's better than ours?"

It was a challenging question, to be sure.

"Our country is huge. It covers an area of nine-point-six million square kilometers," Huahua exclaimed.

"Ours is pretty big too: nine-point-three-six million square kilometers. But we've got more arable land than you, and more forest cover. Those are important things for a country," Benes said solemnly.

"We have lots and lots of oil underground, and lots and lots of coal. And lots and lots of iron," Xiaomeng said.

"So do we. Oil in the Gulf of Mexico, Alaska, and California. And we've got lots of places with coal. Pennsylvania, West Virginia, Kentucky, Illinois, Indiana, and Ohio all have tons of it. And there's lots of iron under the southwestern part of Lake Superior, and copper in Arizona, Utah, Montana, Nevada, and New Mexico, and lead and zinc in Missouri. You haven't got us beat in that area."

"Well . . . we've got the Yangtze River. It's the biggest, longest river in the world!"

"Not true in the slightest. The Mississippi is bigger. And one of its tributaries, the Ohio River, is over a thousand meters wide at its widest point. Have you ever seen a thousand-meter-wide river?"

"Does the Mississippi River have the Three Gorges?"

"No, but the Colorado does. We call it the Grand Canyon, and it's magnificent!"

CIXIN LIU

"You just memorized a geography textbook and came here to challenge us, is that it?" Huahua said angrily.

Now Benes squatted down beside the long roll of paper, untied the green ribbon holding it together, and gently unrolled it. It was a world map, one so big that when fully unrolled it occupied half of the floor space in the hall, but it was a peculiar one: the United States and China were the only two countries drawn, and the remainder of the map was water, giving them the look of two islands floating in a vast ocean. Benes jumped onto the map into the middle of the Pacific, and pointed a hand at each territory.

"Look at our two countries. We're in opposition on either side of the globe, practically equal in area, more or less the same shape. It's like we're a pair of images reflected onto the Earth. And there really are so many things that are mirror images. For example, the two are the world's oldest and the world's youngest countries; one whose people have deep roots and ancient heritage, the other made up almost entirely of immigrants; one that stresses tradition, one that prizes innovation; one quiet and introverted, one outgoing and expansive. My Chinese friends, God put two such countries on the Earth. Don't you think there's a certain mystical connection between them?"

The words captivated her listeners, and they waited silently for her to show her final card.

The president walked across the map to the United States. From a pocket she pulled out a small, gleaming pair of scissors, and then, crawling on the map like a lizard on a wall, cut out first the United States, and then China. The map was so big that it took her quite a while to snip around the borders

386

of the two countries under the astonished gaze of the Chinese children. Then she took the China cutout, crossed the map, and handed it to Huahua.

"This is your territory. Take care of it."

Then she retrieved the cutout of the United States, and returned to the Chinese children. Holding it out in front of her, she said, "Look, this is our territory."

Now the president passed the US cutout into one of Huahua's hands, and with her other hand took hold of the China cutout. She said, "*We exchange them.*"

The Chinese interpreter stared at her in shock. "*Sorry, I beg your pardon?*"

Benes did not repeat her statement—words meant for the history books cannot be repeated. Besides, she knew that not only had the interpreter understood her, but that even Huahua, with only two semesters of English study, had also grasped that simple sentence. She simply nodded at the Chinese children, confirming the unbelievable proposition she had just made.

The Exchange

"What? An exchange?" they asked.

"All Chinese children will move to our territory, and all American children will move to yours," Benes said.

"So that means our territory would belong to you?"

"That's right. And our territory would be yours."

"But . . . what about all the stuff on the territory? You can't ship whole cities across the Pacific!"

"We'll exchange everything in the two countries."

"You mean, you come empty-handed, and we leave empty-handed?"

"Exactly! It's the territorial-exchange game!"

Wide-eyed, the Chinese children looked at each other in total disbelief.

"But . . . that means all of your—" Huahua said.

"All of our factories," Benes said quickly, cutting him off. "And all of our farms. All of our delicacies and entertainments. Everything in America will be yours! Of course, that means everything in China will be ours."

The Chinese children stared at the president like she was a madwoman. Then the foreign minister cracked up laughing, and soon all of the Chinese children were laughing along with him.

"You've taken the joke a little too far," Xiaomeng said.

"Your interpretation is understandable, but I can solemnly declare in my role as national leader that this suggestion is the task I have flown across the Pacific to accomplish. I do realize that it may be hard to prove it isn't a joke, but we are willing to do whatever it takes," Benes said with sincerity.

"How do you plan to do that?" Huahua asked.

"That will fall to Mr. Vaughn," she said, gesturing to invite him over from behind the crowd, where he had been admiring one of the hall's huge hanging carpets. Upon hearing the president mention his name, he slowly turned and came over and stood in the empty space on the map the United States had once occupied. He said, "To prove this ambition would be like proving the international politics equivalent of quantum mechanics or the theory of relativity. You'd need a superhuman mind and intelligence. There's only one person here I can talk to."

Specs had remained silent throughout all of this, but now he stood up and went over to the space on the map formerly occupied by China. Now the two young thinkers stared at each other across the Pacific Ocean.

Vaughn said impassively, "The only heroes in the world are you and me. A tremendous peal of thunder."*

"You're very familiar with Chinese culture," Specs replied, similarly impassively.

"More familiar than you know," Vaughn said, to the astonishment of the children. Not the words themselves, but the fact that they came not through the translator device but from Vaughn himself, speaking Mandarin Chinese.

Vaughn was unfazed by their shock. "I always wanted to learn an Eastern language, but dithered for a long time among Japanese, Sanskrit, and Mandarin before deciding."

Specs said, "We need to be candid."

Vaughn nodded. "Frankness is essential for proving our intentions."

"Then proceed with your proof."

Vaughn paused for a few seconds, and then said, "First, the new world is an abandoned child. It will never grow up; or perhaps more accurately, it's already grown, and this is its shape."

Specs nodded.

"Second, you have your strength, and we have ours. Each of us needs to awaken our strength." Then he paused to give Specs time to reflect on his words.

Specs nodded again.

---

* A paraphrase of Cao Cao's shocking statement to Liu Bei in *Romance of the Three Kingdoms*, chapter 21.

"The next point is critical, and one that only a superior thinker can understand. The difference in our two strengths is . . ." Vaughn cast a look of challenge at Specs.

"Our strength draws from our ancient native land; yours from new frontiers," Specs said.

The two children stared long and hard at each other from their respective continents.

Vaughn asked, "Do you need further proof?"

Specs shook his head gently. Then he walked off the map and said to his companions, "They're for real."

"Talking with you has truly been a refreshing experience," Vaughn said to Specs, bowing slightly from his cut-out spot on the map.

Specs returned the bow. "I have the deepest respect for your idea. Such a profound and audacious idea deserves to be called great."

"We believe that once the game is made public, a process will be set in motion that will be difficult to redirect. If anyone here disagrees with the exchange, you may find it impossible to withstand the pressure of a country of children."

Huahua was silent for a moment. Then he said, "Perhaps that is the case. But what about your side? I have my doubts about whether you can realize your plan. Can you convince the American children?"

With confidence, Vaughn said, "We've got a solution. A new world has the same attraction for American kids as it does for Chinese kids. After all, their veins flow with the blood of the pioneers. They are the most curious children in the world, and the most possessive. A reshuffling of society and the nation will be a most welcome development for them."

Xiaomeng asked, "How long do you expect this game to last?"

Vaughn smiled, more noticeably this time. "According to my predictions, in the space of three to five years, we will be facing an undefended country and will easily be able to retake everything that we bartered away."

The Decision

The meeting to discuss the territorial-exchange game was held that night, three hours after the first Sino-US talks. On the top floor of the NIT, under the light of the Rose Nebula, the Chinese children faced a choice far beyond anything they had dreamed.

Xiaomeng said, "Look at the state of the world. We do need strong industry and defense to protect ourselves."

"But can we get all of that simply by going to America?" Specs asked.

Pacing back and forth, Huahua said, "Why should we let Vaughn scare us? Why not think of another possibility? Once we've crossed the Pacific, can't we maintain our current organization and discipline? Can't we devote our efforts to work and study? Can't Chinese children get those huge factories operating to produce steel and cars and aircraft carriers and spaceships? Can't we put those huge farms to work growing wheat and corn? We can make those cities boom even more than they did in the Common Era. So long as we work hard, we'll become the most powerful country in the world in no time! Why do we look down on ourselves? We showed such bravery and resolve in the war we just fought. Now we're facing a new battle. So long as we put all our energy into it, there's no obstacle we can't overcome!"

His statement drew general praise from the children.

Xiaomeng said, "But the souls of our mothers and fathers will ask us, 'How could you lose the land of generations of your ancestors?' What will we tell them?"

Huahua gave her a look of disbelief. "What do you mean, 'lose'? If an enemy invaded and we surrendered without a fight and lost the country, well then damn us to hell! But we're making an exchange with another party, and it's a fair exchange. Whatever they can do, we can do too. If the adults were here, we could stand before them righteous and confident!"

"But it's not only about the trade. We're swapping not just our territory, but something else even more important," Specs said.

"Is our strength really tied to our ancestral land?"

Specs nodded silently.

"Do you think there will be serious consequences?"

Again he nodded.

Xiaomeng asked, "What's going to happen?"

Specs shook his head. "I don't know. I don't think Vaughn knows either, and he's thought about the question on a much deeper level. America has many times our reserves of goods and resources, so children will be able to lead rich lives for an incredibly long time without needing to work. It's a sweet-smelling, rainbow-hued quagmire. Just like in Candytown, we may see history moving in a particular direction but be powerless to stop it."

The mention of Candytown sobered everyone up for a moment, and they looked in silence out the window at the night lights.

Huahua said, "We have no other choice. The American children are sure to disclose the nature of the games, and when that happens our own kids will want to play. We won't be able to stop them."

Xiaomeng said, "It's a diabolical move."

Specs nodded. "We really don't have any choice. I've got to admit that Vaughn is an exceptional thinker and strategist."

The next day, the American children were informed that they could return home and await word of the Chinese children's decision. This outcome was not unexpected; such a weighty matter could not be decided overnight by a handful of people.

The first thing they did when they got back to America was to reveal the plan for the territorial-exchange game. This raised huge waves as rumors of the trade reached the Chinese children, their initial disbelief turning to elation and banishing from their minds the depression of Candytown and the dejection of the Antarctic Games. The marvelous world of their dreams beckoned. The vast majority of them were enthusiastic supporters of the exchange, and they passionately made their opinion known on Digital Domain. Just as Vaughn had predicted, the process would be difficult to redirect.

One month later, just as the American children were unable to wait any longer, Benes received a call from Huahua.

A pair of dark eyes from across the globe stared out of the screen into a pair of blue eyes for so excruciatingly long the air crystallized. At last, Huahua said, "We'll do the exchange."

An American delegation flew to China the following day. The main purpose of its visit was to discuss the details of the territory exchange, and to formally sign an exchange agreement. Talks took place once again in that ancient hall, and many young experts from both sides were in attendance.

The talks were originally intended to hammer out all the important details, but the biggest international effort in history concerned an endless ocean of details, so after three days of feverish debate, the children found that they could only sketch out the outlines of an exchange plan. All the remaining details would have to be addressed once the exchange was under way. After this reorientation, the talks entered a fourth day. The children had their own way of resolving international issues and were able to quickly and easily dispense with certain problems that diplomats and heads of state kept their distance from in the adults' time, often so quickly that the most seasoned diplomats of that age would have been left speechless. The issues resolved and agreements reached during that week were the equal of a hundred Yalta or Potsdam conferences. At the end of it all, the children of the two countries signed a territorial-exchange agreement known as the "Supernova Agreement":

SUPERNOVA AGREEMENT

1. China and the United States resolve to exchange all their respective territory.

2. The children of the two countries will leave their own territory, and will relinquish sovereignty over that territory; the children of the two countries will resettle in their counterpart's territory, and will obtain sovereignty over it.

3. When the children of the two countries leave their own territory, they may only take with them the following:

      a. Basic necessities for migration, limited to 10 kilograms per child.

      b. All government documents.

4. A China-US Territory Exchange Commission will be formed to exercise leadership over the exchange process.

5. The two sides will conduct the exchange on a state and province basis. When the exchange takes place, all of the current residents of a state or province shall vacate that region at the appointed time. Anyone unable to vacate at the appointed time may temporarily migrate to a neighboring state or province that has not yet undergone the exchange, and then vacate with that region's residents. All states and provinces shall establish state or provincial handover commissions, and shall conduct a handover ceremony when new residents arrive, after which the new residents' country shall assume sovereignty over that state or province.

6. Before the exchange, all state and provincial handover commissions shall deliver an asset inventory to their counterpart, and accept a review by a representative of their counterpart's handover commission.

7. Prior to the exchange, deliberate destruction of agriculture, industry, or national defense equipment within one's own territory is prohibited. If one party discovers its counterpart has taken such acts, it may unilaterally terminate the game, and all consequences shall be the responsibility of the offending party.

8. Transport for the migration shall be resolved jointly, and other countries are invited to lend assistance.

9. Any problems arising during the exchange shall be handled by the China-US Joint Territory Exchange Commission.

10. The China-US Territory Exchange Commission reserves the right of interpretation of this agreement.

Signed by two national leaders
7 November SE 2

The Great Migration

Late at night, the Imperial Palace basked under the blue light of the Rose Nebula. The flock of nocturnal birds that circled Meridian Gate had long since returned to their nests. In the endless stillness, the ancient halls slept soundly and dreamt deep.

Huahua, Specs, and Xiaomeng were the only ones in the palace. The three of them walked slowly down the long exhibition hall. Artifacts that no longer belonged to their country slipped by on either side, ancient bronze and clay made warm and soft by the nebula's light, and they felt almost as if capillaries were showing on their surface, ancient lives and souls made concrete, and that their soundless breathing surrounded them as they moved. The countless bronze vessels and clay pots seemed laden with a liquid as full of vital energy as blood; the long scroll of *Along the River During the Qingming Festival* in a glass case was hazy under the blue light, but they could still hear snatches of the hubbub; a terra-cotta warrior up ahead fluoresced blue-white, and it seemed like they were not walking toward it but that it was floating in their direction. . . . Heading northward from the southernmost premodern section, they crossed the galleries one by one, and time and history flowed back past them under the blue light of the nebula, dynasty by dynasty into the distant past. . . .

The great migration of the two continents had begun.

The children were being swiftly moved off the first two areas to be exchanged, Shaanxi and South Dakota, transferring to various ports on the coast by land and air transport, or temporarily moving to neighboring states or provinces if they missed their chance to go. Each of the two handover commissions had arrived in its counterpart's region to oversee the migration's progress. Young migrants assembled at major ports as oceangoing ships arrived in increasing numbers, war vessels and oil tankers, Chinese and American, as well as from other countries, mainly Europe and Japan. The rest of the world's children buzzed with enthusiasm over this new game between the world's two biggest countries, and they did everything within their power to aid the biggest human intercontinental migration in history. What prompted them to dispatch ships to the two countries, they couldn't properly say themselves. Huge ocean fleets were assembled on either side of the Pacific, but no handover ceremony had taken place in Shaanxi or South Dakota, and the migrants had yet to climb aboard their passage across the ocean.

Up in the artifact exhibition, the three young leaders continued toward the northernmost gallery. Huahua let out a gentle sigh, and said to Specs and Xiaomeng, "I spoke with the American kids again at the airport this afternoon, but they still refused."

After the third round, the two sides had held a series of

negotiations over details, during which the Chinese side had proposed on multiple occasions that the Chinese children should be allowed to take the most precious artifacts and ancient books with them during the exchange. This suggestion had been firmly rejected by the American children. Benes and her entourage were skilled negotiators who usually expressed their opposition using various evasive approaches rather than saying no directly, but they broke with precedent when it came to this question. No sooner did the Chinese children mention artifacts and books than they stood up from their chairs and repeated "No! No!" while shaking their heads.

At first, the Chinese children thought this was just stinginess, since such artifacts were extremely valuable if not priceless, but they later discovered this was not the case. The American children would have the same right to carry off their own artifacts as the Chinese children, and if the United States did not have many truly ancient artifacts from its few centuries of history, apart from some Native American artworks, institutions like the Metropolitan Museum of Art were chock-full of art and artifacts from around the world worth a king's ransom. But when the Chinese children proposed allowing American children to take objects from their territory equal in value to the artifacts the Chinese children took, the Americans still flat-out refused.

During preparations for the Shaanxi migration, American members of the Exchange Commission proposed starting with the Shaanxi Museum of History, built in the 1980s, and the location of the Terra-cotta Army, both of which were far more interesting to them than aircraft factories or space-launch centers. They had an astonishingly detailed awareness of the holdings of all of China's metropolitan libraries and museums, and could easily produce a printed-out inventory of cultural relics.

In a later incident, the Chinese side proposed allowing some American children fluent in both English and Chinese (mostly Chinese-Americans) to remain in the US temporarily to teach English to the Chinese children. Benes agreed, but on one condition: that American children be allowed to take with them many of the Chinese artifacts in the collections of major American museums, particularly scriptures and murals stolen from Dunhuang by nineteenth-century adventurers. This, they claimed, was due to their enthusiasm for Chinese culture, but it was expressed so effusively that the Chinese children rejected it out of hand.

But if the Chinese children were confused by these developments, what often transpired during the ongoing territorial handovers was even more baffling.

Three of Huahua's classmates, Li Zhiping the letter carrier, Chang Huidong the barber, and Zhang Xiaole the cook, were part of the first group of children to leave their homeland. The three of them had made their way together ever since Candytown. This particular group of kids from the capital were relatively fortunate, since they could ride one of the two Hercules cargo planes and avoid the bumpy torture of the seas. The young pilots had just earned their wings and flew almost drunkenly, making the air journey highly dangerous, but this mattered little to children impatient to arrive in a new world. As soon as they received notice, the three boys raced to pack their things as a wonderful, mysterious future blossomed like a flower in their imaginations.

Li Zhiping stopped off at home on the way to the airport

to retrieve a few articles of clothing. He was still in a good mood when he went in the door, but the moment he was about to leave he grew thoughtful. The feeling came so suddenly that he didn't know what to do. Like those of countless other families living in Beijing's courtyard homes, his was a sparsely furnished house. The air still held that familiar scent; a calendar from the Common Era was still hanging on the wall.

In a rush the warmth of his childhood days flooded his mind, and the faded images of his mom and dad materialized lifelike before his eyes. It was as if the nightmare of the supernova had never existed, and he had returned to one of those countless afternoons in the Common Era where his mom and dad were about to come home from work. It was all so real that he could practically imagine that the present day was but a dream, that in no way was he about to leave home forever. Then, steeling himself, he brushed aside his tears, slammed the door closed, and dashed over to the bus headed to the airport.

All along the way, he felt as if something was locked up at home, some invisible piece of clothing that he had an urge to go back and retrieve, but he knew that it had become one with the home and could not be carried off. Without the invisible clothing, he felt a sudden bone-chilling cold that disappeared as soon as he looked for something to dispel it, only to stealthily return as soon as his attention was distracted.

The first generation of Chinese children in the Supernova Era were never able to banish that chill from their souls.

The three boys remained in a poor mood all the way to the airport. As they got close, the other children's jokes tapered off, replaced by silent contemplation. The bus stopped beneath the enormous black body of a Hercules; other huge planes were waiting farther out. The long range of the Hercules meant their next fueling stop would be in Hawaii.

Picking up their few belongings, Li Zhiping, Chang Huidong, and Zhang Xiaole followed the long file of people that led toward the rear entrance of the aircraft and into its dark interior. A few American kids from the Exchange Commission were standing beside the door, white IDs around their necks, carefully inspecting everything the Chinese children carried for compliance with the scope permitted under the rules of the exchange agreement. When Li Zhiping was just a few steps away from the entrance, a spot of green caught his attention, a few blades of grass poking through a crack in the cement of the tarmac. Without a second thought he set down his bag, ran over, and plucked the clump and put it in his shirt pocket before returning to the line.

All at once a few American kids were in his face, pointing at the pocket and shouting "No! No!" followed by a string of English words, which an interpreter translated: The Americans were telling him to leave the grass behind, since it didn't fall into the category of travel necessities and thus was not covered in the carry-on items described in the exchange agreement. Li Zhiping and the kids around him erupted. Were these punks so petty that they'd stop you from taking a clump of grass as a memento from the land of your grandparents? That's just being mean!

Li Zhiping shouted out, "I'm gonna take this grass. You're not gonna stop me! Acting like you're in charge? This is still Chinese soil!" He held his pocket closed and refused to give up the grass, but the American kids didn't budge. The stalemate was broken by Zhang Xiaole, who noticed a kid who had just boarded the plane and who was playing with a game system. He shouted to the American kids, "You don't care that someone's brought a game with them. What does a clump of grass matter?"

The American kids took a look, and then bent their heads together and exchanged a few words before turning back to Li Zhiping and saying what the Chinese children thought for sure was a mistaken translation: "You can go back home, or someplace else, right now and get your own game system, but the grass has to stay here!" Li Zhiping couldn't figure out their sense of values, but there was nothing else he could do but silently put the grass back where he had found it.

As the children stepped through the entrance, they felt as if something inseparable had been left on the ground behind them, and when they turned around and saw the grass fluttering in a light breeze as if beckoning them back, at last their self-control gave way and their tears came. The interior of the military cargo plane was cavernous, equipped with long rows of seats and illuminated only by a dim fluorescent bulb high overhead. There were no windows; the children were now cut off from their land.

Their tears flowed freely once they were in their seats, and some jumped up and flung themselves toward the entrance, which was now closed and had only a single small window to crowd round. It was some time before the American cabin crew could get them seated and buckled in. Half an hour later, the engines rumbled to life and the plane began taxiing. The ground beneath sent subtle tremors up through the wheels, like a mother's hand gently patting her children on the back. Then with a slight bump the vibrations ceased, and the last thread connecting the children to their motherland was severed. Some cried out "Mama!" as others whimpered. Someone tugged at Li Zhiping's sleeve. A little girl sitting next to him stealthily passed a few blades of grass into his hands that she must have plucked from the tarmac during the chaos just before. Their eyes locked for a moment, and he started to cry again.

That was how Li Zhiping came to leave his ancestral land carrying a clump of grass with him. It remained with him throughout his peripatetic life in North America, and on innumerable nights he would wake up from dreaming about his homeland and look at it, its long-dried-out form plated with a layer of living green by the light of the Rose Nebula. On those occasions he would feel a rush of warmth surge through his numb body, and under the tender, watchful gaze of his mom and dad from the beyond, his weary heart would start to sing the songs of his childhood. . . .

Such situations were commonplace throughout the first round of territory exchange. Whenever Chinese children sought to carry with them the most insignificant objects of their homeland—grasses, leaves, flowers, or even rocks and dirt—the American children reacted with horror, and submitted repeated requests to hold discussions aimed at preventing migrants from taking any mementos with them from the land. Their stated motivation was disease control, and most Chinese children believed them, apart from a few who understood the American children's true reason.

The first two areas up for exchange were vacated on June 7, and prior to the arrival of the new immigrants, the areas held handover ceremonies.

The Shaanxi handover ceremony was not held in the provincial capital but outside a small village. All around us were loess hills and gullies edged with the terraced fields left by our ancestors' tilling. The hills extended off into the distance as far as the horizon. This deep and benevolent soil had nurtured untold Chinese generations across the ages, but now the last group of children to be brought up here were bidding it farewell.

Ten children from the handover commission, five Chinese and five Americans, took part in the ceremony. It was a simple affair. We took down our flag, and then the American children raised theirs, and then both sides signed the agreement. The American kids were all dressed as cowboys, evidently taking this as their new Wild West.

The ceremony lasted ten minutes. As my hands shook, I lowered our flag and clasped it to my chest. The five of us were foreigners now. We said nothing, numbed from the exhausting work during the migration. It would take time to fully understand it all. The vast yellow land was like my grandfather's weathered face, and now that giant face that stretched to the horizon was staring silently up at the heavens. There was not a whisper of sound. All of the many things the earth may have wanted to tell us were buried beneath it forever, and in silence it watched us depart.

Not far off a Chinese helicopter was waiting to carry us to Gansu, the second province scheduled for exchange, and away from this land that was no longer ours. I had a sudden impulse and asked the American children if we could be allowed to walk there. The little cowboys were shocked: "It's over two hundred kilometers away!" But in the end they agreed, issued us special travel permits, and wished us good luck.

Then a puppy came running over from the now-uninhabited village, nipping incessantly at our legs. I bent down and took him in my arms. The helicopter flew off with an empty cabin, its thunder receding into the distance. The five of us, plus a puppy born on this very land, began our arduous journey. We couldn't say why. Was it longing? Or penance? We just felt that so long as our feet still were on this soil, no matter how hungry or thirsty or tired we got, our spirits still had sustenance. . . .

From *A Chronicle of the Great Migration, China Edition*, vol. 6. China-US Territory Exchange Commission, New Shanghai, SE 7.

The handover ceremony in South Dakota took place beneath Mount Rushmore. Giant faces of four of the greatest presidents in US history watched in silence as a red five-star flag was raised; later, people would remember a different set of expressions on those faces, but that wasn't the focus of our attention at the time.

Unlike the chilly loneliness on the other side of the world, here several hundred American kids watched the ceremony, and a military band played the two national anthems. Once the Chinese children had raised their flag, representatives of the two sides came to sign the agreement. The Chinese representative signed, and then it was time for George Steven, governor of South Dakota. As several hundred kids watched intently, he ambled over to the signing table, slung a backpack off his shoulder, and took from it a stack of pens, fountain pens and ballpoints both, over a hundred in all. Then he began signing, using each pen for only a dot or two before setting it aside and picking up another. He signed for fifteen minutes, and it was only when the crowd's protests grew too loud that he straightened up from the table. He had signed with nearly one hundred pens, and apparently was somewhat annoyed that his parents hadn't seen fit to give him a longer name. Then he launched into a loud auction of the pens, with an opening bid of $500 each. As I watched the price skyrocket, I was seized with anxiety, and in a flash I thought of the signing table! But I was too slow; a few other kids had already rushed over to dismember it, and in the blink of an eye the poor table had been reduced to splinters of wood in the hands of dozens of kids. I glanced down at the flag in my own hands, but it did not belong to me. Looking about me for something else, I had an idea. I turned and raced into Carvers Café, and as luck would have it in a side room I found the tool I wanted: a saw. By the time I came back out, the bidding had climbed above $5,000 on George Steven's last few pens! Two flagpoles towered before me; on one fluttered the brilliant red Chinese flag, which clearly was untouchable. But the other, which once held the Stars and Stripes, was empty. I hurried over and started sawing, and in a matter of seconds I had cut it through. As it fell, a crowd of kids ran over hoping to take it for themselves, and then fought to break it into pieces, no matter that the wood was too thick to snap. My saw managed to get me two segments, each about a meter long, but I was too tired to fight for any more. But two was enough! I sold the saw for a couple thousand to another boy, who immediately joined the pack tussling over the flagpole like they were in some ferocious football game. I auctioned off one of my pieces for $45,000 but kept the other to sell later for a higher price. Then the army band members starting selling off their instruments, and it was havoc for a while as things got out of control. Some kids who hadn't claimed anything, and who had no money for the auctions, began crowding around the Chinese flagpole, and it was only when soldiers with machine guns from the Chinese Navy vowed to defend the flag and the territory it stood on with their lives that the kids finally left in dejection. Later, everyone regretted auctioning things off on-site, since memorabilia from the first territorial handover quickly rose in value tenfold. Luckily I held on to one piece of flagpole; I used it later for seed capital to open a transport company in Xinjiang.

> From *A Chronicle of the Great Migration,*
> *China Edition*, vol. 6. Sino-American Territory
> Exchange Commission, New New York, SE 7.

Now the three leaders had reached the end of the exhibit, the prehistoric gallery of the origins of Chinese civilization. In the previous galleries they had felt in awe of the finely crafted objects from earlier ages, but also perplexed, since it seemed as if an invisible wall kept them separated. The estrangement had been most acute when they had entered the premodern gallery, and it had almost sapped their courage to go on. If even the not-so-distant Qing Dynasty was an entirely unknown world to them, had they any hope of understanding any earlier age?

But contrary to their expectations, the farther back in civilization they went, the less of a separation they felt, and now that they had reached its remote origins, they had the sudden feeling of being in a familiar, inviting world. As if, after a long voyage through strange, incomprehensible lands, all of them peopled solely by incomprehensible adults speaking incomprehensible languages and living a different kind of life, almost as if they came from a different planet, now they had reached the end of the earth, and had found a children's world just like their own.

Those splendid, exquisite premodern artifacts did not belong to children; the humanity that created them had already grown up. Humanity's childhood may have been more remote, but it spoke to children all the same. The three children stared intently at the Yangshao culture* artifact: a clay pot. The crude object reminded them of a rainstorm from their young childhood, and of forming a similar object out of mud under a rainbow after the storm had passed. The age before them was the age of Pangu separating heaven and earth, of Nüwa mending heaven, of Jingwei filling up the sea, of Kuafu chasing the sun. Humanity grew up, but its courage slackened, and no more did it create such earth-shattering myths.

Huahua slid back the glass of the display case and carefully lifted the pot out. It felt warm, and almost seemed

---

* A Neolithic culture that flourished along the Yellow River 5000–3000 BCE, predominantly in what is now Henan, Shanxi, and Shaanxi.

to vibrate in his hands. It was a being of extraordinary energy. He bent an ear to the opening. "I hear something!" he exclaimed. Xiaomeng pressed her ear to it and listened intently. "It's the sound of wind!" The wind blowing over the primeval wilderness. Huahua lifted the jar up to the Rose Nebula, and the clay had a faint red luster in the blue light. He stared at the fish design, and that combination of the simplest of lines wriggled slightly, and a sudden spirit came into the black circle representing the eye. Shadows flitted across the pot's rough surface; they were too vague to make out, but they had the feeling of naked figures wrestling against something far larger than themselves.

The ancient sun and moon dwelt within the pot and cast gold and silver light over the figures. Its patterns, fish and beasts, were like pairs of eyes looking out over the long millennia, and that first ancestor's gaze met their own and passed to them a rugged energy that made them want to cry out, to weep, to laugh, to tear off their clothes and race through the howling wind in the wilderness. At long last they could feel their ancestors' blood flowing in their veins.

The three of them crossed the age-old palace beneath the light of the Rose Nebula holding the ancient pot, the oldest artifact in the city, left to them from the infancy of Chinese civilization. Walking slowly and carefully, they held it as gingerly as if it were their own eyes, or life itself. When they reached the Golden River Bridge, the last gate of the palace closed behind them with a clang. They knew that no matter where they went, their lives would be forever connected to that clay pot they held. It was their origin and their destination, and the source of their strength.

CIXIN LIU

Genesis

A two-day gale had finally died down, but the waves were still high and the night sky remained overcast. The only things visible on the water in the dead of night were endless churning whitecaps.

The first of the migration fleets had left port sixty days ago, and this was the first storm it had encountered. The wind had been strongest on the previous night, and two of the smallest-displacement transport ships, sailing at the rear, had been swallowed up by the gigantic waves. Another twenty-thousand-ton freighter had gone to their aid, but when the captain gave an ill-considered order to turn, putting the ship parallel to the waves, it was capsized by a few huge hits. When two helicopters that took off from another military vessel disappeared without a trace into the ocean, fleet command had to abandon the rescue effort, consigning more than twelve thousand children to the inky depths of the Pacific.

The remaining thirty-eight ships continued their arduous passage through the wind and waves. But the children were already used to the harshness of the voyage. First the wretched cabin conditions and the torment of seasickness, then food shortages, with daily rations only enough for one full meal, no vegetables. Even vitamin tablets were limited. Half the children came down with night blindness, and a growing number were septic, but they maintained discipline under adverse conditions. Organization was sustained in small, medium, and large groups, and leaders at all levels remained in their posts, carrying out their duty with fearless dedication. Once they reached the Americas, sustaining that discipline and organization would be for the Chinese children a trial far more difficult than any storm or hunger.

Two days ago they had crossed paths with the American migration fleet. The two fleets followed their own path in silence, neither acknowledging the other's presence. The American children did not appear to be much better off.

At last the waves receded. They had diverted from their route for two days in order to follow the safest line through the storm, and now the entire fleet was attempting an arduous change of heading. Waves thundered off the bow and port side, and the side-to-side rocking intensified.

The dark clouds overhead had scattered, and the light of the Rose Nebula hit the waves and scattered into a thousand directions, turning the Pacific into a marvelous ocean of blue fire. The children ran out onto the deck, their footsteps shaky from seasickness and hunger, and flocked to the sides of the ship as if sleepwalking. But there was no stopping the cheers when they saw the majestic sight before them.

It was the last day of the second year of the Supernova Era.

Midnight.

A few destroyers fired ship guns into the air, and strings of flares and fireworks rose from other ships. The explosions and the waves and the children's excited shouts blended into one, resounding through the air and across the sea.

The first rays of dawn peeked out from the eastern horizon and mingled with the Rose Nebula into the most magnificent riot of color in the entire universe.

Now it was January 1, the third year of the Supernova Era.

Epilogue
Blue Planet

Finished at last! Time to take a deep breath, like a diver breaking the surface. For the half a year I spent underwater, this book has occupied my entire life. Now I can truly say that I am finished "writing," since the power's out again—the government says it's another problem with the solar batteries—and I've had to take up that ancient pen. Yesterday it was clogged from the cold and I couldn't write; today it isn't, and I'm sitting here sweating in the heat and dripping onto the pages. The climate varies day to day, sometimes hour to hour, and without the AC it's intolerable.

Out the window is a swath of verdant grass adorned with the pale yellow cottages of the immigrant village. Beyond them—god, don't look out there—is nothing but desert, a red desolation frequented by raging dust storms that blot out the dim red sky and the sun that provides little heat in the first place.

Such a god-awful place. Such a god-awful place!

"You said that when you finished the book, you'd watch the kid," Verené says.

I say I'm writing the afterword. I'll be done soon.

"It's all a waste of energy. Too fringe to be proper history, and too realistic to be fiction."

She's right. That's what the book agents said, too. But what can I do? It's the current state of historiography that's landed me in this dilemma!

It's my misfortune to be a superhistorian in this era. A little over three decades into the Supernova Era, the period has been the focus of a mountain of research, putting it well beyond the scope of historiography and into a sort of sensationalized commercialism. Book after book, most just playing to the crowd. A few of the duller so-called historians even parcel out the three decades into smaller periods, measured by the day and more numerous than the dynasties of the Presupernova period, and publish studies for each to rake in the cash.

Most historians of the Supernova Era currently follow one of two major schools of thought, alternate history and psychology.

The alternate history approach is currently in vogue. This school poses historical hypotheses. What if, for example, the supernova rays were a bit stronger and killed off everyone over the age of eight? Or a bit weaker and allowed anyone under twenty to survive? What would that have done to the history of the Supernova Era? If the Supernova War had been fought not as games but as conventional battles in the Common Era meaning of the term? So on and so forth.

The school had its reasons for being: the outbreak of the Supernova War brought humanity to the understanding that from a cosmic perspective there is an element of randomness to the march of history. In the words of noted alternate historian Dr. Liu Jing, "History is a little tree branch carried along a stream. It might whirl in an eddy for a while, or get caught on a rock poking above the surface, or any number of other possibilities. For history as a discipline to study just one of those possibilities is as ridiculous as playing cards with a deck consisting entirely of aces."

The development of this school is tied to the proof in recent years of the parallel universe theory, whose far-reaching implications for all disciplines, history included, are only beginning to be felt.

I won't deny that there are a few serious alternate historians, such as Alexander Levenson (*The Direction of the Section*) and Matsumoto Taro (*Unlimited Branching*), whose research uses a unique perspective on another potential pathway as a way to expound an innate law of actual history. These scholars have my respect; that their work has been ignored is historiography's tragedy. On the other hand, the school has provided a wonderful stage for showy crowd-pleasers who are far more interested in alternate history than in the real thing, and for whom the name "historian" is less appropriate than "alternate history novelist."

The aforementioned Liu Jing is their chief exponent. She pops up in the media these days flogging her fifth book, for which she was reportedly paid an advance of 3.5 million Martian dollars. From its title, *The Big If,* you can pretty much guess at the contents. Liu Jing's father from back in the Common Era must be mentioned in any discussion of her scholarship, not, I assure you, because I'm trying to make a bloodline argument, but simply due to the fact that Dr. Liu has repeatedly acknowledged her great father's influence on her academic approach. I feel I ought to understand him a little. This has been no easy task. I scanned through materials from the Common Era and searched through all the ancient databases I could find, but came up with nothing.

Fortunately, Liu Jing was Verené's graduate advisor, and so I had her ask Dr. Liu directly. I learned as a result that Liu Jing's nobody of a father, Liu Cixin, had written a few science fiction stories back in the Common Era, most of them published in a magazine called *SFW* (I checked this out; *Science Fiction World* was a previous incarnation of the Precision Dream Group that has a monopoly on hypermedia arts on two worlds). Verené even brought back three of his stories. I got halfway through the first one and had to throw it away; what utter trash! The whales in that story even grew teeth! Under the influence of a father like that, it's no wonder Liu Jing has the attitude toward scholarship and the methods she does.

The psychological school of superhistory is a far more serious pursuit. Its adherents believe that the great divergence in the Supernova Era from the track of prior human history was due to child psychology in SE society. In *Germ Cell Society,* Von Svensker systematically expounds on the unique implications of the family-free society at the start of the era; Zhang Fengyun goes further in the somewhat controversial *Asexual World,* providing a sober yet brilliant analysis of a society in which sex is basically absent. But to my mind, the psychological school is built atop a shaky foundation, for in actual fact, the psychological state of SE children was entirely different from that of CE children. In some ways they were far more naïve, but in other ways they were more mature than even CE adults. Whether SE history created this psychology or vice versa is a true chicken-and-egg question.

A few serious scholars who do not adhere to any school have made valuable contributions to superhistory. In *Classroom Society*, A. G. Hopkins provides a comprehensive study of the forms of government in the children's world. This monumental work was attacked from many sides, mostly on ideological grounds rather than for any questions of scholarship, which, given the scope of the book, is hardly surprising. Yamanaka Keiko's *Raising Oneself* and Lin Mingzhu's *A Candle in the Cold Night* are two books on the history of SE education that, despite being a bit heavy on sentimentality, nevertheless have value as comprehensive, objective historical documents. Zeng Yulin's magnum opus *To Sing Again* is a rigorous yet poetic systematic study of the art of the children's world, and one of the few works of superhistory with both critical and popular appeal. The results of these scholars' research must still stand the test of time, but their research itself is serious, at least compared to the stuff in *The Big If....*

"You lose your cool whenever you mention my advisor," Verené says, looking over my shoulder.

Can I keep cool? Can Liu Jing? My book's not even published, and already she's mocking it in the media as "unfictionlike fiction, reportage that doesn't report, ahistorical history. It's unclassifiable." An attempt to bolster oneself by belittling others will in no way have a positive effect on the academic climate of superhistory that's polluted already.

I wrote this way out of desperation. A prerequisite for

historical research is to let history cool down first, but has the Supernova Era cooled down in thirty-odd years? Not one whit. We are the witnesses to that history, and the terror of the supernova, the loneliness of the Epoch Clock running out, the torpor of Candytown, the great tragedy of the Supernova War, all of it is deeply imprinted in our minds.

Before migrating here, I lived beside the railroad tracks, and every night I was tormented by nightmares in which I was running through the wilderness in the dark surrounded by terrifying noises—floods, earthquakes, the howls of hordes of giant beasts, the thunder of nuclear bombs. And then one night, I awoke with a start from that nightmare and dashed to the window. No stars, no moon, only the Rose Nebula shining over the land, and a night train making its slow passage. Can one do research at a theoretic level in such a state? No, we lack the dispassionate detachment that theoretic research requires. It will need to wait until there's enough distance between the early Supernova Era and the researchers, which may leave it in the hands of the next generation. All our generation can do is descriptive writing, giving our descendants records of the period from the perspective of eyewitnesses and of historians. That is all that superhistory can do for the time being, in my opinion.

But even this isn't easy. My initial approach was to write from the perspective of an ordinary individual, making the book feel more like a novel, and deal with high-level national and world developments by incorporating quotations from source documents. But I am a historian, not a litterateur, and have not a drop of literary talent in a huge ocean. And so I went the other way, depicting the national leadership directly and incorporating details about the experiences of ordinary people as quotations. Most of the child leaders from that time are no longer in their posts, giving them plenty of time to take my interviews, and as a result I have written what Liu Jing calls an "unclassifiable" book.

"Daddy Daddy, come quick! It's going to get cold outside soon!" Jingjing shouts, rapping on the window. His face is pressed up against the glass, squishing his nose to one side. In the distance the strange, isolated peaks cast long shadows across the red sands. The sun is going down. Of course it's going to get cold.

But I am, after all, a historian, and I can't help but do my job. The study of superhistory is currently concentrated in a debate over a few key questions, a debate that has spilled over into the media, where it has only become more sensationalized. However, far fewer serious superhistorians than laypeople have put forth opinions, and so I will take this opportunity to explain my position on a few of the hottest topics.

1. Dating the start of the Supernova Era. There are two extreme positions on this question, one holding that the era began with the supernova blast, reasoning that a universal symbol carries the most authority for the start of an era. This clearly is untenable, since while human calendars may be tied to cosmic symbols, eras are only marked in history. The second position holds that the era did not begin until the start of the Great

Migration, which doesn't hold up because prior to the migration, or even prior to the Supernova War, history had already progressed away from the Common Era model. The starting point I find most appropriate is the extinguishing of the Epoch Clock. Although critics may point out that the Common Era model still held then, there is an inertia to history, and you can't, say, argue that the whole world became Christian at the birth of Jesus. In both historical and philosophical significance, the Epoch Clock is inarguably a highly meaningful symbol.

2. The success or failure of the use at the close of the Common Era of country simulations as a means of selecting child leaders, and in particular whether this was legal. I don't want to comment too much on this issue, since those who believe this method to be unacceptable have not to this day come up with any better solution, much less in those grim days when every country was on the verge of extinction. There are many self-opinionated people in the field of history these days, and the best way to clue them in is to make them walk a train rail set between two tall buildings.

3. Whether the goal of the world war games was play or a fight for Antarctica. It's hard to answer this question now with an adult mind. In Presupernova war, politics, economics, nationalism, and religion blended into one and are hard to tease apart; so too with the Antarctic Games. In the children's world, play and national politics were inseparable, two sides of the same coin. This ties into the next issue:

4. The strategies of the Chinese and American children in the Supernova War. It has been proposed that the substantial military advantage commanded by the American children meant they would have easily occupied Antarctica in a conventional war. In such a war, the American children could have used their navy to break the enemies' sea transport lines, making it impossible for any other country to send troops to the continent. This notion displays a basic ignorance of world politics and considers the Supernova Era world from a shallow, Common Era geopolitical view. Its proponents fail to understand a fundamental rule of world politics: the balance of power principle. In such a situation, the other countries would have immediately set up alliances, and any group counting China, Russia, the EU, and Japan among its members would be powerful enough to stand against the US. The resulting world order would be little different from that of the war games, except that countries would be exchanged for alliances, and politics would have a slightly more Common Era feel to them.

5. Whether the Great Migration was a historical inevitability. This is a profound question. After the exchange of Chinese and American territory, children from other countries joined in the game—Russia swapping with the countries of South America, and Japan with the Middle East—and then it swept the globe as the main driver of postwar world history, essentially performing a hard reformat of global geopolitics. Regrettably, this extremely worthy subject has not yet been studied in any depth; interest remains focused

on the outcome of the migration. And no wonder: people are always more interested in the unexpected, which the consequences of the Great Migration certainly were. Before it began, children came up with various possible outcomes, sometimes from the minds of great thinkers and strategists like Vaughn and Specs, but more often from ordinary people. But time proved all of these predictions incorrect. The actual outcome took everyone by surprise, and was beyond the boldest imagination of any of the children of that period . . .

"Daddy Daddy, come out! Didn't you promise to look at the blue planet with us? It's about to come up!"

With a sigh I put down my pen, realizing that once again I've unconsciously started into a futile theoretical discussion. And so I decide to end it here. I stand up and go out onto the lawn. The sun is almost below the horizon, and the Rose Nebula is getting light.

"God, the sky's clean!" I exclaim. The motionless, filthy clouds you used to see every time you went out have vanished, and the sky is a pure, pale red.

"You just noticed? It's been a week already!" Verené says, tugging at Jingjing.

"Didn't the government say it couldn't afford to clean the safety dome?"

"It was volunteers! I went too. I cleaned four hundred square meters!" Jingjing says proudly.

I look up at the top of the dome two thousand meters high, where people are scrubbing away the last of the dirt, looking like so many black dots against the bright blue backdrop of the nebula.

It's gotten cold, and it's starting to snow. The verdant grass underfoot, the red sands outside the bubble, the glittering Rose Nebula out in space, and the swirling white snowflakes paint an intoxicatingly gorgeous picture.

"They never get the right adjustments to the climate-control system," Verené says.

"It'll get better. Everything's going to get better . . ." I say from my heart.

"Come up! Come up!" Jingjing cries.

Over the eastern horizon a blue planet rises like a sapphire set into the pale red veil of the sky.

"Dad, is that where we came from?" Jingjing asks.

I nod. "That's right."

"And our grandparents still live there?"

"Yes. They've always lived there."

"Is that Earth?"

Looking at the Earth is like staring into my mother's pupil, and tears swim in my eyes as I choke out, "That's right, my child. That's Earth."

Afterword

My home lies more than six hundred miles from Beijing, and for at least three decades the journey by train took over seven hours. One day a few years ago, however, I bought a ticket on a futuristic, streamlined high-speed train that had a top speed of 300 kilometers per hour, and I gaped in wonder at the unfamiliar scenery flying by, since the train was traveling a brand new route. The whole trip ended in Beijing just two hours later. A high-speed rail line had appeared on the outskirts of my city, but as for when ground had been broken, and when construction had been completed, I was totally unaware. It was as if it had come into being overnight. Along its journey the train had passed through a tunnel, spending a full ten minutes at nearly two hundred kilometers per hour in what I later learned was the country's longest rail tunnel. I can remember back to my childhood, and how the digging of the country's longest rail tunnel (probably not even a tenth the length of this new one) was a huge national news story. Now it doesn't even make an impression.

That's how fast China is changing.

Countless tall buildings, hypermarkets, and factories

spring up like magic all around you. But the biggest changes are invisible: a wired China is expanding rapidly, and people spend at least half, if not more, of their personal lives online. They interact socially, purchase practically every good imaginable from Taobao up to and including hamsters, and huge groups of them can make their opinions and requests known directly online for events large and small, forming a powerful force of public opinion that is overwhelming traditional media and is rapidly becoming a major determiner of China's future. The scene in *Supernova Era* where the internet and a quantum computer facilitate a national dialogue has already basically come to pass in China. The other day I went to Xiong'an New Area in Baoding and visited a brand new city under construction where the supermarkets have no attendants, the hotels are unstaffed, and the vast majority of the cars on the streets are driverless. AI has replaced humanity.

China used to have no sense of the future. In our subconscious, today was the same as yesterday, and tomorrow was going to be the same as today. The future as a concept doesn't really appear in traditional Chinese culture.

But today, "futuristic" is the most salient impression one gets from China. With everything changing at a blinding pace, a breathtaking future rises like the sun from the horizon, fully compelling, yet suffused with terrifying uncertainty and danger. This provides fertile ground to science fiction, which has been thrust suddenly into the spotlight from its former position on the margins in China; today even a non-governmental science fiction convention can boast the attendance of a national vice president.

The first draft of *Supernova Era* was written thirty years

ago. One night that year when I was in Beijing on a work trip, I had a dream: a limitless expanse of snow, whipped up by the wind into a ground blizzard, and an object—perhaps the sun or a star—glowing with a blinding blue light that painted the sky an eerie color between purple and green. And beneath that dim glow, a formation of children advanced across the snowy ground, white scarves wrapped around their heads, rifles fitted with gleaming bayonets, singing some unrecognizable song as they moved forward in unison. . . . When I recall the horror of that grim scene it still gives me palpitations. I awoke in a cold sweat and couldn't get back to sleep, and that's when the germ of the idea for *Supernova Era* first took shape.

Back then, if someone had predicted China as it is today, thirty years later, even I, a science fiction writer, would have found it hard to believe.

Nevertheless, the novel accurately depicts the reaction of Chinese people today in the face of a world that's brand-new and getting newer every day, the reaction to a time when old faiths and supports collapsed before new ones could be erected: utter confusion. Or more correctly, this is the reaction of the middle-aged and elderly—people like myself. China's new generation is wholly integrated into this new world as native inhabitants of the information age. They are deft users of the internet with no need for instruction, and have quickly adopted it as an inseparable external organ. To them, this is the way the world ought to be, and change is a matter of course; put them in the world of the novel, and they'd adapt to reality even more readily once the adults depart.

Fear of abandonment is an eternal human constant. In the

dark, you advance slowly in a particular direction holding hands with your mom and dad, and even though you can't see them, those two hands keep your soul firmly anchored. All of a sudden they let go, and you grope helplessly around for them in the darkness, and you scream in desperation, but the infinite blackness swallows up your voice. . . . It's a dream that everyone probably had in their childhood, something every child fears.

And it is also the greatest fear of humanity as a whole, a terror deeply rooted in human civilization, one that occupies a key place in our spiritual life. Staring into the endless darkness of the cosmos, humanity futilely grasps for a pair of nonexistent hands, but we have so far been unable to find any signs of other intelligent civilizations from our vantage point on a planet that's no more than a speck of dust in outer space, even as the gods of religion grow ever harder to make out. And therefore our world today is already that of the children in the novel: humanity is an orphan unable to find its parents' hands, its mind full of terror and confusion even as sparks of naivete and unruliness flicker into flame. . . . We may not even be as lucky as those children, since in our course of study there is no one to instruct us.

With that in mind, the story told in this novel is a fairly unremarkable one.